A Memoir in Letters

A Memoir in Letters

◆

My Life on Both Sides of the Iron Curtain

Hadwig Gofferje

iUniverse, Inc.

New York Lincoln Shanghai

A Memoir in Letters
My Life on Both Sides of the Iron Curtain

Copyright © 2005 by Hadwig Gofferje

iUniverse books may be ordered through booksellers or by contacting:

iUniverse
2021 Pine Lake Road, Suite 100
Lincoln, NE 68512
www.iuniverse.com
1-800-Authors (1-800-288-4677)

ISBN-13: 978-0-595-34271-6 (pbk)
ISBN-13: 978-0-595-79040-1 (ebk)
ISBN-10: 0-595-34271-X (pbk)
ISBN-10: 0-595-79040-2 (ebk)

Printed in the United States of America

For my family and my friends, who stood by me during hard times.

Contents

Preface

Initially I intended my autobiography for my children and grandchildren. As I considered the historical background of my personal narrative, I realized that my story deserves to be told to a larger audience.

World War II and its repercussions influenced my early childhood and my youth until I came to the United States in 1960. Fleeing west in 1945 from the approaching Red Army, growing up under Communism, and escaping to West Germany in 1955 were the result of the war and the division of Germany.

As in all wars, justified or not, the innocent are the victims—the population and especially the children. Every child deserves to grow up in peace and under the protection of responsible adults. Unfortunately this is not possible during war.

Acknowledgments

I was lucky during the early stages of my writing to have had the support and constructive advice of my late husband Michael Dertouzos. I owe many thanks to Marlys Saltzer and Silvie Thierry for reading the drafts of my manuscript and for their suggestions and encouragement.

I thank Dr. Hans Gofferje, who supplied much interesting information about my Huguenot ancestors. Thanks to my son, Leo Dertouzos for designing the maps and to my daughter, Alexandra Rowe for her help with editing, designing the cover, and marketing ideas. Finally, I am grateful to Dave Baldwin for enduring my constant preoccupation with this project, for his technical support, and for rescuing me from the erratic behavior of my computer.

For My Children

✦

My Reason for Writing This Book

My father had died in 1966, and when my mother died in September 1978, I was suddenly overcome with the loss—not only with the loss of my mother, who was my support in life, but also with the lost opportunity of asking my parents the many questions I did not ask when they were still alive.

I was twenty-nine when my father died, and I did not feel the same urgency as I do now to find out what kind of people my parents were. I think that it takes maturity and a certain amount of life experience before one is confronted with this question. No doubt, some day both of you will feel the same way about your parents. This is why I want to give you some answers about your mother. In doing this, I want to show the person and the woman I am, rather than the image you have of me as a parent.

This is the purpose of writing this "opus." If you get bored reading this, put it down and wait a few years. Chances are, you are not ready for it. I was in my forties before I started wondering about what kind of people my parents were. The curiosity became increasingly urgent as I got older.

When I was planning to write these memoirs many years ago, I often thought about it but never started. It is no coincidence that I finally write it now. I have reached a stage in my life where I am free to be myself again.

Some people become self-centered as they grow older. Perhaps there is no way to avoid this process. It is the consequence of life's continuous disappointments and unfulfilled expectations. But we are controlling this aging process to a great extent, both mentally and spiritually. The body starts to disintegrate, but the mind does not lose its ability to expand. Aging gracefully is a very difficult task. It requires the adjustment to the slowing down of the body and the realization that the spiritual development is just beginning. Perhaps it was meant this way, to offset the disadvantages of one with the benefits of the other. I hope I will age gracefully.

The ability of people to learn does not diminish in old age. The process of learning slows down, but the capacity for learning is still there and any success becomes so much more satisfying. I think when we stop learning we may as well be in the grave. I am referring not only to learning new skills, such as playing a musical instrument or learning a new language, but also to growing spiritually and to becoming wiser.

It is the increased loneliness that comes with old age that is so conducive to spiritual growth. We start asking ourselves: What are we here for, and where do we go? The answers to these questions are different for everyone. This is the reason why I sit here asking the question, Where did I come from?

Keep in mind that this is not meant to be a literary masterpiece, but more a search for the self. The process of this search has had a positive effect on me. It forces me to look back on my life and put it in perspective, and it also changes me back to the person I was before marriage and childbearing. I was strong then, happy and full of ambitions. As time went by, I stayed strong, even ambitious, but the goals have changed.

Germaine Greer writes about aging as a "rite of passage, a celebration of what could be regarded as the restoration of a woman to herself—by threading her way back to childhood and catching hold of a girl she could draw strength from and rely on matured."

As I am editing this manuscript, I find that I am still the strong girl with all her dreams and ambitions intact. Pain has taught me important lessons. The events in my life made me grow and helped me reach my present strength.

Having recently learned about the powerful influence parents have over their children, especially when they are very young, I began to wonder whether I gave you all the love and tools you need to deal with the adversities of life. I want you to know that I took my role as parent very seriously and did my best. I hope that I have been a good mother to you.

Carl Jung wrote about writing an autobiography: "I can only tell stories. Whether or not the stories are true is not the problem. The only question is whether what I tell is my truth. An autobiography is difficult to write because we possess no standards, no objective foundation from which to judge our selves." I am not writing these memoirs to judge myself. That is something you will do. All I want to do here is to tell you my story, my truth.

How Do You Pronounce That Name?

✦

The Origin of My Name and the Story of My Ancestors

My paternal ancestors were Huguenots who had moved to Kleve, just across the border from Belgium, then belonging to Prussia. My mother's ancestors were Bavarians. Prussians and Bavarians did not get along too well throughout German history, but I am the product of a marriage between a Prussian and a Bavarian.

The early Protestants in France, called Huguenots, were followers of John Calvin (1509–64). Although the French Crown opposed Protestantism and John Calvin fled to Geneva, the numbers of the Huguenots grew steadily. There were Huguenots among all classes from nobles to merchants to peasants. France had more than two thousand Huguenot congregations in 1561. By 1662 there were more than a million Protestants in France. The Crown was under the influence of the Catholic Guises, and the country was embroiled in religious wars. Cardinal Richelieu was particularly notorious for the persecution of the Huguenots.

The persecution of the Protestants culminated in the Massacre of St. Bartholomew in 1572. Three thousand Huguenots were killed in Paris and a total of twenty thousand across France. Four hundred thousand Huguenots fled the country. They settled often just across the border, hoping to be able to return to their homeland.

Henry of Navarre became the first Huguenot king of France (Henry IV) in 1589, but he converted to Catholicism in 1593 in the hope of pacifying his subjects. He proclaimed the Edict of Nantes in 1598. France was now Catholic but granted freedom of worship to the Huguenots. The religious wars seemed to have ended until Louis XIV (1643–1715) opened the religious question again. He prevented the Huguenots from holding public offices and excluded them from certain professions (medicine, for example). They had to pay special taxes, and they were often disowned. He revoked the Edict of Nantes in 1685, and Protestantism became illegal in France until the French Revolution.

My father's ancestors immigrated in 1546 from Meaux, France, to Mons, Belgium, and later to Kleve, Germany, just across the border between Belgium and Germany. Kleve, although on the western border of Germany, was a Prussian possession. Protestant Prussia welcomed the Huguenots after they were forced out of Catholic France. Berlin had a large Huguenot population. They were valued for their skills, craftsmanship, and industriousness. They had their own church in Berlin, which still exists, the Hugenotten Dom.

The first Huguenot generation in Germany probably spoke French and German; later generations spoke only German. The name "Goverié" can be found in the birth and death registers in Kleve in 1749 and in Amaregnon near Mons since 1628.

My father did most of the ancestor research in the 1920s and 1930s. He visited a "Goffriér" in Eberswalde near Berlin who had all kinds of records and oral information about our ancestors. From him he heard the following story: Five Goverié brothers, silk weavers by profession, fled around 1683 by boat from their new hometown Mons. They went down the river Maas (Meuse in France) toward Maastricht. Two brothers drowned on the way, but two other brothers landed in Amsterdam and went from there to Hamburg. The government of the electoral prince Frederic III of Prussia granted asylum to the brothers in Hamburg and settled them in Prussian Pommerania. The last of the five brothers, who is the ancestor of our family branch, stayed in Kleve.

Joannes de Govriér is the oldest documented ancestor in Kleve. He is registered as Jean de Goverié; as Johannes de Goverié at his first marriage in 1749; and as Joannes Goverié at his second marriage in 1775. His son Jacobus de Goverié, my great-great-grandfather, lived from 1750 to 1827. He was also a silk weaver and was wealthy. After the second marriage of his father in 1775, he moved from Kleve to Emmerich and took his younger siblings Petronella (born in 1752) and Ludovic (born in 1754) with him. In 1783 he became officially "Burgher of Emmerich."

The spelling of our name changes from record to record. This is explained by the fact that most people were illiterate three hundred years ago and orally reported names led to many spellings of the same name. Over time the spelling of the name evolved to the German form "Gofferje" with or without accent, and the "de" disappeared. A name with "de" usually indicates nobility. It is believed that my ancestors were poor nobility and sold their title. This was often done to raise money for the poor nobles and was a way for the wealthy and prominent burghers to acquire a title.

Again and again I came across stories about some of my ancestors, but we know them only from hearsay. Antonie Gofferjé in Isselburg, Germany, talks in 1902 with certainty about being related to a Vicomte de Turenne, a field marshal of France. However, nobody knows how we are related to him. Antonie did not explain her assertion.

This is what we know about Henry de la Tour d'Auvergne: He was a Calvinist and supporter of Henry IV of Navarre, and he became Duke of Bouillion and sovereign of Sedan. He had two sons and five daughters. The second of his sons, Henry de la Tour, was the Vicomte de Turenne. He was known as one of the greatest military commanders in France and was the highest-ranking Huguenot until his conversion to Catholicism in 1668. He was a respected diplomat and was described as noble, reliable, generous, and faithful. Voltaire said about him: "He was one of the great men of our time." He was married but had no children. He conquered all of Flanders, but a cannonball killed him in Baden, Germany, in 1675. Napoleon buried him in 1800 in the Dome des Invalides in Paris. My uncle Paul Gofferjè in Erfurt received a copy of an etching of the Vicomte from the Louvre in Paris. I think he looks rather forbidding, and I would not like to be his enemy.

Two of my ancestors fought in the Battle of Waterloo (1815). Peter Paul Gofferjé fought on the side of the French, while his brother Ludwig Josef fought on the side of the Prussians under Field Marshal Blücher. Ludwig Josef was wounded twice, and Peter Paul ended up as a prisoner of war in Berlin.

The next three generations after Jacobus de Goverié were born and lived in Emmerich or Krefeld. My paternal grandfather, Karl Heinrich Gofferje, was born in Krefeld in 1855. He was a medical doctor and married my grandmother, Anna Friedericke Zierler, in 1888. Anna was born in 1861 in Bad Ischl, Austria. My father was born in 1893 in Niederbreisig.

In the maternal line, my mother's earliest documented ancestor is Althans Schmidt, born in 1550. "Schmidt" or "*Schmied*" means "blacksmith" in German. The next three generations were also blacksmiths, but Althans' great-grandson (1637–1720) was also "Gottesvater"—some kind of "church father." After the Reformation, all of my mother's ancestors were Protestants. Many of them were Lutheran ministers, and their daughters were married to Lutheran ministers. The family tradition was carried to my grandfather and uncle, who both had a PhD in theology. Thus a strong Protestant line of clerics emerged. It is surprising that after the Reformation they stayed in Catholic Bavaria where the Protestants were persecuted and often lost their lands and property. One unlucky ancestor was participating in a rebellion, where he was caught and hanged in the town square of Ulm.

Fifteen years after the death of J. S. Bach, Georg Simon Löhlein (1725–81), a relative of my maternal grandmother, became well-known in the music community of Leipzig. He was director of the "Grosse Konzert," a precursor of today's Gewandhaus, a composer, a teacher, and an author of popular music textbooks. Uncle Friedrich, my mother's cousin, sent me a copy of the following article, which appeared in the *Augsburger Abendzeitung* in March 1945:

Goethe's first published poem appeared 175 years ago in the cultural magazine, *Hamburger Unterhaltungen*. Goethe was not personally involved in the publication, although it was probably not published against his wishes. It was a slightly risqué New Year's poem, which Goethe had written in merry company in 1768. Goethe met in this circle of friends on repeated occasions the composer and "father of the German Piano School," Georg Simon Löhlein of Neustadt, near Koburg, who had a very adventurous life. As a young man, on a trip to Kopenhagen, he encountered recruiters for the Prussian Army, who put him into the famous "Long Guard" of the Prussian King because of his extraordinary height. He was wounded in 1757 during the battle of Kollin and was taken as prisoner of war to a military hospital in Vienna. Here he played his violin so sweetly for the Empress Maria Theresia of Austria that she freed him and sent him home. He went to live in Leipzig where he became conductor of the "Gewandhaus." Here he met the young Goethe at the publishing house of Breitkopf. He composed a lovely melody for Goethe's risqué poem, matching nicely with Goethe's humor. Löhlein published the song with Goethe's lyrics in the *Hamburger Unterhaltungen*. Thus Goethe's name appeared for the first time in public. Throughout his life, Löhlein set many more of Goethe's poems to music.

Friedrich Schmidt, my grandfather's brother, immigrated to the United States in 1890, when he was only twenty two years old. He had studied theology at the university in Erlangen, Germany, and continued his studies in Baltimore at Johns Hopkins University. In 1897 he became professor and later head of the Department for Modern Languages at the State University of Oregon. According to an article in the *Oregon Daily Emerald,* he published a dozen books and 50 articles in German and English. Included in his books are *Famous Germans of Recent Times,* and his most important work was the translation of Goethe's *Faust* into English. It was the first English edition ever made. He also wrote a biography of Gerhart Hauptmann, a German poet who was given a Nobel Prize for literature, and a college textbook designed for the use of German students. He lived in Eugene,

Oregon, until his death in 1945. He had no children, otherwise I would have had relatives in the United States.

Henry de la Tour

Nr. 1981 a/b

Collegium musicum

Nr. 80

G. S. Loehlein

Konzert

für Cembalo (Klavier), 2 Violinen und Bass

Op. 7 Nr. 1

Verlag von
BREITKOPF & HÄRTEL
in
LEIPZIG.

Printed in Germany

NETHERLANDS

Amsterdam

Kleve

Krefeld

Dusseldorf

Bruxelles

Maastricht

Aachen

BELGIUM

Mons

GERMANY

Luxemburg

Paris

Meaux

FRANCE

Jacob de Goveriè (1750–1827).
My paternal great-great-grandfather.

Anna Maria Huebers, married to Jacob de Goverié in 1776.

Friedrich, Andreas, Benjamin Schmidt (1800–82).
My maternal great-great grandfather.

Ernst, Friedrich, Benjamin Schmidt (1830–96).
My maternal great-grandfather.

Theodor Schmidt (1867–1942).
My maternal grandfather.

Luise Schmidt, my maternal grandmother.

Anna Zierler, my paternal grandmother.

There Was Always Music

✦

My Grandparents and Parents

I know very little about my grandparents. My mother's father, Dr. Theodor Schmidt (1867–1943), was "Kirchenrat," a church official in Augsburg. I was too young to have any memory of him, but I loved listening to my mother's stories about him. He liked to go fishing for relaxation and often took his son and three daughters along. One hot summer day, his daughters—Edith, Klara, and Irmgard—wanted to go swimming while he was fishing in the river Kessel. For lack of bathing suits, he told them to go into the water with their little aprons on. Their mother would have been horrified to hear about this and was never told. The girls, meanwhile, had fun and kept the secret. I wish I had known Grandfather Schmidt; it seems that he was a very generous and open-minded man. My mother always spoke of him with great respect and love.

I never knew my grandmother Luise Schmidt, since she died in 1932 before I was born. All I have are some photographs and a few cherished recipes, which I will hand down to my daughter and granddaughter.

I remember being in my maternal grandparents' house in Augsburg after my grandfather had died. My mother and her two sisters were emptying the house, and while they divided the silver and the jewelry, I looked on. One of them gave me a little brooch with stones and told me they were diamonds. That brooch, really a pretty piece of custom jewelry, is still somewhere amongst my memorabilia. I remember only this incident along with a terribly cold night at that house. These were not familiar surroundings for me, and I was not at ease. Later, that house was totally destroyed by bombs during World War II.

My paternal grandfather, Dr. Karl Heinrich Gofferje (1855–94), was married to Anna Zierler (1861–1935). Karl Heinrich Gofferje had a medical practice in Niederbreisig (Bad Breisig today). He died when my father was only one year old. My father became the ward of his uncle Heinrich Zierler, a dentist living in Hamburg. My grandmother Anna Zierler made her living with a tailoring business after her husband's death. Both Anna and Karl Heinrich were very musical. Karl Heinrich played violin, cello, and flute and his wife sang. Grandmother Anna did not want her son to become a musician and wanted him to concentrate on his schoolwork. My father was sent to a boarding school in Rothenburg. After tenth grade he enrolled at the *Humanistisches Gymnasium,* a high school in Würzburg, where he graduated in 1912. While in Würzburg, my father was allowed to study at the conservatory free of charge. He had already studied the violin in boarding school against the wishes of his mother. He played piano and violin and taught himself later to play the lute and recorder. At his graduation, someone played variations for solo violin behind a screen of plants. When his mother asked who the talented violinist was, she was told that it was her son. She must have made her peace then with her son's music playing. Grandmother Anna was living sometimes with my parents, but later mostly near my parents in Frankfurt/Oder. My sister Ute told me that she loved to visit her and would bring her food that my mother had cooked. They often read books together. Once, they had a window open when it was raining as they read under an umbrella. Anna Zierler died in 1935 of cancer. Because I was born in 1937, I knew neither my paternal nor my maternal grandmother.

Uncle Heinrich Zierler funded my father's education and wanted him to go to medical school at the University of Würzburg. During this time, my father also continued his musical studies at the conservatory. He served as a medic with the Bavarian artillery during World War I, during which time he sustained a leg injury and was dismissed from service.

My father continued his studies after the war but switched to dental medicine. He received his MDD in 1919. He married a teacher, Margarete Koltermann, in 1917 in Würzburg. My stepsister Brigith was born in 1919. He opened a dental practice in Ochsenfurth near Würzburg in 1922. His marriage to Margarete ended in divorce in 1926, and in 1927 he married my mother, Edith Schmidt.

My mother was educated at the *Stetten Institute,* a women's finishing school in Augsburg. Some of her classmates became her lifelong friends. After she graduated, she entered a tailoring apprenticeship. She was always artistically talented and designed the clothes she made with great skill. She spent two years as a nanny with an artist's family in Amsterdam. While she was there, she took courses at the Art Academy in the textile field. After her return to Augsburg, she opened a boutique with her younger sister Klara.

My mother was not only a musician but also a mountain climber and a good skier. She tells me that there were no athletic clothes available for women, and she and her sisters had to make them. It sounds like they were ahead of their time.

After returning from Amsterdam, she joined the *Alpenverein*, an alpine society, which promoted hiking, climbing, and skiing. She also became a member of the *Wandervogel*. This was the youth music organization where my parents met, while attending workshops on singing, music courses, or lectures.

The *Wandervogel* was founded in 1901. The name means "migratory birds." It was formed in reaction to formality, superficiality, and mechanization of life. The organization also offered young people freedom from adult authority. Activities included camping, hiking, folk dancing, singing, reciting poetry, and staging plays. Music and song were the focus of the group. Several songbooks were published, and many of the songs are still sung today in Germany. My parents' friend Fritz Jöde founded the *Neudeutsche Musikergilde* (the New German Music Guild) in 1919. The purpose was to raise the level of the youth music. *Die Laute* was a publication of vocal and instrumental music. *Die Musikergilde* was a yearly publication with different contributors. My father's work appeared in both of these publications.

My parents were married in 1927 and lived in Ochsenfurth, where my father had his dental practice. My father's passion was music and not dentistry. While his patients were waiting with a toothache to be treated by him, my father played the violin in the back room and let them wait. Thankfully for those neglected patients, my father gave up his dental practice and studied music at the Würzburg Conservatory. Soon he was called to teach at the *Musikheim* in Frankfurt/Oder, which was a music academy founded by the Prussian Minister of Culture in 1929. Its mission was the formation of a community for the common practice of music and choral singing. It offered courses for the musically trained, as well as for teachers, ministers, and youth group leaders. In 1930 the *Musikheim* sponsored a conference for the "Awakening of Baroque Instruments (lutes and recorders) and Their Use in the Present Time."

My father was a musician, musicologist, and composer. Much of his work influenced musicology and music teaching in Germany. Music historians, musicians, and instrument builders worked together in the beginning of the twentieth century for the revival of the recorder and the lute. My father criticized the new mass production of recorders and occupied himself with the construction of an improved recorder. His design combined historical accuracy and technical advances and was patented in 1932. He cooperated with instrument builders, and the Merzdorf-König-Gofferje Recorder was created. His recorder method was published in 1932. My father was also involved in the revival of the lute. He had a reproduction of a Renaissance lute built from an original in a museum in München. I remember the sweet music he played on this instrument. I have his lute and took lessons for several years. He composed solo music for the lute and wrote accompaniments for various instruments to German folk songs and old hymns. Some of his compositions were recently played in a concert performed in the cloisters of a monastery close to Stuttgart, Germany.

After my parents moved to Frankfurt/Oder, their four children were born. My father was teaching and practicing music at the *Musikheim*, which evolved into a kind of musicians' colony. These must have been my parents' happiest years. I remember hearing stories and seeing pictures of parties and good times with singing, playing music, and performing theater.

My father in 1926.

Mother in 1925.

Mother in 1969.

Father playing his Renaissance lute.

Father tending his garden in 1961.

Playing recorder with Father.

DIE BLOCKFLÖTE

EINE ANWEISUNG

DIE BLOCKFLÖTE ZU SPIELEN

GEGEBEN VON

KARL GOFFERJE

ERSTER TEIL:

DIE GRUNDLEGUNG

1 9 3 2

GEORG KALLMEYER VERLAG   BÄRENREITER-VERLAG
WOLFENBÜTTEL-BERLIN   KASSEL-WILHELMSHÖHE

A Child Experiences War

✦

The Last Years of World War II in Frankfurt/ Oder

I was born on September 4, 1937, into a family of four: my father and mother, my older brother, Dieter, and my sister, Ute. My family lived in a penthouse apartment at Lindenstrasse in Frankfurt on the Oder River. I remember it as a spacious apartment with large rooms. There was my father's study with a balcony. It was a great privilege for us to sit quietly in my father's study while he was working at his desk. The shelves were filled with books containing illustrations, and we used them carefully as picture books. My favorite book was an illuminated book showing the troubadours of the Middle Ages. I also liked to sit under the desk, pretending it was a little hut. It must have been quite crowded next to my father's feet. I gather that he liked it because he never chased us out.

One night, when a thunderstorm was approaching, we watched it from the balcony. The swallows were circling around and lightning flashed in the distance. My father taught us to count until the thunder started and thus to determine how far away the storm was. He explained the lightning and thunder, and from that time on I was never afraid of a storm. Understanding the nature of things is the best cure for fear.

Adjoining my father's study was the music room. It was a large and airy room that contained walls of sheet music, a two-manual harpsichord, and a collection of other musical instruments. This room was also used for special occasions, when guests came, or on holidays.

At Christmastime the tree was set up in this room. We children were not allowed to enter the room while the tree was decorated. We never saw the tree before Christmas Eve. The day before we got to see the tree seemed like the longest day in the year. We could hardly wait until we were allowed to enter the room. When a bell rang in the early evening, the door opened, and we admired the tree ablaze with real candles. We were always so stunned by the tree that it took us a while to realize that there were presents for us under it. I remember that my mother had made a bride's outfit for one of my dolls one year. My doll was beautiful in all that lace. We had our dollhouses set up in the room. Since I was still younger, my dollhouse was a very simple wooden shell with primitive furniture but no fancy things. On the other hand, Ute had a "palace" for a dollhouse with "running" water and electric lights. A family of little mice lived in it. I remember that the "lady" of the house was called "Mausi." Her husband was a bunny and was called "Hasi."

The furniture in Ute's dollhouse was rather delicate, and I was not allowed to play with it. Of course, I played with Ute's house whenever I could get away with it. One day I caused a disaster, and my sister was very angry with me. I took all the delicate cups from the cupboards and somehow broke their handles off and floated them like little boats in a big puddle of water in the middle of the kitchen. This was the end of my playing with the house, even behind my sister's back.

My brother had his electric train, which was as much my father's toy as it was my brother's. The inhabitants of our dollhouses were small enough to get rides on the train. I also had a wooden truck, which I took to the kitchen for grocery shopping. My mother filled it up with little goodies like raisins, nuts, and cookies.

Unfortunately when we had to escape from the approaching Soviet army in 1945 at the end of the war, we had to leave all these wonderful things behind. This must be the reason that to this day I still like to play with dollhouses and electric trains with my granddaughter Kiera. Attached to the music room was our family room, which was a dining and living room in one. At the end of a long, dark corridor were the kitchen, the pantry, and a back entrance. The bedrooms and the bathroom were situated off this corridor.

We children used mainly the back entrance and stairs, which led to a brick courtyard where we spent many hours playing with other children. We played "catch" and "hide and seek" and jumped ropes. One of our favorite games was to spin a top for as long as we could and keep it going by hitting it with a string attached to a stick. If the ground on which the top spun was smooth, the top would spin for a long time. We often had competitions, and the kid whose top would spin the longest won. Another favorite activity was rolling a wooden hoop in front of us. We kept it rolling by hitting it at the right moment with a short stick. We became very skillful and managed to negotiate a path with obstacles like trees or people. And there were the usual ball games.

I remember feeling superior to the children with whom we played in the courtyard of our apartment building. We called them *Hofkinder*—children of the courtyard. I suspect that thinking ourselves to be better had something to do with the level of my parents' education. It was certainly not wealth that gave us this feeling.

My earliest memory was the birth of my sister Gisla, on April 20, 1940. A friend of the family took me to the clinic, where we found my mother cheerful in bed and a little baby in a crib. I was told that this was my little sister. I did not have much understanding of this information since I was only a little more than three years old. Evidently I did not remember my mother having been pregnant and had no idea about childbirth.

I stayed in the home of friends while my mother was in the clinic. They seemed much older to me than my parents. One of their two sons was the best friend of my brother, Dieter. At that time, both sons were gone from home. One of them served at the Russian front and was killed in action. These kind people tried to make me feel at home, but to no avail. I was hopelessly homesick and cried myself to sleep every night. They gave me a monster of a stuffed animal, a dog many times bigger than I, but he did not make me feel any better. Later there were several occasions when my parents left me with friends while they were vacationing or during the terminal illness of my brother. I remember being terribly homesick on every occasion and hating the idea of living in someone else's house. These feelings were so powerful that I still become homesick today.

I have hardly any memories of my brother, Dieter. I was told that he was a wonderful babysitter. I remember going to a railroad depot—one of our favorite hangouts—not far from our house. Dieter loved to watch the trains. He took me there along with Gisla, who was in a stroller, as she was still too young to walk. Standing on top of a steep embankment, we clung to a chicken wire fence with our faces pressed against it and watched the steam locomotives going back and forth. Whistles blew and engineers yelled; black smoke and steam were everywhere. It was heaven! We spent hours up there, or so it seemed. When we got home, our mother found us dirty, complete with the black imprint of the chicken wire fence on our faces. I am still fascinated by trains—real ones, model trains, and streetcars, anything that rides on rails.

I asked our family friend Dietlinde, who knew Dieter well, what she remembered about him. Ute and Dieter were planning to spend the end of their summer vacation in 1941 in the country at the parsonage in Obertopfstedt (Thuringia), where Dietlinde's father was minister. Both Ute and Dieter became sick at the end of the summer and could not make the trip to Obertopfstedt. Dietlinde wrote in 1996 about my brother:

Although Dieter was a year younger than I, he was very mature and intelligent. He was very critical of his father without being disrespectful. Your father was very cautious in the way he interacted with him and treated him like an adult. I wrote into my diary in June 1942 about Dieter's death, still very much in shock. I had been with him only one year before and we had been so happy and had gotten along so well. I am enclosing your mother's letters, but I don't have the date of his death.

I also asked Ute to tell me what she remembers about her brother, but she only told me that he paid no attention to her, that he had better things to do than to play with her. I have heard that Dieter was a very good student in school and my father taught him to play the violin. Dietlinde told me that when he practiced, he had to play in the kitchen far away from my father's study because he could not stand to listen to it. I don't know if this is true. I remember my father as a very patient teacher. When I was nine years old, he gave me violin lessons. My practicing must have also sounded horrible to him. I did not practice too often, since I wanted to be outside and play. When I did not know the music in the lessons, my father would tell me that I was playing *Stiefel* (it means "boot" in English but gets lost in translation), which was his way of telling us we were playing wrong notes and out of tune. An easy way out for me was to cry. If I had had a teacher other than my father, I would have been too embarrassed to cry and would have tried harder. I might even have learned to play the violin. When I was fifty years old, I decided to learn how to play my father's viola, which I had by then inherited. I still take lessons and enjoy playing in my amateur quartet, although I still do occasionally play *Stiefel*.

Dieter became very ill in 1942. He had both diphtheria and scarlet fever. He was then fourteen years old and had had a great growth spurt. His heart had not yet caught up with his size and was too weak to fight the disease. Scarlet fever is a streptococcus infection and could have been cured with antibiotics. Penicillin was brand-new but not available to the public. My brother could have lived with the right medication, but he died in June of 1942.

This is a letter from my mother to Dietlinde's parents:

Frankfurt/Oder, July 1942

Dear Mariele and dear Arthur,

Thank you from the bottom of my heart for your condolences. The sorrow for the loved one who passed away too soon is indescribable. I am again and again thinking of ways to find him. But there are only memories—a few things made by his skillful hands, his toys, and school things. What is the purpose of life?

Dieter is lying in a bed of flowers in the music room, where he spent his last days and where he died. We covered him with my bridal veil. At his head are branches of jasmine, delphiniums, peonies, and spirea; at his feet are roses and candles burning in our heirloom candlesticks.

On June 24 at 5 PM, friends came for a memorial service. A friend played one of Bach's Three-Part Inventions on the harpsichord. A young friend of Dieter, who knew him since 1929, spoke wonderful words. Afterwards we listened to the hymn "Herzlich tut mich verlangen" *[a Bach chorale]*. Thus we said good-bye to him here at the house. In the meantime grandmother Zierler's grave is closed again after having received the urn with his ashes.

The intellect knows that the end was inevitable because his heart gave up, but the loving heart is unable to understand. Mariele, you know how much he meant to me, how close we were. I am grateful for having been able to care for him for 26 days and nights, but all the motherly love in the world could not have kept him alive. He was such a blossoming, talented, and honest boy. Is it at all possible to understand why it had to end?

Our plans for the summer: We sent Ute to Nürnberg and Augsburg *[to stay with relatives]*. She will be back for the beginning of school. Around Aug. 6, Friedel *[my father's nickname]* wants to travel with me to Augsburg and München, and then for 3 weeks to Bad Ischl, Austria, to the home of his mother. Ute and Hadwig will stay here with friends. The Polish girl *[our maid]* will be on vacation for three weeks. I will take Gisla with us and leave her with my sister Irml in Augsburg where they don't know yet our youngest one. If it suits you, I could visit you with my two little ones in the fall. We send you our love, grief stricken and humbled.

With sorrow,
Edith

Here is a letter from my mother to Dietlinde. It describes the last and difficult days of my brother's life.

Frankfurt/Oder, July 1942

Dear Linde,

Your loving letter brought me your kind thoughts of our beloved Dieter. I thank you very much. You got to know him here still in his last healthy days. It has already been 14 days since he closed his eyes, and I still cannot believe it. He suffered very much in the last ten days. The end was forecast by restlessness, great agitation, and crying attacks. Unfortunately the morphine injections did not help, so that the poor boy had to experience the bitter end in full consciousness. He noticed how he lost his eyesight and he could hardly speak. And yet, it seems that he is only gone on vacation and would return. Thank you again, dear Linde. I hope you enjoy your vacations at home.

Your Aunt Edith.

Dieter in 1942.

In spite of all the people around me, I pretty much lived in my own world. I could occupy myself for hours on end with drawing, cutting papers, and playing with my dolls or with my imaginary playmates. I had wonderful conversations with these imaginary children. When an adult asked to whom I was talking, my answer was *meine Luftkinder*, my imaginary friends. I was not sure that they understood what I was talking about, but these *Luftkinder* were very real to me. From this phantom world of mine came a word that nobody understood. The word was *Kaffala*. I have no idea what I meant by it, but I remember being asked about it many times. My secret word is even secret to me.

In our living room was an antique cabinet with glass doors high enough so that I could see my reflection in it. Often, I danced in front of it and watched myself in my "mirror." When asked what I would like to be when I grow up, I answered *Seiltänzerin*, tightrope walker. Somehow I must have associated dancing with acrobatics. Having observed my antics, my father composed a dance for me as a birthday present. It was written for harpsichord, and my mother played it for me while I danced.

My parents had friends who had a large farm in Grossgandern, a village not far from Frankfurt. We loved to visit there. I remember playing outside in the gardens and making the messiest mud pies. My favorite place was the large cow stable. On a cold fall day, it was very warm and cozy inside. We watched the cows munching on hay and dared each other to go up close to the bull. Sometimes we sat on a low roof and watched all the activities of the farmyard, which was exciting for us kids from the city. In the house were comforts like big feather beds for cold nights, and the breakfasts were delicious. Everybody gathered around the large table. It must have already been wartime, since the food was very simple. We had a watery soup made from rye flour and bread, which the woman of the house sliced directly from large rustic loaves. She also nursed the smallest child while we ate. Everything, although simple, tasted so good and must have been very healthful too. Their oldest son, Theo, was a border with us later when he went to school in the city.

Occasionally, I was quite adventurous. In the mornings, my mother went grocery shopping or did errands. A house helper was usually around to keep an eye on us. Sometimes my mother would take me along, but one day she disappointed me and left me at home. I missed her intensely and decided to go out on my own and look for her. I secretly went down the back staircase and started walking toward the center of the city.

I had no idea where my mother went, but I was confident that I would find her. I remember walking on and on, and I began to get tired. I always thought that she would appear at the next intersection. As I was crossing the busiest bridge across the river Oder, a woman noticed me unaccompanied in heavy traffic. She talked to me and probably got some information from me as to where I lived and managed to get me home. My worried mother was upset at what I had done, but I thought that my deed was heroic. It was just unfortunate that my mother and I had missed each other on the streets. When it was mentioned that I had gone all the way to a bridge across the Oder, I was very proud of my feat and never really understood the danger of the situation.

There was a fairground on the way to the river, and once a year a circus set up its tents. The most exciting part about the circus performance was that one could view the animals in their cages during intermission. I loved the animals, but when I went to a circus as an adult, I felt sorry for those animals, which had lost their freedom and were forced to do tricks for the public.

When a fair was in town, I tried to take as many rides as possible. My favorite ride was a carousel with chairs suspended from chains, which were twirled around and around, and one could even add one's own movement like on a swing. If I could manage to get some coins, I would sneak down there all by myself. I was only six years old, and I headed straight to my favorite ride. I must have had a hard time getting up on the seats. Perhaps someone lifted me or I learned to pull myself up on the chains. I flew around and around, and it was simply heaven. The pleasure was not at all diminished when, without fail, I threw up as soon as I got off the ride. That was all part of the deal.

Since we lived close to the river, we could easily walk down to the riverbank. The river was often overflowing, and in the winter we could skate for long distances on the flooded meadows. In the summer we swam in an area specially designated for swimming. To go swimming was one of the highlights in my life, although I did not know yet how to swim.

At one time or another, we all caught the usual children's diseases such as chicken pox and whooping cough. When I was sick in my room and left alone, I played with my doll, Mieke. She had hair painted on her head, and I always wanted her to have real hair. With a pair of scissors I cut my own hair and put it on her head, but it would not stay in place. When my mother came to check on me, she was shocked and asked what I was doing. She did not understand how beautiful Mieke was with my hair. I was very hurt because she didn't appreciate my resourcefulness. Another time, I threw my throat lozenges out the window into the courtyard where the kids ate them for candy. They kept asking for more and eventually all my medications ended up in the courtyard. It must have made me very popular, unless somebody got sick from it, but I never found out.

Meanwhile the war was part of our life, and we endured many bombing raids by the Allied Forces on our city, mostly at night. One late evening toward the end of the war, the sirens signaled an imminent attack. We were usually given a warning, but this was the only siren signal before the bombs started to fall. My mother woke me from a feverish sleep. We children had been sick with the flu and were sleepy and groggy. We had to dress in a hurry and run into the basement. My mother was busy with dressing my younger sister and could not help me, and I never had a chance to get dressed. The bombs were falling all around us. Confused and in a panic with only an undershirt on, bare-bottomed and bare-foot, I ran downstairs, and instead of taking the stairs into the basement, I ran into the street. Nineteen forty-four was a particularly cold winter, and it was January. A red sky and "fireworks" surrounded me. I did not know where to run, and an adult must have caught up with me and brought me to the basement of our house. My poor mother was probably beside herself with anxiety.

Frightened, we waited patiently in our basement "room," which had been made livable as a bomb shelter. Boards over coal crates made makeshift beds. I don't remember how many nights we spent there, but this night we experienced a particularly vicious attack. When it was over, we ventured back upstairs, crept back into bed, and inspected the damage the next morning. All the windowpanes were shattered, but we were much luckier than our neighbors, whose houses had been hit. We walked around in the neighborhood the next day and saw a house cut in half, furniture hanging over the edge. Other places were burned out. This was the end of the war, and our city had never been hit to such an extent. Soon afterward we packed what we could carry and joined the refugees who were leaving the city in droves.

I was seven years old and did not understand that the Germans had started the war and had bombed other cities. Frankfurt was a site for air defense and therefore a target for bombing raids by the Allied Forces. Phosphor bombs were dropped and made the river burn for days. A bomb fell in front of our house but did not explode. Fortunately it was defused, but if it had exploded, we might all have been gone. As a child, one does not see beyond one's immediate suffering and fear. No child should ever have such experiences.

The winters of 1944 and 1945 were very cold. The flooded meadows on the banks of the Oder and the ponds were frozen. On a cold winter's night when I was almost asleep, my mother came to my room and asked me to come and look out of the window with her. The sky was clear and was glittering with stars. My mother showed me the *Milchstrasse* (Milky Way), but I could not understand why there should be milk in the sky. I remember what it looked like to this day but did not understand what the Milky Way was until many years later.

Ice skates materialized from somewhere, and my sister Ute took me skating. The skates were the kind that attached to the shoes and had to be fastened with a special key. I was not yet able to do this myself, but somebody was always helping me to get my skates on and off. I remember the exhilaration of gliding on the ice. The frozen meadows had valleys, and it was great to just slide down one side and come up on the other. I must have also fallen quite a bit, but I have no memories of falling or hurting. It was lots of fun.

One day when Ute and I came back from spending an afternoon skating on a pond, we walked home with our skates slung over our shoulders. We saw columns of people in rags, wandering in the street carrying a few belongings. These were refugees from the east where the Russian army had already invaded Germany. The refugees found shelter in the schools, since all schools were closed. The windows were pasted with newspapers to keep out the cold and for privacy. I was only seven years old then and did not really understand what was happening to these people, but I had a very uneasy feeling witnessing their misery. Ute told me that she helped these people to find shelter and get settled.

During a night in early January 1945, we heard footsteps in the attic over our penthouse apartment. My courageous mother went upstairs to see who was walking up and down over our heads. She found a young man hiding from the Nazis. It was so cold that had he not walked all night, he would have frozen to death. My mother brought him a blanket and some food but asked him to leave as soon as it was safe. When she told us this, we all knew that if we only breathed a word to anyone we could all end up in a concentration camp for hiding someone, even though he had found his way into our attic by himself. He was probably a deserter. The war was practically lost, and he was very young and wanted to save himself. Had he been found, he would most certainly have been shot.

Across from our apartment building was a large park. We often watched Hitler Youth rallies taking place there. On holidays, particularly on April 20, Hitler's birthday, we had to fly the swastika flag or we could be arrested. Gisla's birthday is on April 20, and naturally she believed that the flags were flying for her. The park across from us was converted to a Russian military cemetery as soon as the Red Army entered the city.

My father had a teaching position at the music academy in Lauenburg, Pommerania, and was not living with us in January 1945. When it was only a matter of time until the Russians arrived in Frankfurt, my mother decided it was time for us to leave, the sooner the better. We packed what we could carry. We children carried a backpack on our backs, our school satchel in front, and a piece of luggage in every hand. I was carrying a violin case, which was also packed with a lot of things besides a violin. We were so loaded that if the weight had not been evenly distributed back and front, a slight nudge would have made us fall over. We were allowed to take one favorite toy, and I decided to take a doll. My favorite doll, Mieke, I put to sleep in my bed, since she was the worse for wear. I told her we would be back soon. We never came back, and I missed Mieke very much.

We had a boarder at the time, and he helped my mother, my two sisters, and me to the train. It was January 30, 1945, and it must have been one of the last trains leaving the city. The train was filled to the brim with people trying to get out of Frankfurt before the Russians came. We had heard horror stories about the Russian army and feared for our lives. My sister Gisla and I were lifted through the window into a compartment. There was no other way for us to get into the train. I don't know how my mother and Ute got in and found Gisla and me. We rode the train all night, and all I remember is that it was very crowded, scary, cold, and uncomfortable. We were going to a small village in Thuringia where the minister and his wife were friends of my mother, and we hoped to stay with them until all this was over.

Hitler's total war meant suffering and tribulation for a lot of European people. This included the German population. If Hitler had not insisted on his *Endsieg* (final victory), a lot of misery could have been avoided and lives could have been spared. On October 21, 1944, the Red Army crossed the border into East Prussia. Two and one-half million Germans lived in East Prussia, almost two million Germans lived in East Pommerania, and almost five million Germans lived in Silesia. There would have been plenty of time for them to leave for safety, but "running away" was forbidden by the Nazis and preparations to flee were considered sabotage. Officials were asked to report anybody who was planning to leave. Nevertheless, wagons and horses were secretly prepared. The mayor of Insterburg, East Prussia, was given a secret order to have merchants and craftsmen send machinery and surplus on the trains to the west. Only the army—not the people—was allowed to use the trains. A request by the mayor of Insterburg to transport refugees by train was denied by Nazi officials. The only way out was by horse and wagon or by foot. The train stations were overrun by people waiting for trains to take them westward. They were mostly women and children. The men were at the front, and old men and young boys were forced to serve in the *Volkssturm,* a paramilitary group, which was supposed to hold German territory until the end.

Empty farms and fields and abandoned and lost animals wandering around were signs of a coming catastrophe. Contrary to orders, people were leaving everything behind and moving in treks slowly westward. The treks were in the way of army movements and military transports cut off the road, thus holding up the treks for hours, especially at river crossings. Some of these treks made it to Frankfurt/Oder, from where they moved on further west. The winter of 1944 was severe, and many children and old people froze to death. Eventually Russian tanks ran directly into the refugee treks. Unimaginable terror such as rapes, torture, murder, arson, and general chaos ensued. Many families got separated, and if they found each other again, it took years.

The last transport by train to safety across the Oder was on January 18; after that, it was only on foot. Many refugees were cut off and hoped to get out via the Baltic Sea. Ships were overcrowded, and not every ship made it to safety. An example was the ship "Wilhelm Gustloff," which was packed with refugees, mostly women and children. A Russian submarine sank it with three torpedoes on January 30, 1945. Nine thousand passengers died and twelve hundred survived. The tragedy was worse than the sinking of the Titanic. The commander of the Russian U-boat was celebrated as a national hero. Over two million Germans disappeared at the end of the war and twelve million were absorbed into postwar Germany, where they contributed to bring about the German *Wirtschaftswunder*, the miraculous economic recovery.

My family in 1941.
From left to right: Dieter, Mother with Gisla, Father, me, Ute.

Running from the Russians

✦

Settling as Refugees in Obertopfstedt

Considering the chaos and the panic, we were lucky to be able to leave Frankfurt in time and to find a train that would take us to relative safety. We came to Obertopfstedt for several reasons: We chose the countryside because there were no bombing raids, food was still available, and it was not too far away, since my mother always hoped that she could go back to the home we left. Otherwise she could have gone to her relatives in Bavaria. Some of our relatives had already lost everything. Bombs had hit their houses. Had we gone a little farther, we would not have been caught in what would later become the Soviet Occupied Zone and then East Germany. The war was not officially over until May 1945, and nobody knew what lay in the future for our country.

It was still dark when we arrived at our destination. Dietlinde came to the train station to greet us with a horse and buggy. We had arrived in Greussen, a small town in Thuringia. We could load either our luggage or ourselves into the buggy. There was not room enough for both, so we left the luggage stored at the train station. Squeezed into the carriage, we rattled toward Obertopfstedt, a village with no more than 200 native inhabitants and as many refugees. Dietlinde told me that I was traumatized by all the previous events and could not be talked to. I would turn away when addressed and did not talk to anyone for a long time. Gisla, who was only four years old at the time, seemed to take things in stride, but I remember her having nightmares. It became a nightly occurrence that she would wake up screaming and nobody could quiet her down. Nobody ever found out what her nightmares were about, but they must have eventually abated.

Prewar Obertopfstedt.

The parsonage, where we were to stay, was a large brick house that was already filled with the minister's family and refugees. Some refugees were relatives of the minister, some were people who were assigned to live there, and we were the last ones to arrive. We had one single room at first for the four of us—my mother, my two sisters, and me—but later we had two adjoining rooms. We used one room as a bedroom without heat and the other as a kitchen, living room, and dining room all in one. I had to sleep on the couch. There was no indoor plumbing, although the parsonage was the "fanciest" house in the village. It had a water pump in the downstairs kitchen and an indoor toilet, which was really an indoor privy on the first and second floor. This was luxury. The farmers had to carry their water from public water pumps in the village square and used privies, which were usually at the edge of the manure piles. It was a wonder that we had electricity.

The parsonage today.

With Gisla in 1946.

Water was available for the villagers from several iron pumps. The village center was a place for socializing, and the women came to fill their buckets, which some carried on a "yoke." The women stood next to their water buckets and gossiped. All the latest news could be heard here. We usually hung out in front of the *Schenke,* the village tavern. There was a pump in front of it and a wooden bin with salt in the entrance of the *Schenke.* We took handfuls of salt and dropped it secretly into the unsuspecting women's water buckets, intending to teach them not to gossip. It is a wonder that we never got caught.

The *Schenke* was also a general store and a bakery. In the back of the building was a large beehive oven, and bread was baked there once a week. The farmer's wives brought their casseroles and cakes to be baked. They carried their wares to be baked on large circular baking sheets, which they carried on their heads. The delicious smell of everything made us very hungry. We wished that some of those baked goodies were for us, but we did not have enough food to even think about baking.

The years in Obertopfstedt brought a lot of hardships, but as children we made the best of it. We managed to have some good times and even some fun. The most pressing problem was getting food. Money had lost its value, and food was bartered for luxury goods, which other people with food wanted. The farmers were the only ones who had plenty of food. Over time, they must have become almost wealthy exchanging food for jewelry, fine china, cameras, and other luxury articles. Since we had to leave most of our possessions behind, we had nothing to exchange for food.

My mother, who was a very accomplished seamstress, spent the days in the houses of the farmers sewing for them. In exchange for food, she mended and sewed clothes from their fabrics, which had been acquired through bartering. When there was a wedding in the village, my mother spent many days and nights sewing for the wedding party. I was sleeping in the same room where she worked, and when I awoke in the morning she was often still sitting at her sewing machine.

Meanwhile, we had no news of my father and did not know where he was. My mother must have somehow communicated with him and told him where he could find us after the war. One day, we received a message from my father that he was in the next village and was waiting for a safe time to come home. He was tired and hungry and looked terrible. He was very sick with pneumonia. Because there was no transportation in Germany at that time, he had walked more than one thousand miles from Lauenburg (on the Baltic Sea) to Obertopfstedt. He told us that he had a soldier as a companion and they walked mostly at night when the roads were free. A group of Czechoslovakians attacked them and forced them to take their clothes off. They gave my father a green forester's uniform, which was much too small for him since he was a tall man. He must have had many stories to tell, but understandably he did not talk much about his ordeal.

With my father home again, there was yet one more person in our tight quarters, and we were lucky to have gotten the room next to the one we occupied. He had been home for just a few days when the Americans politely asked my father to come with them to Greussen for a "conversation." He came back a few hours later. Someone in the village had denounced him. He had been a member of the Nazi party, but they could not find that he was guilty of any war crimes. On the contrary, he was a very idealistic man, and as a musicologist he had been working to revive the German folk songs and traditions, which was one of the Nazis' projects. He believed in the culture of his country.

Since the whole family was cramped into one room, Ute and I slept in a room in the farmer's house next door. I was seven years old and Ute was fifteen. Since all the schools were still closed, Ute was working at a farm where she was well fed, and we often got some food when we visited her. At the time of Germany's surrender, the American army occupied Thuringia, the "land," where we now lived. There were American soldiers in the village square who played with us children. Sometimes they gave us chewing gum or chocolate. This was the first time that I had seen chocolate. We did not speak English, and I don't know how we communicated, but the soldiers seemed to enjoy our company. The armistice had a provision that the Americans gave up some of their occupied territory in exchange for a section of Berlin. The Russians had conquered Berlin, and the Allied Forces wanted to share our capital. The Americans moved out from Thuringia, and we were sorry to see them go.

There was a rumor on one evening in July 1945 that the Russian army would move in. We were all terrified. We had heard terrible stories of the Russian army looting and raping even old women. It all came true. We played in the neighbor's yard on that evening, but in the back of our minds we were very uneasy and scared of the approaching Soviet army.

Eventually we went to sleep, but we were awoken during the night by havoc in the house. I awoke and saw two soldiers wrestling with my fifteen-year-old sister. When I tried to get out of my bed and go over to her to help her—I don't know what I could have done—one of the soldiers put a gun on my chest and I froze. I probably did not even understand that they were trying to rape my sister. She fought them heroically until a shot was heard downstairs. The soldiers left in a panic. While all this was going on, they had locked the old farmers in their room.

They stole what they could find and started to harass the women in the house. We found out the next day that this scenario had been repeated in many houses throughout the whole village and that a lot of women ran in their nightgowns into the fields to get away from the raping soldiers.

I don't remember ever having been as frightened as we were during that night. I couldn't understand why nobody came to help us. The Russians were armed and we were helpless civilians. What could anybody do? As soon as the soldiers left, we opened the windows and screamed, "Help, help!" as loud as we could. My parents were in the parsonage next door and heard us. They were safe since the Russians did not enter the parsonage. Later I found out that the men in the house next door, the minister and his brother, had armed themselves with sticks to come and help us. They asked my father to join them, but he told them that they were crazy and would get shot. They were appalled that my father did not want to help his daughters. In retrospect, he was right: What could three men with sticks do against soldiers with guns? They also had no idea how many soldiers there were. They would have surely gotten shot and possibly killed. From that night on, every time that I came across a Russian soldier, I felt afraid. After many years, in 1969, my husband and I entered the Soviet Union in Leningrad as part of an IEE (Institute of Electrical Engineers) delegation. Soviet soldiers entered the plane with machine guns after we landed, and all my memories and my fears came back. It was a very eerie feeling, and I had to use all my intellect not to lose control.

Sometime later, I came home from playing outside when Dietlinde took me aside and told me that the Russians had arrested my father. I was stunned and wondered if he would ever come back. They held him for four weeks in the prison of a nearby town. He used the time to read everything in the prison library and to learn Russian. He heard that someone in the village had denounced him as a member of the SA, which of course was not true. They let him go because they could not find him guilty of anything. He brought back a few books from the prison. When I later read these books, I found in them a big stamp saying "Gefängnis Nordhausen"—Prison of Nordhausen.

The Russian army entered our houses frequently and without warning. They looked in every cabinet and every corner and took anything they fancied, often not even knowing what they had taken. They were astonished to see the luxuries in the German cities. Where they came from, they had no electricity and no running water. We heard them say with wonder, "Licht aus Wand, Wasser aus Wand"—light from the wall and water from the wall. We also heard that they washed everything including potatoes in the toilet, since they had never seen such a thing. The Russians loved bicycles and stole many of them. When the bike had a flat tire, they merely stole another bike and left the one with the flat tire behind. Many people thus got their bicycles exchanged, and if they were lucky, they found a better one instead of the one that was taken from them.

As a precaution at the end of the war, we had buried any precious articles like silver, jewelry, and cameras. A great place for this was the dirt floor in the tower of the village church. Nobody ever found our "treasures," but the moisture damaged many things. When we dug them out several years later, we found mostly rusted items.

Any goods we had for barter were gone, and we had to find food somewhere. We could buy a few basics with ration cards at the general store in the village, but that was not enough to feed us. I remember being constantly hungry, and when we saw the farmer's kids eating large sandwiches, it made us not only hungrier but also very envious.

A plot of land behind the cemetery belonged to the church, and the minister divided it up between the parties in his house to grow vegetables. My parents were great gardeners, and the project was very successful. My father built a bench and a table in a shady corner. Sometimes he sat there in the evenings and relaxed after the hard gardening work. One summer night, I awoke from my sleep hearing some strange noises and scratches in the kitchen/living room where I slept. I called my parents, and my father came to explain to me that he had found a hedgehog while he was sitting in the garden and had brought it home. Since hedgehogs are nocturnal, this little fellow walked around the room, probably searching for food. He was about ten inches long with a little snout and was very cute. He looked just like the hedgehogs in Beatrix Potter's stories. The next day we got live worms for him and placed them on a saucer. We now had not only a hedgehog roaming around but also various worms crawling on the floor. When we thought the hedgehog needed some fresh air, we put him in a doll carriage and took him for rides. He lived with us for two or three days. Eventually my mother got tired of worms everywhere, and we took the hedgehog back to the garden where my father had found him. Every time thereafter when my father sat on his garden bench, the same hedgehog came out from where he lived and settled between my father's feet. He became his friend for the whole summer.

Rabbits were our only meat source. We collected weeds along the side of the road to feed our rabbits. Clover and dandelions were favorite rabbit food, and there were plenty of them. Gisla and I also had pet rabbits. Naturally we did not eat our pets. When one of the rabbit mothers died, we took her litter into the kitchen where the cute little rabbits lived in a cardboard box next to the warm stove. We fed them with a medicine dropper and, as far as I can remember, they all survived. Soon they jumped out of the box and ran and played all through the kitchen. We sat watching them and were very much amused by their performance every evening.

After the farmers of the village had brought in their harvest, we grazed the fields for leftovers. We collected ears of wheat, sugar beets, and potatoes. My mother had fitted us out with aprons, which had big pockets into which we collected what we found on the field. We hated this activity. It was usually very hot, and after a short time our backs ached from constantly bending over. We also understood that mother needed our help to feed the family, so we went grudgingly with her into the fields. We thrashed the wheat with sticks, blew out the chaff, and took the grain to a mill and received flour in return. Sometimes my mother ground the grain by hand in an old-fashioned coffee mill and made hearty cracked wheat rolls, which were delicious.

A lot of sugar beets were grown in our area, and we took our collected sugar beets to a sugar factory. We brought back the syrup, which had to be boiled down. We did this over a coal fire in a large copper kettle, which was usually used to boil the laundry. Everybody in the family took turns stirring since it had to be stirred constantly. The resulting syrup was our only source of sugar except for an occasional jar of honey. The minister kept bees, and we helped with turning the centrifuge when the honey was harvested. The minister parted with his honey only reluctantly. Unfortunately there were always casualties in the summer when we suffered bee stings. Once I got stung on my foot. It swelled so much that I could not fit my foot into any shoe and I had to walk barefoot for several days.

With our ration cards we got *Marmeladenpulver*, a brownish powder that when mixed with water should make jam. The stuff was fairly disgusting. Even though we could get berries, we had no sugar to make jam. The margarine we had was a yucky, yellowish mass. To this day, I never buy margarine. I buy only real butter, which together with cream was an unknown commodity then. We could occasionally get a pitcher of milk from a farmer. My mother sent me often to go and ask for it. I hated to do it, because for me it was a form of begging. Potatoes were our staple. Since there was no fat, we grated the potatoes, added an egg if we had one, and put the mass directly on the cooking stove to make potato pancakes. We called them *Hungerfladen*, "hunger cakes."

The only sweet we had was *Pflaumenmus*—prune butter. Prune trees were everywhere—they almost grew wild—and we collected prune plums in the fall. We pitted and cut the plums and boiled them down in the same copper kettle in which we had boiled the sugar beet syrup and the laundry. With a bit of sugar beet syrup added, it made a delicious spread, not unlike apple butter.

In the spring, when the farmers needed help in their fields, they hired kids from our school. The school often closed since we all preferred to work in the fields rather than go to school. We had good food while we worked and even made a few pennies for pocket money, but food was the more desirable reward.

Meanwhile our clothes and shoes would get worn out or we would outgrow them. There was no place where we could get clothes or shoes. Sometimes we received used clothing from the relief organization, Caritas, which the minister distributed. Since I was so tall for my age, I wore adult dresses, which sometimes were so low cut that my mother would have to attach some lace or fabric at the neckline in order for me to be proper. I was so young, however, that I did not have anything to show anyway. My mother was also very resourceful in lengthening dresses with whatever fabric she had. My schoolmates always made fun of my "two-tone" dresses. In the winter, we wore Dutch wooden clogs for shoes. Our socks were long gone, and all the mending in the world could not save them. We wrapped our feet in rags and stuck foot and rags into the clogs. At home or in school, we left the clogs at the door. All the children's clogs were neatly lined up in the hallway of the school. Once I got a pair of penny loafers from Caritas. They were my pride and joy, and everyone was envious of my beautiful shoes, the only pair I owned. We also received from war surplus long gray-green soldiers' coats and parachute silk. My mother made lovely blouses from the silk and everything else from the soldiers' coats. She even made shoes from the heavy fabric. They were beautifully stitched onto felt soles. My doll Mieke II still has her little shoes made by my mother from the same material.

We had no toilet paper and no candles. The few "candles" available in stores looked like a wick stuck into shoe polish. We had many blackouts after the war, and candles were precious items. I don't know where my father found old train schedules, which were printed on very strong but thin paper. This made the best toilet paper, and I remember my father sitting for hours and cutting the pages precisely with a knife and just about large enough for what they were intended. Matches were also in short supply. We had a constant fire going in our coal stove, which we used for heat and for cooking. My father called a thin, tightly rolled piece of paper "Fidibus," and he used it to light candles, his pipe, or a homemade cigar from the fire in the stove.

All our hardships did not keep us children from having fun. When it snowed in the winter and we didn't have sleds, we improvised. We went to the village dump and picked out pots or pans that were large enough to sit in and to slide down a hill in the village. I had found an oblong roasting pan, and with an old sack for cushioning, it made the best "sled," although it was a little difficult to steer. We fell often, particularly when the hill became all ice, but our young bodies did not mind. There was always a group of adult spectators at the bottom of the hill. We must have been a very amusing sight, since I remember much laughter.

Gardens, orchards, and fields surrounded the parsonage where we lived, and we loved to play outside in the summer. When it got dark, the excitement grew, and we dreaded the time when our parents called us inside. We all had rabbits, and the minister had goats for milk and also some chickens. Gisla and I together with the minister's sons often made mischief. We soaked some pieces of bread in wine and fed it to the chickens. To our amusement, the poor chickens got drunk and staggered around. I don't remember if any adults saw what we were doing, but we did not get reprimanded. Fortunately the chickens survived.

The parish in Obertopfstedt did not have a sexton. Some of the duties such as ringing the bells and winding and setting the church clock in the tower were performed by the sons of the minister, and we often tagged along to help or just for company. Our favorite activity was ringing the bells for holidays, weddings, or funerals. We rang the bells by pulling on heavy ropes. We held on to the ropes, letting the bell pull us up. If at the same time we swung back and forth, it was just as much fun as, if not more fun than, a regular swing. We had become so skilled that it did not interfere with the sound of the bell. The clock in the tower had a square opening on the face. One could see the whole village and surroundings on this side of the tower. The cemetery was in that direction, and one of us had to watch the funeral procession and tell the others when it arrived at the gravesite, so that we could stop the ringing and let the funeral service proceed. I am sure we were not always accurate, and the minister ended up standing at the grave site waiting for the bell to stop ringing before he could finally start speaking.

There was another, older cemetery near the church with old graves. One day we found one of the graves collapsed, leaving a gaping hole. We challenged each other to climb into it, but we found nothing but a couple of snails on the bottom. While we each took turns climbing into the empty grave, we heard some terrible noise, like knocking on the door of the church tower. This frightened us so much that we ran and flew over the cemetery wall. We never played near this particular grave again.

There was no refrigeration in the village, and root vegetables were stored in a *Miete*—a kind of root cellar. Pits were dug deep enough to be below the frost line, and vegetables like potatoes, carrots, and turnips were placed into them and covered with straw and then with soil. In the spring when the vegetables had been dug up for consumption, an empty pit remained. There was an area of such empty pits right next to the parsonage. We used the pits as dugouts for playing war. We had all been living through the war, and now we enacted it in a less dangerous fashion. A feud had been going on for a long time between the upper and lower village. Nobody knew exactly what the feud was about, and it was probably between the adults, but we youngsters used it to find a reason for our war. The field of empty pits became a battlefield. The ammunitions were mud balls on a stick, which we flung at our enemies in the next dugout. When we took over their dugout, we ran to it with lots of howling and war noises. It was the girls' job to form the mud balls from the heavy clay, which was everywhere. Our war went on for weeks, and I don't know if any party actually was victorious. It did not really matter; it was more important that these games occupied us for a long time, and we enjoyed all the excitement. We must have come home from our "battles" covered with mud, which annoyed our parents but did not diminish our fun.

The minister's sons had gotten hold of some tobacco and cigarette paper. They asked me if I was interested to come and smoke with them. I was game, of course, and we sat on the banks of the village creek and felt very adult while we smoked our rolled cigarettes. Afterward we thought it would be a good idea to go to the water pump and thoroughly rinse our mouths, so that we would not get caught. I think the adults were too preoccupied with our survival at the time and never found out that we had our first smoke. Tobacco was very scarce, and most people grew their own tobacco. We had to help our father to harvest it and string it on wire to dry, which was a very messy affair. Our fingers were stained for days. I don't know how he processed the tobacco after that, but he used it as pipe tobacco and made his own cigars. The American GIs often gave us cigarette paper, and since we had no tobacco, we rolled "cigarettes" with crumbled chestnut leaves. It makes for a fairly disgusting smoke, and it is a wonder we did not poison ourselves.

After our father had returned from Lauenburg and lived with us again, he was looking for work. Since he was a musician and musicologist, his services were not in demand when everyone was occupied with their survival. Fortunately, he was unusually skilled and handy. In the past, he had worked with his instrument builder friends. Now, he found that he could use his skills by repairing the farmers' pots and pans in exchange for food. The neighboring villages were all part of the same parish, and some of the village churches had beautiful old organs, which had not been taken care of for years. My father was commissioned to repair these old organs. Most of the work had to be done on location, and we went frequently with him and assisted him in working the bellows. We often did this also for the organist in church services. The bellows were manual; we stood on two steps and pushed one down with our weight while the other step rose. This had to be done very smoothly for the sound of the organ to be even. Sometimes we gave each other rides. One of us worked the bellows while another kid was sitting right in the organ on top of the bellows, going up and down with them. Some of the wooden organ pipes ended up in our place and made our two rooms even more crowded.

Occasionally, I went with my father as he walked around the fields and along the brook. He often sketched or photographed. I still have some of his sketches. He colored in the photographs with special pencils, after which they almost looked like color photographs.

My father's sketch of the Wartburg.

My father taught violin to private students and participated in an orchestra in Greussen. I remember a performance of Bach's Christmas Oratorio in a church. My father was the first violinist and concertmaster. The church was unheated, and I remember him sitting in the front row dressed in a surplus military great-coat. His wool gloves had the fingers cut off. It was a memorable evening, and the cold did not take away from the experience. This oratorio is still my favorite Christmas music. Christmas without Bach is no Christmas for me. I heard a lot of Bach's music in my youth. It is part of my childhood.

Christmas 1945 was unforgettable for most Germans. We were hungry and cold; some of us had lost everything either from having been bombed or, like us, from having to flee while leaving everything behind. The future of our country was very uncertain.

We did not have a Christmas tree, only pine branches decorated with paper stars, which Ute had made. There were not many presents except for what we had made ourselves. But there was a great surprise for Gisla and me. My father had made dollhouse furniture, enough to fill a whole little house, which we borrowed from Dietlinde, who was much older and did not play with her dollhouse anymore. He worked mostly at night when we were asleep. However, I remember my father working with wood and a little coping saw, but I had no idea what he was doing. My mother made little cushions, tablecloths, and any "upholstery." I will never forget the surprise we had, and I loved the beautiful things under our makeshift tree.

When my parents escaped from East to West Germany in 1961, the dollhouse furniture made it across the border. Later it was shipped all the way to Boston. When my own children were five and two years old, we built a house for the furniture. I painted the furniture, which had never been painted since we did not have paint after the war, and I made new curtains and cushions; a family of small bears settled in it when it was ready. My kids loved to play with it. Now, as I write this, the dollhouse is next to me; it has many more things in it, and it delights Kiera, my granddaughter, when she visits me. Sometimes I still play with it a little bit myself. Meanwhile the tenants have changed. There is still a family of animals: Mama Bear with a big hat, Papa Bear who always loses his hat, a little mouse called Stuart Little, and Bobby Bear. The dollhouse gets packed away when the weather gets warmer but comes out every Christmas when it seems brand-new again.

I must have talked a lot about my favorite doll, Mieke, who was left in my bed in Frankfurt/Oder because I hoped to go back for her. I missed her very much, and my mother told me that perhaps some day she would come to me. I was almost nine years old when I received a letter from her. In it, she told me that she would join me again soon and that she had missed me too. On the morning of my ninth birthday, I woke up and on the floor next to the couch, on which I usually slept, was a doll's bed, and in it was Mieke. She was adorable, all new with real hair, and she had a wreath of real flowers in her hair. I was so happy to have her back, not minding at all that she was a new doll and did not look beaten up like my old one. I carried her around in my arms all day, and a photo shows how happy we both were. She slept in my bed next to me every night, but so did our cat. When I was not watching, the cat clawed her legs and arms. I suppose it was jealousy that made her do it. This did not diminish my love for the doll. As dilapidated as she became over the years, she got married, even gave "birth" to children, and had a busy life. Just like the dollhouse furniture, she eventually joined me in Boston. Here she sat for years in the closet of my study. Meanwhile she became fifty-seven years old and looked it. She had not aged well. When I realized that Kiera was interested in my doll, I let her play with her. Kiera and Mieke fell instantly in love. Now she was carried around in public in Kiera's outgrown stroller. She almost lost one of her legs, and I taped up her leg and arms until she looked like an invalid.

I heard from friends that famous Käthe Kruse dolls like Mieke can be repaired. I sent her to the doll hospital in Donauwoerth, Germany, and after four months and a lot of money, she came back looking like new. She had new arms and legs and a new wig (of real hair), and her neck was not wobbly anymore. In spite of her blonder hair and a little makeup on her face, she had not lost her personality. Now she needs a new wardrobe, since she had a somewhat middle-aged spread. Kiera got another doll from me for Christmas. She always wanted one like Mieke with real hair. Mieke now has a new playmate, Kirsten, who came from Sweden (not really; she is an "American Girl" doll). They have matching beds and chairs and have tea together every time they visit with each other, and they even have matching dresses.

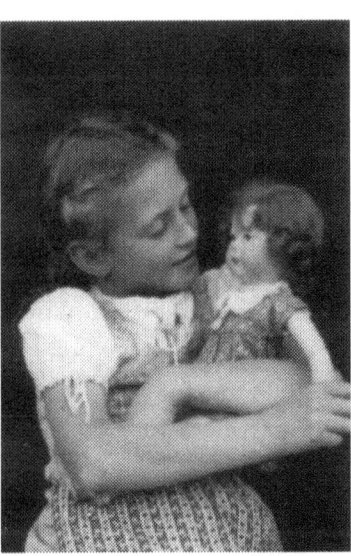

With Mieke in 1947.

When I was not drawing, writing stories about animals, or writing songs and poems, I read books. We had no books, and there was no young people's literature to read. The minister's family had a bookcase full of volumes of classic German literature. Since this was the only reading material available, I read almost all of them over the years. Thus I read the whole works of Gottfried Keller, Wilhelm Hauff, Uhland, Goethe, Schiller, and others. I was much too young for this literature and I don't know what I actually got out of it, but I enjoyed reading it. I am still a voracious reader and never throw out a book.

In 1946 one could still cross the border illegally into West Germany. All my mother's relatives and friends were in the West, mostly in Bavaria. We were all terribly undernourished, Gisla especially, and my mother decided to go across the border with her and leave her at a former classmate's large farm where they had plenty of food. People who lived next to the border separating the Russian zone from the Allied zone took whoever was willing to pay across the border at night. My mother and Gisla made it safely to the West. Mother was given lots of foods we had never seen since the war. She packed it in a large backpack, left Gisla with her friend, and made her way across to the East again. She did not come back when we expected her back. We got very worried, but about three days later she appeared. The Russians had caught her on the border and kept her for three days in their barracks where she had to clean their quarters, after which they let her go. She had fish in her backpack, which began to smell badly so that she had to throw it out, but she brought back blood oranges, dried bananas, chocolates, and other good things. These were the first oranges and bananas we children had ever seen. Naturally all of it was delicious and it was gone very fast. It was a miracle that the Russians did not take away the food.

In about a year after the end of the war, my mother applied for a traveling permit and was issued one by the mayor of Obertopfstedt to return to Frankfurt and see if any of our possessions were left. She took my sister Ute along who recalls the following: The door handle to our apartment was ripped out, and the windows and doors as well as all electrical wires were gone. Nothing was left intact. The floor was covered with inches of rubble. My mother visited a tenant two floors below from where we had lived and found a tailor living there using her sewing machine. He told them that toward the very last days of the war the whole city was plundered and ransacked by Poles. The strings were cut out from our beautiful two-manual harpsichord. The wood of the instrument was used for firewood. An antique secretary from my mother's family could not be unlocked and was thrown out of the window. My father's books, sheet music, and any instruments ended up thrown into Lindenstrasse. Some of my father's friends managed to save the most important musical instruments and either gave them to the conservatory or took them to a monastery in Mühlrose, a town south of Frankfurt. There they were stored in a room the door of which was closed with brick and mortar, and thus the instruments survived. When they were later recovered, they had fallen apart and had to be completely restored. I now own some of these instruments.

One would have expected that the Russian army had done all the damage, but instead it was the Poles, who had been brought into Germany for work. They were taken by the Nazis from the streets in Poland and transported to Germany, where they lived in camps and worked in factories or wherever they were needed. Now the time had come for them to take revenge on the German people. They set the inner city on fire and destroyed everything in their path. In 1946 when the rivers Oder and Neisse became the border between Germany and Poland, part of the city became Polish. Inadvertently, the marauding Poles destroyed even what later became their own territory.

I remember our Polish maid who was assigned to us by the labor ministry when my mother was looking for help. I am sure that my mother treated her decently, but we found that she stole food. She was caught drinking the milk, which was rationed for us little children. She must have been hungry, but nobody had enough food to eat at the end of the war. I have also heard about the Poles having destroyed and burned towns in their own country before the Russians came. They hated the Russians and did not want to leave anything behind for them. I also heard stories of German refugees leaving their land and taking their Polish laborers with them when they fled to the west. They were only too glad to go west with the German refugees. The Poles may have hated the Germans, but they definitely feared the Russians.

My mother's brother was a professor of theology at the university in Erlangen, West Germany. One evening he came home from the university and parked his car in front of his house. A car driven by a drunk American GI struck and dragged him. He was instantly killed. My mother requested permission to go to his funeral. We could not travel freely and especially not across the border into West Germany without such permission. Permission was not granted with the excuse that she was not closely enough related to her brother. This was the usual arbitrary treatment we always got from the Communist authorities.

My father was teacher and later director at the conservatory in Sondershausen, a town nearby. He lived there in rented rooms and was looking for an apartment for us. He never managed to get a place so that we could all be together again. Occasionally I took the train and visited him there. He usually gave me a violin lesson, or I played around on his piano. Sometimes he took me to a concert, which was always a treat. I remember a very talented, young violinist who played beautifully. The E-string on his violin broke in the middle of the concert, but he kept on playing, using the upper positions on the next lower string. I was so impressed. He was an amazing virtuoso and would have had a very successful career, but nobody ever heard about him again soon after that concert. It was said that there was a problem with an embezzled Stradivarius violin.

The schools were eventually reopened. Gisla and I went to the village school in a one-room schoolhouse. Grades 1 through 4 were taught in the morning, and grades 5 through 8 in the afternoons. There was only one teacher. I was not her favorite pupil since I often pointed out mathematical mistakes that she had made on the blackboard. Most children in this school were farmers' children, and after having finished eighth grade (or eight years, whichever came first), they went to work on the farm or entered an apprenticeship. I graduated from the little village school after eighth grade and went on to high school in the next bigger town, Greussen. There were only four of us from Obertopfstedt: the minister's son, two sons of refugees in the village, and myself. We lived a long way from the school. We mostly walked or took our bicycles if the weather was good. Sometimes we met the milk truck and got a ride sitting on top of the milk cans. It was not very comfortable, but it was a lot faster than walking three kilometers on a dirt road.

I liked the new school. It was a lot more challenging than the village school where we had only one teacher for all the subjects. We now had different teachers for various subjects, but very often we had teachers who were not qualified to teach. There was a shortage of teachers, particularly for the new subjects like Russian and social studies, and the latter was actually Communist indoctrination. We had a good math teacher and a good biology teacher, and one of our better teachers was our German teacher. She was not my favorite teacher since she always criticized my essays. I never wrote enough and never used elaborate language. What I wrote was always short and to the point, which does not make an interesting essay. When we had technical papers to write, like for instance in chemistry, the chemistry teacher read my papers to the class as an example of organization and logical thinking. It was clear that I would become a scientist and not a writer.

Our first Russian teacher was a kindly Russian lady who had immigrated to Germany after the October Revolution. Her father was a jeweler and therefore bourgeois and undesirable. We did not learn very much from her. We always asked her to tell us stories about her life and about "Mother Russia." She always obliged very gladly. We listened with great interest about her life in a country we did not know but heard so much about. Later, we had a retired Russian soldier as our teacher. He came to school in his military tunic under which he never wore a shirt, at least not as far as we could tell. We called him "Ivan," of course. His teaching method was very boring, and since we were forced to learn Russian, we learned nothing. We learned the Communist songs phonetically by heart and never knew what they actually meant in German. I still know some of these songs today. Some teachers were Communists. Others did not care about politics. Our young social studies teacher was an agitator. He kept us in class one day and wanted all of us to become members of the Communist youth organization "Freie Deutsche Jugend" (FDJ). Nobody was interested, but he would not let us go until we all "decided." Nobody dared to refuse for fear of mistreatment and no more good grades. We eventually became members, all together, involuntarily.

Socialist ideas cannot be taught with math, physics, chemistry, or biology, and we got a very good education in the sciences. However, in German literature and history, we got a very heavy dose of Socialist indoctrination. We knew about the lives of Karl Marx, Friedrich Engels, Lenin, and Stalin in great detail. Every book we had read or every historical event we discussed was considered socialistically, which meant we had to apply "socialist dialectic" as used by Marx and Engels. We used Communistic slogans and phrases wherever we could fit them in, hoping they would get us better grades. We had become quite good in mouthing those slogans without really knowing what they meant or even caring what they meant. This was presumably what our teachers wanted to hear, but we were never sure whether it meant more to the teachers than to us, or if they were just playing the game as we did. It was basically a matter of survival, just like our membership in the Communist youth organization was just an act of survival. We also had a few token Communists in our class. Their parents had been Socialists and the kids carried on the family tradition. Some of the earlier Socialists were often disenchanted with the Communist state and would become dissidents, who were later persecuted by the Stasi, the secret police of the German Democratic Republic. The rest of us tried to keep as low a profile as possible. In the evenings, we listened with our parents to the BBC on our radios. Even when the broadcasts were jammed, we learned how to get important information from amongst the noises.

We read many Russian Socialist authors in German class, but the German classics could not be ignored and were taught also. We did not get to read any Western contemporary literature. Not only were those works not available in East Germany, but they were also forbidden to be read. If anybody was lucky enough to get hold of a Western book, it was handed around and we all read it with relish. This is what happened for example with Pasternak's *Dr. Shivago*.

We also had classes in current affairs. Communism was praised and we were told that it was the only way to peace, since capitalism always leads to war. We learned that the capitalist economy was always in crisis, but we also knew that our Communist economy was barely surviving. The Russians had dismantled entire German factories after the war and shipped them to the Soviet Union. Consumer goods were the last priority in our economy. Because most of the industry had to be built up again, we were forced to take up professions that were necessary for the Socialist economy, like engineers of all kinds and teachers. We had no choice in picking a career.

Every first of May was a great event for the Communists, and we had to parade to show the world that we were all happy Communists and worked for world peace. We met at our high school and marched from there with flags of the FDJ to a city square, which could hold all the demonstrators from the various schools, factories, and offices. My mother had to march with the colleagues from her workplace. We had to listen to endless propaganda speeches and soon got very tired of it. Slowly we disappeared through the crowds and went home again. Unfortunately the functionaries from our school found out what we were doing, and in the future we had to reassemble at our school again after the demonstration so that every student could be counted.

We had a class reunion in the mid-nineties in Dresden. The reunion almost failed because some classmates wanted to invite the Communists, and others wanted to boycott the meeting if the Communists attended. Finally it was only a small group of friends from my class who met in Dresden. I was the only attendee from outside Germany. I was part of the class only for ninth and tenth grade, after which I moved to Erfurt. I was surprised to hear that after I had left the school, the Communist pressure increased on my classmates. I got the impression from the discussions that the more the Communists became entrenched, the more oppressive the system became.

Playing "wedding" in 1949.

Me in 1949.

Gisla, Ute, and me in 1949.

Reverse Discrimination

✦

Why I Decided to Go to West Germany

I wrote into my journal in May 1952 that I wanted very badly for us to move to Erfurt. I was so tired of life in the miserable village of Obertopfstedt. I missed the companionship of young people of similar social background. My sister Ute was already living in Erfurt and had an office job in the Finance Ministry. I was beside myself with joy when I heard that my mother had found an apartment for us.

In the summer of 1952 we moved from Obertopfstedt to Erfurt. My mother had taken refresher courses in typing and shorthand and had found a job as a secretary with the Ministry of Culture. She knew much of cultural matters, was good at her job, and soon got promoted to administrative assistant.

We moved into an interesting penthouse apartment, which used to be an architect's office, but it was perfectly comfortable and sufficient for us. It was exciting to live in a city again. Erfurt is a beautiful city, famous for its yearly garden shows. It has beautiful old houses, an old university where Martin Luther studied, and a cathedral with bells famous throughout Germany for their sound. The largest and most famous bell, "Gloriosa," is rung only on holidays like Christmas, Easter, and New Year's Eve.

My mother loved her job in the ministry. She met many interesting people on her job, like actors, writers, and artists. One of the benefits was that she got free tickets for the theater in Erfurt and for the National Theater in Weimar, which was not far away. I loved going with her to theater and opera performances. My classmates and I also went often to the *Stadttheater* (city theater) in Erfurt, and we knew all the resident actors. After school we often waited outside the theater, which was close to the school, and tried to get a glimpse of our favorite actors, on which we usually had crushes. I developed my love for the theater in those high school years.

Erfurt had two public high schools. One of them was very prestigious but only for boys. I was determined to go to this school as the only girl and I applied. Of course, I was refused admission and was told to enroll in the girls' school. I had no choice but to go to the girls' school, and I was furious. I was only ahead of my time. The classes in the all-girls school were mixed one year after I entered the school at grade 10. There were no totally coeducational schools in Erfurt when we moved there. I attended the "Königin Luise" school from 1952 to 1954. There were two tenth-grade classes in the school. I did not like my class, because my classmates were either Communists, very religious, or strange. All the popular girls were in the other class. However, two girls in my class, "Schimmel" and "Ottilie," became my closest friends. The three of us were constantly together, and we are still in touch with each other as I write this.

The Erfurt Cathedral, built 1554–1707.

A distant Gofferjè uncle and aunt lived in Erfurt. They had introduced me to a girl of my age who lived next door to them. Her name was Helga, and when we were both seven, we became best friends while we were still living in Obertopfstedt. We would see each other whenever I visited my relatives, or she would come and visit me. Later when we had moved to Erfurt, we lived not far from each other. Helga went to my school but was in the parallel class. I had hoped that then we could be really good friends, but she already had her own group of friends and we did not get together as often as I had hoped. I was very disappointed. Many years later when I was a student at the University of Tübingen, we ran into each other in Stuttgart, waiting for the streetcar. Later she joined me in Tübingen, and we became very close again and even shared boyfriends (but not simultaneously). When I went to Germany during Christmas in 1996, I found Helga again through a common friend. We could not meet then but had a long telephone conversation. More than 30 years had passed since we had seen each other. She told me that I had always been such a "*Power Frau.*" I had no idea that my contemporaries thought of me that way.

While in tenth grade we took dancing classes in the local dancing school. We had dancing lessons one night a week, and every Sunday afternoon we could go there and practice dancing. Usually I went with my friends. I was not one of the popular girls, and the boys whom I liked were not interested in me. The dancing teacher told me that I was dancing very well. But still the "cute" guys did not ask me to dance. Many of them were tall enough not to feel intimidated by my height. Ute told me that I was not approachable, but in reality I was really shy. There was one guy with a cleft palate. He was a great dancer and asked me to go with him to the final ball, but I declined. I wanted a good-looking guy as well as a good dancer. Thus I stayed home, which was not all that bad since I did not have a special dress like all the other girls. I actually met a boy one day at one of our dancing sessions. He invited me to go to the movies with him. We had a good time, but my mother made such a fuss about nothing that I got very upset. I felt that she did not trust me, and from then on I did not bother to go out with anybody. There was still time for that later.

I was participating a good deal in sports like swimming and track and field. I was never a good runner, but I was good at jumping and at shot put. We often traveled with teams from the school to sports meets. We always had a lot of fun, regardless of whether we won or not. At a swimming competition in school, I came in third among all the upper classes. Later, I joined an independent swim club in Erfurt, where I could excel whether I was popular or not. I swam a very good time at the first practice session and went once a week to the pool to train.

After some time, I complained about a chronic sinus infection. I could barely breathe through my nose, and the doctors could not help me. Spending so much time in the pool made it worse, and eventually I had to give up swimming. It was only years afterward that I discovered that I was allergic to the chlorine in the pools.

Occasionally my classmates and I organized hiking or biking trips. We usually took the train to an area that we wanted to explore and then walked or biked through beautiful landscapes and stayed at youth hostels. We also went often to the theater, where Ottilie, Schimmel, and I saw *Tosca*, *Madame Butterfly*, and *La Boheme*, which I loved. Verdi's and Puccini's operas became my favorites.

During summer vacation I took a job in a factory. I worked the early shift from 6 AM to 3 PM. The first day I only watched and was bored to tears. The factory was making radio tubes, and we were threading ceramic insulators into the filaments. One had to have extremely good eyesight for this, but it was very mindless work. The foreman in my shift did not like me and picked on me constantly. This made the job even less endurable. I was asked to replace my friend who worked the night shift, and I liked it so much better. From then on, I switched to the late shift for good and had a different foreman. Then I was almost having fun. Working at this factory made me realize that I would never want to make a living in this way and that a good education is very important. I started to really concentrate on my schoolwork and was angry with myself about every "B" I got, which could have been an "A."

Another summer I worked as a camp counselor. It was actually a volunteer job. The Communist regime expected the young people to work during summer vacations, either on a farm, in a camp, or in a factory. The pay was minimal if there was any at all. I liked being a counselor. The kids whom I supervised were boys and girls about eight or nine years old. We swam, played games, and participated in sports events. We had a lot of fun, and it was a nice change to be in the countryside. In the evenings, we socialized with the other counselors and our "superiors," among which there were some very interesting people.

The windows of our apartment in Erfurt looked into the courtyard of the headquarters of the "People's Police." On June 16, 1953, we noticed great unrest in and outside the headquarters, but we had no idea what was happening all over East Germany. Eventually the newspapers reported that a popular revolt had broken out. We were required to stay home during the next two days and did not witness any of the important events. Our only sources of information were newspapers and the radio, both of which were censored, but we had learned to read between the lines.

After Stalin's death in March of 1953, we hoped that there would be a relaxation of the conditions in East Germany and the Eastern Block countries. When the work quotas in the factories were increased, an uprising of factory workers started to spread spontaneously throughout East Germany. On June 16, five thousand workers marched to the Alexander Platz in Berlin. The number rose to seventeen thousand the next day, and workers in Magdeburg, Rostock, Dresden, Görlitz, Halle, Leipzig, and other cities joined the general strike. Work also stopped at the Olympia works (manufacturer of business machines) in Erfurt. The demonstrators removed Communist flags, set buildings and prisons on fire, and destroyed Communist party offices. The East German government declared a state of emergency, and in the afternoon of June 17, East German and Soviet armies fired into the crowds and arrested six thousand people. On the evening of June 17, the uprising was crushed, which would not have been possible without the intervention of Soviet troops and their tanks. President Walter Ulbricht used the revolt to eliminate all opposing forces to his regime in the future. Life in East Germany was "back to normal," which meant oppression not only continued but also intensified.

I graduated from high school in June 1954. I had been so looking forward to this point in my life, but now I was almost sad that the time in school was over. I did not have a great social life in Erfurt, but I grew to like the school and my friends. I wanted to go on to a university in order to study chemistry. I applied at the university in Jena but was rejected because I was "politically undesirable." The Communist regime of East Germany wanted to educate only the "proletariat," the farmers and factory workers. My father was a music professor, which made me ineligible for a college education, no matter how good my grades were. I was crushed by the rejection but decided to work for a year and then try again.

My father had become director of the conservatory in Sondershausen. He was not a member of the Communist party, and the leading positions were usually given to party members only. When the pressure on him to join the party increased and he refused, he lost his job. In 1953 he found work as the director of the library in a research facility of the Academy of Sciences in Gatersleben, near Halle. My mother worked with him there, and we finally had an opportunity to all live together again.

The good news was that the institute gave us a new house with a garden, which was a great luxury for us. The bad news was that the institute was in a remote village in the middle of nowhere. The institute was a community of scientists and support staff and did not have much to do with the village. The region was mostly agrarian, growing sugar beets and producing sugar in the local factory.

Soon after I graduated, we moved to Gatersleben, which was not what I had in mind when I felt my independent life was just starting. We never stayed in one place long enough to put down roots or to have a place where we belonged. This had always bothered me, and my frustration was caused by our having been refugees in 1945. I wanted a stable family, the same friends, and a place to call home. We were not so lucky. These constant moves are perhaps the reason why I became so settled later in life.

Our tomcat "Tiger" did not want to move either. We had all our things packed and the moving truck was about to leave, but Tiger was nowhere to be found. We called him and looked for him and waited some time, but he did not show up. We finally gave up and told our neighbors, who had a big German shepherd and loved animals, to forward Tiger when he came back. We almost forgot about the cat for the next few days. We were busy getting settled in Gatersleben when we got a message from the train station. The message was to come immediately and pick up a box with an animal in it. It was Tiger. We rushed and picked him up. The trip did not seem to have upset him too much. After a time of adjustment, he was a happy cat and enjoyed roaming in the garden. The only problem was that he attracted other tomcats that howled at night and kept my father from sleeping. Father had a pile of little rocks on his bedroom windowsill. He used to throw them at the cats, but since it was dark, I hope that he did not actually hit the cats.

My sister Gisla went to high school in nearby Quedlinburg, and I found a job in the laboratory in the research institute where my parents worked. I started writing a journal while we lived in Erfurt.

I wrote into my journal in July 1954:

The earnestness of life begins for me when I have to start working instead of going to a university, which was my plan.

The worst of all is the unavoidable move to Gatersleben on August 31. I feel nostalgic about the beautiful days of school, which seem to lie so far in the past. At the time the school days seemed to be full of problems. Going to college has become an illusion, or it lies much further in the future. The rejection of my application to the University of Jena brought me to the brink of desperation.

According to the analysis of my handwriting, I am supposed to have great inner strength. I could use that strength now. I manage to deal with the problem. What else can I do but to resign myself to fate for the moment? I can always fight later.

I don't look forward to life in this godforsaken place, Gatersleben.

In spite of disappointments in the past and much hated boredom at times, I developed a love for the town where I spent my last two years of high school. It will be hard to leave this place and leave all my friends behind. I remember how happy I was when we moved here two years ago in July. Yesterday we had a last gathering, all of us, the class 12 B of '54. From now on everyone will go her own way, after we have been together for so long and after we shared so many problems. We will be scattered and everyone will follow her own goals and will not think much about old classmates. We planned our first reunion for the day after Christmas, here in Erfurt. Will everybody come? Or will we forget our friends soon? The thought of leaving here is a nightmare. I wish the move and my first day of work were already behind me.

My work was tolerable but not very exciting. I was working in a laboratory with an older, very strange scientist who spent most of his time looking into the microscope. I had to mix solutions for his cultures, clean the lab dishes, make photocopies of scientific publications, and make coffee for him. Whatever he did not want to do, I had to do. I did not learn a thing, and it did not take long before I got tired of the daily routine. After a few months, I was transferred to a larger lab next door. There were two younger scientists and several younger assistants working. We isolated alkaloids from plant materials so that they could be studied. Here I learned laboratory techniques that became useful in my later chemical studies. The company of other young people made the work less lonely. But soon I began looking for more social contacts and diversions.

I had my own room at the institute now, but that did not make me much happier. I was complaining about a wretched life: boring work, no girlfriend or young people for company. I felt lonely and forlorn in this muddy, remote village where only cows should live. I still had hope that in a year I would be able to go to college.

Other young people working here were also waiting to go to a university. Meanwhile they worked in the labs like I did. They also felt cut off from the world in this place. We decided to make our own fun. I was made director of sports and hiking in the FDJ (the Communist youth organization). None of us were Communists, but all of us had been forced to join. Now it seemed that the organization was the only possibility to find other young people. We decided to use the organization for an excuse to have a social life, and we used the available money for activities. In this remote place, nobody knew what we were doing anyway. We organized hiking and ski trips and used the gym in the local school for gymnastics. This gave us all something to do with our free time, and soon we were all friends and had our own "club." We used the bus of the institute for day trips and went to the theater in Halle or Dessau. I also started swimming again and swam my best time in the 100-meter breaststroke at a swim meet in the next biggest town, Aschersleben.

On a beautiful summer day we decided to have a campfire on a hill at some distance from the village. We loaded our bicycles with food and blankets and set out in the evening after work. We collected branches and made a great fire. We all sat around and had fun until it started to rain. It was not just a shower, but a relentless rain. First we tried to tough it out, but when it became late we packed our things and started back home. Needless to say, we got very cold and were drenched by the time we got home. This was our first and last campfire.

The institute organized botanical excursions in the summer. One such excursion went to a research station on the island of Hiddensee on the Baltic Sea. Most of our gang signed up. We stayed on the island in tents and had a great time. During the day, we dove into the sea to collect various seaweeds and any other plant life. We studied our finds under microscopes and drew them. We also took excursions around the island and studied plants. We all had terrible sunburns from spending so much time on the beach. One of the scientists had wisely made up a zinc ointment back in the lab, and soon we all had white faces and noses and looked like strange warriors. In the evenings, we usually made our own excursions. One night we got a little scared coming upon soldiers guarding the borders, but we continued to walk all around the island, which we did in two trips. One night we walked the southern circumference; another night we walked the northern one. There was much camaraderie, and we had fun but also learned much at the same time. It was really a great study vacation.

I got a camera and took many pictures. I could use the darkroom in the institute in the evenings, and photography became my new hobby. Not every picture I took was a success, but I learned much, particularly in film processing and making copies. Of course, all this was black-and-white photography. The wife of the institute's director was an art historian and was interested in old churches. There were beautiful old Romanesque and Gothic churches in the area. She organized field trips to some of these, which was a great opportunity for my amateur photography. On one of these trips, we went to Magdeburg and visited the great cathedral.

When we had not planned an activity, I was very content to listen to my radio and to read a good book, which has gotten me through many a boring time. However, I was happy to make the following entry into my journal:

I finally met a girl who lives next door and we became friends. Her name is "Gisi." She is a lab assistant in the institute and is happy that we met.

Time passes faster now, but I am very much upset about the uncertainty of my future. Will I be able to study at a university or not? I think of it all the time and feel very lonely and hopeless, since my prospects are not very good. I cannot expect any help in this matter and I have to rely on my own resources. If I get another rejection from the University in Halle or in Jena, I will freak out.

In May 1955 I received again negative replies from the universities in Jena and Halle. I was devastated. Getting a higher education was my goal, and even after a year working in the institute, I was not any closer to it.

This is what I wrote in my journal:

Much has happened in the last days. I was too upset to write anything down, but I am a little calmer now. I have received my second rejection from the university. It felt like a slap in the face. I must succeed and have taken up again my plan to leave for West Germany. I worry about how I can support myself and the decision is difficult, but I have pretty much decided that I will leave.

Two from our group have already left for the West for the same reason. My decision is difficult and the uncertainty of it all scares me. I will have to make it on my own since my parents will not be able to support me. I don't know how tough I am and what difficulties I can master. If I want a college education, there is no other way for me than to leave. There is only one way to find out if I am able to make it on my own: grit my teeth and go for it.

The major problem was that in West Germany our high school diploma from East Germany was not recognized, and I had to get a high school diploma in the West before I could apply at any university there. Once I left, I could not go back to the East to visit my parents. I was making a serious break with my past and with my family. They could also not finance me because the exchange rate for ten East Mark was only one West Mark. It was also illegal to bring money across the border.

I went for a short vacation to Erfurt and stayed with my high school friend Schimmel, whose family was already settled in Bielefeld, West Germany. I had a permit to go to West Germany for a short time for vacations, and the East German authorities expected me to return.

While we were waiting for our departure in Erfurt, Schimmel and I lived a very unstructured life and enjoyed the town we both loved so much. We tanned ourselves on the roof garden, went to see a garden show, and saw movies. On Wednesday we started our journey to the West and arrived there without any problems. My mother sent a package with all my things after I arrived.

When I said good-bye to my father, he was upset, and I wrote in my journal that he made a "scene." I don't remember what it was that he said, but he was most probably upset that I left and could not express his feelings any better than to make a "scene."

Turning Point

✦

Working and Studying to Get into a University

Our train trip across the border to Bielefeld was uneventful. Schimmel's family had invited me to stay with them until I could be on my own. I was looking for a job. I needed to make some money so that I could give Schimmel's family a weekly sum for my board. I liked staying with them, and it was perfect that Schimmel and I could study together. Soon I wrote my first letter home.

Bielefeld, August 1955

Dear Mother,

I am already here since Wednesday and have not yet written home. The time after my arrival here was very exciting and I had no peace of mind to write letters. It is very nice in Schimmel's home. They have a beautiful modern apartment. Her father is very kind to his children and also to me. He wants to help me very much, and for the time being I can stay here. Schimmel and her siblings can be grateful for having a father who is willing to help his children with everything. The package with all my things arrived safely, I thank you.

I began to plan my future yesterday. I was looking for a job but was still unsuccessful. I believe that the situation is not hopeless and I am confident that I will make it. Schimmel and I are waiting for a friend to take us to Göttingen either today or tomorrow. We will investigate the possibility of going to the university there.

I have not yet spent any money. I have only 10 Marks, which I want to keep for a day when I really need it.

Love,

Hadwig

My first problem in Bielefeld was to get a high school diploma, which was necessary for studying at a university in West Germany, since my East German diploma was not acceptable. There were courses given for students from East Germany to review high school material and study subjects that were not taught in East Germany. We had to relearn history, which had been taught to us only from the Communist viewpoint. We had to have enough credits of another European language like English or French. We had learned mostly Russian or in some cases Polish in the East. We had to be familiar with Western literature, which we had been forbidden to read in the East. In short, we had to be reeducated. Luckily our math and science knowledge was superior to that of the Western students. My friend Schimmel had already taken such a course and was about to take her final exam. I applied for a preparation course, although I had no money for tuition and had to make a living at the same time.

Bielefeld, September 1, 1955

Dear Mother,

I thank you for the letter and the birth certificate, which came just in time. In just two days I was able to take care of many things. I will start a job in a factory on Monday. I can stay here with Schimmel until November. After that I want to go to Wuppertal to take a special preparation course for the Abitur *[the German high school diploma]*, which I plan to take at Easter.

I was very lucky so far. I have already a new passport and managed to keep my East German passport, which should have been confiscated *[why did I want to keep it?]*. I need transcripts from the 8th, 9th, and 10th grades for my foreign language credits.

The trip to Göttingen was canceled. I wrote instead to the university there and am waiting for an answer.

Everybody here is extremely nice to me. I get so much attention, and I am not at all used to it. But I am grateful for being liked. Perhaps you can mention to your sister in Augsburg that I would like to visit them during Christmas vacation. I don't know if they will have me and I don't want to beg them.

Please give my love to Gisla and Ute.

Thank you again,

Hadwig

Bielefeld, September 6, 1955

My dear Mother,

I thank you for your letter and the wonderful birthday greetings, which arrived in time. You asked me how I spent my birthday. It could not have been more beautiful. Everybody here cared so much that it was almost embarrassing to have a birthday. I got so many presents: towels, stockings, books, and chocolates. They gave me a party in the afternoon with pastries, cakes, and whipped cream (you know we did not have these things in East Germany and for us they are a treat). The whole day was very much like a holiday, and at night we went to the movies.

My serious life continued yesterday. I have now spent my two first days at work. I have a job at "Eilers," a company that specializes in advertising articles, pocket calendars, writing pads, and the like. My work is very dull. I have to package products or check them for printing mistakes. Alas, this mindless work has to be endured so that I may realize my plans for the future. I expect to make about 10 Marks a day.

My friend Siegfried, a member of our gang in Gatersleben, who had also left for West Germany, came to visit me here. He is having a much harder time getting started. He thinks that I will be able to take the preparation course free of tuition. Arthur, another one of us, has also left for the West. Some day we may have a "Gatersloch" reunion. *[We used to call Gatersleben "Gatersloch," since it was such a "loch," a hole, meaning a backward place.]* I thank Ute and Gisla for their letters. Please explain to them why I don't answer them separately. I don't want to write everything twice. I am sure they read my letters. They should consider my letters to you as also addressed to them. Could Gisla find my pen pal George's address in England for me?
Love,
Hadwig

Bielefeld, September 25, 1955

My dear Mother,

Thank you for your long letter. I also received the transcripts. I still need one from the 8th grade, in order to prove that I had at least four years of English. I did not yet hear anything about the preparation course.

For a vacation you want to go to Augsburg to visit your sister? I hope that you can get a permit to cross the border. I will cross my fingers for you. Perhaps we could meet in Augsburg?

I would like to spend Christmas with our Augsburg relatives, instead of in some boarding school, where I might be to prepare for my high school diploma. I am also dying to see my cousins Ossi and Walter again.

I don't need the summer clothes now, but a winter coat is very necessary. When we go out, like last Sunday, I am dressed well, but all with borrowed clothes. I don't have enough money to buy a raincoat. It is probably better anyway to wait for the winter sale.

I am surprised to hear that you are studying English again. Are you doing it by yourself or do you take classes?

Schimmel's mother will like the present you are sending. She loves handmade things, and it will look great in their apartment *[she was planning to send a tea cozy]*. Gisla should write me a letter soon.

Lots of love,

Hadwig

Bielefeld, October 10, 1955

Dear Mother,

Thank you for the package with the winter coat and the stationery, which is very useful for writing all those letters home. I could also use some envelopes.

The work in the factory is very monotonous, but everybody likes me including the stern foreman. A coworker invited me to her house the other day. She has a daughter of my age and a son who studies at the Technical University in Aachen. He was very nice and helpful with advice for my studies in the future. I received another invitation from a coworker and everybody gives me presents. They feel sorry for the poor young girl from East Germany.

I have had no news about the preparation course and it makes me quite nervous. I hate the uncertainty. I will take the train on Saturday and visit the university in Göttingen. Perhaps this will be useful, and I don't want to put it off any longer.

I went for the first time to a large and new department store. It is a terrible feeling to see all the beautiful things and not be able to buy anything. I resisted temptation as much as I could and bought nothing.

I did not even look too much at all the goods. I have no money to spend, but that does not mean that I am suffering. I am saving my money for the fare to Göttingen and perhaps for a trip to Augsburg.

Time passes very fast, particularly in the evenings. I go to bed very late, since I study Latin, explain math to Schimmel, and explain chemistry and physics to her sister. There is little time left for myself and for writing letters home.

A few days ago I strolled through the city. It was marvelous to watch all the lights, the richly decorated windows, the elegant people, and the fancy cars. It was such a contrast to the scene in East Germany where there is nothing in the windows, hardly any lights, hardly any cars, and only people in grubby clothes. It was such an uplifting experience, not that I needed to be uplifted. I am very happy and confident that a better life is within my reach. All the people who I have met so far have been very nice to me, and that helps much.

Enough writing for today! I will write you in detail about Göttingen.

Lots of love,

Hadwig

Bielefeld, October 17, 1955

Dear Mother,

I did not yet go to Göttingen. It would have been a miracle if it had worked out. Our friend and family doctor, Dr. Lezius, told me not to come because nobody would have been there to meet me. I will go on the following weekend.

Today came the rejection for the preparation course in Wuppertal. It seems that I am getting rejections from everywhere, but I will not give up. Both courses, one in Münster and one in Wuppertal, are filled. It was quite a shock to me. It might be best if I go there in person. This means that I will have to spend my saved money, but it cannot be helped. In spite of it all, I am planning to pass the "Abitur" exams by Easter. I will prepare myself for it while I am working. The problem is what to do until then? The job I have now is seasonal and will end after Christmas. Until then, I am working 13 hours each day of the week. It is no fun to work on Sundays as well. I keep in mind that there are people who have a harder time than I have.

Otherwise everything is the same. Schimmel will take her exams next week. I hope she will pass. I wish her success since she studied so much harder than I ever could.

Schimmel did not pass. She planned to take the exams again, the next time with me. She was able to tell me what I needed to study, since she had been through it already. I, on the other hand, could help her with her studies. We made a good team.

Ute sent me a nice letter. How does she manage her MS *[it was just diagnosed]* and how does she take it, when she knows that her disease is incurable? I cannot imagine how difficult that must be for her. Why do we have so much bad luck in our family? We will not give up. Never! Things don't come to us easily. Please don't worry about me. I will find a way to reach my goal. It is late again and I dread tomorrow's drudgery.
Lots of love, also to Gisla and Ute,
Hadwig

Bielefeld, November 3, 1955
My dear Mother and dear Gisla,
   I want to give you good news today: I received a letter from Tante Schneider *[family friends living in Lahr in the Black Forest]*. They offered to let me live in their house in return for housework. I would also be an apprentice in a pharmacy for the required 2 years, if I decided to study pharmacology instead of chemistry. My good luck seems unreal. I will answer the letter tonight and can hardly wait for the answer.

It turned out later that it was not such a good deal, after all. The apprenticeship did not exist, and our "friends" took advantage of me with the housework.

I am still trying to get into one of the prep courses. The courses in Münster and Wuppertal run from the first of November to the end of March. Both courses are oversubscribed. My application was forwarded from Münster to Wuppertal, but the decisions are made in Düsseldorf. I don't believe that I have a chance to attend. Besides, the course began already. It may be better if I earn some money while I prepare for the exams. Schimmel's family invited me to stay. They also want me to stay here for Christmas. I don't have any other option and I like it here. I have not heard anything from my Augsburg relatives.

Schimmel did not pass the examinations because of German, but we believe there was also some malice from the teachers. We will now take the exams together around Easter. I will have to manage it somehow, while I work to earn a living.

Gisla, don't be upset that I have not yet answered your letter. I have no time to write, I worked 76 hours last week. We now work every weekend as well. The work hours will go back to normal after Christmas. I make more money with all this overtime, and since I am not going to Augsburg, I have the money to spend on other things. I would like to buy some fabric for a dress. Perhaps mother could sew it for me?

I have a terrible cold and have not had enough sleep for a long time. I cannot even sleep late on Sundays.

I wish mother success in her English studies. I will have to brush up my English also. It is late and I must go to bed now.

Lots of love to all of you,

Hadwig

Bielefeld, November 14, 1955

My dear Mother,

Thank you for your letter. I am surprised that you have time to write me such long letters. It makes me very happy to have letters from you so often. Meanwhile I received an answer from Tante *[aunt]* Schneider. I enclose the letter so that you can read it. You can imagine how much I look forward to staying with them. They will expect me in Lahr after Easter.

I have hardly any time to study because of so much overtime at my job. There is no weekend and no holiday for me.

I accept your offer of making me a dress, if you can afford the money to buy fabric and the time of sewing it. I have enough clothes except for a better outfit, like a nice dress. I cannot walk around in sweatpants all the time like in "Gatersloch." Does the pattern for the dress have a full skirt? You don't have to finish it completely. I can finish it here. I will take some time off between Christmas and New Year.

Dr. Lezius told me that I could come and visit him when you will be there. I will not have enough money for the fare before January. It would be so great to see you again.

I went to the theater by myself yesterday. It was a great luxury for me, but I was starving to see an opera again. It was beautiful and I wish I could afford to go more often.

It is late again. I never get enough sleep anymore. But these are the sacrifices for my future.

Love,

Hadwig

Bielefeld, December 12, 1955

Dear Mother,

Your long letter just arrived. I will answer it immediately, since the seasonal work in my job is finished. I also finished my daily English studies and have time to write this letter.

From today on, I don't have to work overtime anymore. This means that I finish work now at 4:15 PM. It is wonderful, but I don't make very much money either. Next week many workers will quit. I talked to my boss about staying on. I am allowed to stay and work until spring. I will be transferred to another department, although the foreman would have liked to keep me in his group. He is always very nice and friendly to me. I don't have to worry about a new job now. Who knows if I would have found another job in such a short time? There is very little work available after Christmas in this company. This is because we produce mainly calendars.

I will send a small package tomorrow with Christmas presents for all of you. Please promise me not to open it before Christmas Eve. The things in it are not perishable. The tea cozy for Schimmel's mother has arrived. We have put it away until Christmas, so that it will be a surprise.

December 6 was St. Nicolas Day. Santa Claus was very generous with me. He brought me so many sweets that I got sick from them. Are the many presents not proof of my good behavior?

I also got many presents at work, particularly from a very nice woman, Frau Finke. She is a coworker and would have liked to have a daughter. She likes me very much and kind of adopted me. After Christmas many coworkers wanted me to visit them, which I will do.

I will have to stop now and prepare dinner. Schimmel and her sister Elke are not home. I help here more around the house than I did at home. It would be very bad form to be lazy, when the family is so generous to me. There is a lot of work with nine people in the household, and so many of them men.

Lots of love,

Hadwig

Bielefeld, December 21, 1955

My dear Mother,

I send you all the warmest Christmas greetings and wish you restful holidays. Are you, like me, looking forward to a few days without work?

I will take a vacation between Christmas and New Year and will take a little rest before the exams. I can stay on at my present job, but I wonder if I should have looked for a better job. I make very little money without working overtime. After I pay for room and board, I am left with only 15 Marks per week. This is not much money considering that I must save for an emergency. We may even work only on alternate weeks, which will be a very meager situation. However, I will have more time to study.

Thank you very much for the package. Homemade cookies always taste best. I am so very pleased with the new dress and like it a lot. I finished the last stitches here last weekend. I bought for it a new leather belt in a very fashionable color. I also bought a beautiful button and wear a salmon-colored scarf with the dress. It looks really good and I will wear it on Christmas. Gisi *[friend from Gatersleben]* sent me a pretty silver pin and Ottilie *[friend from high school]* a book. When you receive my package, please don't open it before Christmas Eve. I hope that you will like the presents.

It is now very boring at my job. All the nice women who worked only for the Christmas season are gone. I miss them very much, particularly Frau Finke. She became a great friend. I was her "Herzchen" *[little heart]*. She invited me for after Christmas and I look forward to this visit. I have received many invitations and a lot of presents. I was never so spoiled.

Schimmel and I made a study plan for after the holidays. The serious work will then begin. We do not have much time left. I hope

Tante Schneider found a position for me in a pharmacy. I have not heard anything again from her.

Ute wrote me a long letter. I am always impressed with her optimism. How does Gisla do in school? Tell her to learn languages. They will always be very useful in life.

Christmas will be an eating orgy here. You cannot imagine the splurging around here for the holidays. I think often how happy we were with so much less. My opinion is so much different, often too radical for these surroundings. Everybody's ambition is to make much money. The temptations to spend it are too great. There are not many scruples, and every young person wants to make money without much effort. I have already noticed that the West German youth has become very superficial. I have yet to meet a person with a serious and profound attitude. The ambitions are for amusement and sensations. This is very foreign to us who come from the East. I don't feel comfortable at all among Elke's *[Schimmel's sister]* classmates. They are all pompous little fashion dolls.

It sounds like I was a "Goody Two-Shoes," or I was still very much under the influence of East German deprivations. The latter is probably true.

I have to vacuum the apartment and cook dinner again. The girls are not home and the boys are screaming for food. Good luck to all of you and have a trouble-free New Year.
With much love,
Hadwig

Bielefeld, December 28, 1955

My dear Mother,

I had beautiful and very nutritious holidays here. I received many presents. The best, of course, was the dress from you. Everybody thought that it looked great. I got towels, nylons, cologne, chocolates, and many books.

I visited Frau Finke yesterday. She is very nice to me and is a wonderful hostess. I came back loaded with presents and a book, which her husband had bound for me in leather *[I still have that book]*. It is so heartwarming that so many people thought of me.

The presents in this family were very expensive and luxurious. Schimmel received a gold watch and her mother expensive wineglasses. Life is not bad here.

I knitted during the holidays, sometimes until late at night. Every once in a while I become totally involved with a project. I went for a walk on Boxing Day and daydreamed about spending my life with you. How I would have my own little house and a black Mercedes. I will achieve all this yet.

I still have a week of vacation, which is great. Friends are invited for New Year's Eve and we will celebrate at home. A young man invited me to go out, but we don't know each other well yet and I found it awkward to go out with him while I am here. I declined and nothing came of it. Except for Schimmel's brothers and their friends, I don't have much contact with young people. Occasionally I get a letter from one of our "gang" in Gatersleben.

I manage very well by myself and have not been really homesick, but I think very often of our family. I would love to go home for next Christmas. It would be nice for all of us to be together again. Ute, who is now in the hospital, will perhaps be able to come home also. I wonder how father was over the holidays. Does he read my letters? I am happy for Gisla that she went to Jena over Christmas. She will manage well in her life, and when I am able to help her, I would like to do that.

I am often very silly here and they shake their head about me. Sometimes I don't know why I am so happy. I just have to laugh my head off. And sometimes I get a little blue, but it passes fast.

Where will I be in about one year? I have to reach my goals, no matter what happens. It is wonderful to make plans for the future, even if one knows that things may turn out quite differently. It is fun to live with fantasies.

Be well and let me thank you for all your love.

Hadwig

Bielefeld, January 8, 1955

Dear Mother,

We had a wonderful New Year's celebration at which I drank my first champagne. We were many people with all the invited friends. I was a little tipsy and had a wonderful time. This was my first really enjoyable New Year's Eve.

After this holiday season, the serious life will go on. I study according to the plan that I made so that I will be able to finish all the subjects by March 10. We still don't know the exact date for the examination. I have lots of subjects to study: German, history, math, and English. Unfortunately I cannot begin to study until after 8 PM. With so many people in the house, there is no quiet time in this family. I work long hours every night and never go to bed before one in the morning. Fortunately we have very little work to do now in the factory. Today is Sunday and I am taking the day off. I share a room with Schimmel. Sometimes I miss my own room in which I could study undisturbed. I still need a lot of textbooks and my logarithm tables. Can you please send them to me?

We had a young man visiting today. He also has to retake the Abitur exams. He does this in Hannover where the requirements are altogether different.

Schimmel's mother is always very nice to me, but I don't think she likes me very much. She is jealous of me because I have her daughter's confidence. I am always very helpful. Often I bring breakfast to her bed, help cleaning the house in whatever little time I have left, and always help preparing dinner. She does not seem to appreciate it much. I have to be grateful that she lets me stay with her family. I just want to pass those exams and then I will be off on my own. Please send my ski boots, I could use them here.

Until my next letter lots of love,

Hadwig

Bielefeld, January 15, 1956

My dear Mother and Gisla,

A letter to you is on its way, but I have to write more things.

I hope that you will not go bankrupt, having to pay so much for my postage *[I sent all letters home without stamps in order to save money]*.

I wear my hair long now. This way I don't have to pay for haircuts. Schimmel gives me a haircut when I need one. She is very good at it.

My studies are progressing nicely. I have fun studying and I look forward to taking the examinations. I still have to get used to working at night. This is my only "night life." In order to catch up with lost sleep, I slept almost all the time last weekend. I had a horrific headache, which would not go away. Now I am well again.

I studied until 2 AM yesterday and consequently overslept this morning. I have to read and study so much literature for German. I went to the library today and brought back five books, which I will have to read during the following week. My schedule is very tight.
Love to both of you,
Hadwig

Bielefeld, January 25, 1956

Dear Ute,

When I received your letter, I had a very bad conscience, because I should have written a long time ago. I will answer your letter immediately. It is already 11 PM and I still have to study German, but I do not want you to have to wait so long for my answer. Thank you for the compliment on my "youthful charm" in the picture I sent you. There are now dark circles under my eyes and not much "youthful charm" is visible. I have not lost weight, it seems only so in the picture.

A big winter sale began last Monday in the stores. Everything is very inexpensive, but not inexpensive enough for those who don't have money, like me. It does not matter. I am much too preoccupied with my studies at this time and don't have time to go around the stores to even just look at things. It is very sweet of you to send me stationery. I can always use some. I prefer a large pad with plain white envelopes.

For now I say good night. I still have to study German. I would like to close with Fontane's quotation: "The subject is much too vast." For me the subject is German, and it is certainly too vast!
Lots of love,
Hadwig

Bielefeld, February 13, 1956

Dear Mother,

Tante Schneider wrote a very nice letter. They expect me right after the exams. They have not yet found an apprenticeship for me, but think that I may work in the hospital pharmacy in Lahr where Prof. Schneider is a surgeon. I send the letter to you, because I don't have much time to explain.

We had our company party last Saturday. We were driven out to Lemgo, a pretty old town close to Bielefeld. Originally I was not in the mood to go, but I went anyway and had such a good time that I didn't get home until 6:30 the next morning. I drank only champagne, which is my new passion. The company paid for everything; the trip, the dinner, and the drinks.

I went to a dance at the YMCA last Wednesday. There were lots of young Englishmen *[Bielefeld was in the zone occupied by the British]*. We had to speak English since they, of course, did not speak German. I had a good time and taught Michael how to dance. We had a very pleasant, yet somewhat halting conversation. Now I have to go back to my studies.

Monetarily I am very badly off. I was planning to send a package home, but I am broke. I work only forty eight hours a week now and earn thirty Marks. I pay twenty Marks every week for room and board and need at least five Marks for pocket money. Not much is left for saving.

Love,

Hadwig

Bielefeld, February 20, 1956

My dear Mother,

Thank you for the package with the boots. I wore them several times already when we went sledding.

Regarding your suggestion for me to go to England for a while: That sounds interesting, but I would rather go to France and learn French. Many people told me that they were disappointed in England, but others liked it very much.

I assume that I will be an apprentice in the hospital pharmacy in Lahr. If I study pharmacology I need 3 years of Latin, which is a lot if one considers that I never learned it in high school. During the apprenticeship I will not have much time to study Latin. I will try everything and see what is best for me.

My orientation in German literature has already been westernized, but I believe that my own personal opinion has not yet been jeopardized.

I presume that I meant by this my socialistic attitude, which I must have had after so many years of Communist indoctrination.

Schimmel and Elke cannot help me, since they are not very good in this subject. To study German literature takes most of my time, because I have to read so much, which is also a lot of fun. We did not get to know much Western literature in our East German high school, and I have to make up for much of what we missed.

I am exhausted and my power of concentration is beginning to suffer. I have to take it a little easier this week. I sent my application to Münster today and hope to have the date of the exams soon.
Much love,
Hadwig

Bielefeld, March 4, 1956

My loved ones at home,

The uncertainty about the date of the exams is driving Schimmel and me crazy. We finally called Münster and found out that the exams will not be given before the middle of April. What a nuisance! On the other hand, we will have more time to study. The "labor camp work" at the factory is beginning to get on my nerves.

I had to say good-bye to Michael, my British friend from the YMCA. He is leaving Bielefeld, which is a pity because he was such a pleasant and dependable fellow. He always took me home to my doorstep. However, I had to stress my brain to keep up a conversation in English with him.

During Easter vacation Schimmel and I would like to go hitchhiking to Hamburg. I wonder if you know someone in Hamburg with whom we could possibly stay. I hope that our plans will materialize. We want to go as cheaply as possible.

Please send this letter to Ute so that she can read my news. I thank her very much for the beautiful stationery. I will also write a letter to Gisla soon. After the exams I will go to Lahr. The exams will last about a week, and I wish they were already behind me.
Lots of love,
Hadwig

Bielefeld, March 23, 1956

My dear Mother,

I wrote a letter to Richters [my mother's friends in Hamburg]. I wrote to ask them if we could stay with them for a few days. They told me that they are too tired. I always feel that when people know I come from "the other side" *[East Germany]*, they believe that they have to take care of me or give me something for nothing. This makes me feel like a second-class citizen. When I will be in Lahr, I will tell nobody where I came from. It serves no purpose to even talk about it. Schimmel and I will go to Hamburg anyway. We will stay in a youth hostel.

I have been trying to write a letter home, but it is already 1 AM. I studied math for five hours and need a break and will use it to write a letter. I have time to sleep late tomorrow.

It is great not to have to go back to work until after Easter. Then I hope to work for only three more weeks. I am also not in the mood to take exams, but it will be good to have them behind me.

I saw a slide show recently as part of a promotion for a travel agency. They showed beautiful pictures of Germany and Northern Italy, which put me in the mood for traveling. They gave away prizes, like a free two-week trip to Lake Garda. As usual, I was not the lucky one to win the trip.

When I have to go to Lahr, it will be just like moving. I have already accumulated too much stuff. How shall I pack all these things?

I will go with Schimmel to Hamburg on Monday morning. It will be such a relief not to have to work for a while. I am sick and tired of the "stimulating work" and my "intelligent" coworkers. What surprises me is that every working girl between 14 and 40 "goes steady" with someone. Although the atmosphere at work is not very beneficial for me, it is important to get to know the working folks.

It is getting late and I have to quit. I will write you from Hamburg. Are you going to be able to make a trip to South Germany? We could meet there and I would like that very much.

Lots of love to all of you,

Hadwig

I don't have any journal entries about our stay in Hamburg. I remember that we had no trouble finding rides there and that we had a wonderful time. Large cities always excited me. A young friend of Schimmel's family took us out dancing at a club on the famous "Reeperbahn" (a street with plenty of restaurants, clubs, and prostitutes). We stayed at the youth hostel, and someone stole all my money from my coat pocket. They couldn't have taken it from a poorer person.

It had taken me months to save up that money. From then on, we lived on Schimmel's funds and had to be very frugal.

Dortmund, April 19, 1956

My dear ones at home,

I am happy and the exams are behind me. I don't yet have the final results, but it really looks like I passed. Please excuse me if this letter sounds a little bit distracted. I have not been able to catch my breath. This is our lunch break, after which the exams will continue. Schimmel just took history. They asked her about the Contract of Versailles. She is now cramming for German. I hope that she will make it.

We found room and board in the Catholic mission for less than five Marks per day. We are four girls and twelve boys and get along very well. There are also students who live in Dortmund and environs. On Monday we had to report at the Stadt Gymnasium *[city high school]* and started immediately with writing essays in German. We sat two to a table, which made it easy for me to help Schimmel, although we had different topics and problems so that we could not copy from each other.

On Tuesday I took English and Schimmel took Russian. In English we had to write about "the economic effects of war." It was easy for me.

We took the math test on Wednesday. They gave us four problems, but we had to solve only two. I solved three of them correctly. The fourth one I could not do because we did not learn about compounded interest *[a capitalistic concept]*. Today we had orals. We had to talk about the French Revolution. I was one of the first to finish. I am now sitting here at 1:30 PM. I am waiting for the results, which will be announced tonight. After that we will take the late train home.

I started to write the letter in Dortmund, but I continue it after we returned to Bielefeld. We had to wait a long time for the results. We "hung out" together, and the tension was high. In order to relax, we sang Russian and East German songs. Some boys told funny stories in a local East German dialect. It was a wonderful camaraderie. We all felt like we belonged together. Everybody was just great. Some of the students had already been studying for several semesters in East Germany. In spite of the age difference, we got along well with each other. Even the teachers were very nice. Only four in our group flunked. The headmaster congratulated us lucky ones who passed, and we presented him with flowers. The teachers were very moved. Afterwards, we all went to the post office to send telegrams home. Then we accompanied each other to the trains. The boys knotted many handkerchiefs together and waved good-bye. We had just met and must already part. I wrote one of the best math exams of the group, and after the written exams I was sure that I had passed.

It felt so good to be together with people of one's own level of intellect. Schimmel passed also. She was much less nervous this time. I think that my presence was a great help to her. I helped her with her essay and solved a math problem for her. When we arrived back in Bielefeld, there were tears of joy. I felt that by helping Schimmel I had paid back some of the kindness that her family had extended to me. Now I have to pack my things, do some errands, and go on with my life.

I may have to take an additional exam in Latin. I will begin to study Latin as soon as I arrive in Lahr. I have such a feeling of accomplishment, much more so than after the Abitur exams in Erfurt. This time it was a well-deserved success. Next time you hear from me, it will be from Lahr. I leave here on April 24.

Lots of love,

Your very happy Hadwig.

A Wrong Turn

✦

My Short Interlude in Lahr

This is a letter from Tante Schneider about what awaited me in Lahr:

Lahr, February 8, 1956

Dear Hadwig,

I did not write for such a long time because I could not find a position for you in a pharmacy for April 1956, only for April 1957. You can work in the hospital pharmacy for pocket money. You can have room and board with us for free. This will, of course, not give you any credits toward your studies.

Did you pass the exams? I will send you money for the fare to Lahr. Or could you be in Frankfurt on Feb. 28, from where we could bring you here by car?

Please write soon and let me know what you decide to do. I hope that you will come anyway. You could learn much in the hospital. No experience is wasted and you are still so young *[I was by then 18 years old]*. Come to Lahr, to a cozy home and a beautiful garden.

Yours always,

Mutti Schneider

Lahr was a sleepy little town in the foothills of the Black Forest. The center of town had attractive little shops, but nothing was happening here. The Schneiders were my parents' friends from our time in Frankfurt/Oder. Their only daughter, Ute, was close to me in age and we had been playmates. I stayed with them in Frankfurt whenever my parents traveled. I got invariably very homesick while staying in their house. Their lifestyle was so very different from ours. Dr. Schneider was a surgeon, and when I lived with them in Lahr, he was the director of the local hospital. Tante Schneider was a frustrated actress and organized frequent amateur plays.

Originally I wanted to study chemistry and not pharmacology. I did get on that sidetrack only because it does not take as many semesters at the university, but then I would have to spend the two years of apprenticeship, during which I would be paid some money. When I heard that there was no apprenticeship for me as promised, I changed my plans back to studying chemistry. Meanwhile I was committed to go to Lahr but also had no other place to stay until I would try to get into a university and until I could apply for scholarships.

Lahr, April 4, 1956

My dear Mother,

The first mail I received here was your long letter. I was so happy about it. This is the first time since I left home that I feel really alone. I am so out of place here and very lonesome. I miss young people most of all.

I live with the two Schneiders, their 86-year-old mother, and a middle-aged housekeeper. Their daughter, Ute, studies in München. She also takes acting lessons on the side.

I left Bielefeld on Monday morning. A friend of Bernd [*Schimmel's brother*], who owns a factory in Lahr, just happened to be in Bielefeld. Thus I had a ride to Lahr in their car. They delivered me in front of the Schneiders' house. They gave me their telephone number and told me to call them. They liked me and would like to invite me to their house.

When I arrived, the Schneiders were astonished about my height, as usual. They have a picture of their son's wedding in which I was a flower girl, and nobody would have recognized me as the same person.

They made me polish silver and iron clothes today, which is not my favorite occupation. I am not much interested in housework. However, I did not admit my aversion and already received much praise. I have a little room of my own upstairs. I have to get used to living alone again, since I shared a room with Schimmel for so long.

I miss the family life. I felt very much at home in Bielefeld. Everything is different here, but everybody is very nice. The Schneiders own an old villa with a beautiful garden. The house seems much too large for them. The place is stuffed with antiques like a museum, just like their house in Frankfurt/Oder was. Schimmel's family lived in a very modern apartment, which I prefer. One does not dare to sit down here on the precious Biedermeier chairs. The garden is like a park.

They took me to town today in their car. Lahr has cozy, narrow streets, and the town feels very rural. I will start to work in a boutique in May. The owner is expecting a child and needs someone to tend the store before, during, and after delivery. I will make 100 Marks a month, which I can keep.

We also went to the local pharmacy to ask about an apprenticeship. They have no openings. Perhaps they will take me in the fall as an assistant. The owner of the pharmacy was very nice, and I believe that she wanted to hire me. I seem to make a good impression on people, even if I don't curtsy like old-fashioned Tante Schneider wants me to do. I don't even know how to curtsy.

I heard that the apprenticeship for pharmacology will be shortened from two to one and one-half years, but the time required to study at a university will be lengthened instead. If this were true, it would be easier for me. I start now to learn Latin seriously. The Schneiders will help me find a tutor.

I would love to go home for Christmas if the East German authorities would give me a permit to reenter East Germany. Perhaps I should try to come in the summer. Gatersleben is more pleasant in the summer anyway, and I cannot afford the money for two trips. Perhaps we will be able to spend our lives together some day. It does not look as if I will get married, in spite of an abundance of men *[little did I know]*.

I hiked in the surrounding mountains this afternoon and brought back a bunch of anemones for my room. I am very tired. I hardly slept last night in the foreign bed.

Lots of love to you and all the others,
Hadwig

Lahr, April 30, 1956

My dear ones left behind in "Gatersloch,"

Thank you very much for your collective letter. I am looking forward to the arrival of the package.

It is raining today. That is why I have time to write. Otherwise I would have to split wood. Yes, these are my jobs here: to mow the lawn, to iron, to clean bicycles and silver, to clean the house, and to work in the kitchen. It is a life filled with hard work. I don't mind the work, but what bothers me is that they treat me like an immature child. I am not 5 or 6 years old anymore as I was when they knew me in Frankfurt/Oder. However, I keep my thoughts to myself and I am always polite.

I finally found time to unpack today and to iron my own clothes. They were very wrinkled from having been packed for so long. I would love to buy you some beautiful fabrics, which I see here in the stores. I cannot afford to buy them, only look at them. I need underwear very badly. Can you send me some? Also my watch broke down, and since it is very hard to be without a watch, I walk around with my alarm clock in my pocket.

Adolf Köberle *[my mother's childhood friend and professor of theology at the University of Tübingen]* is very nice to offer his help. My plans are still very much in the air. I want to see if I can start to work in the pharmacy in the fall. If I go to a foreign country as they suggested, I would have to go as an au pair, and I just realized how much I hate housework. If I don't have work that challenges me intellectually, I am not happy. To do some housework every now and then is all right, but not as a life's occupation. I hope that life will be more interesting in the future than it is now.

Lots of love to all of you,

Hadwig

Lahr, May 2, 1956

My dear Mother,

You will probably be surprised that I am writing again, but there is so much to tell. I thank you for the package. At this moment I am eating some of your delicious chocolates. It is already 9 PM, and I still have to study Latin after having worked for others since 6 AM without interruption. I don't want to do this for the long term. I will have even less time for myself if I am working in a pharmacy. I learned during the last months in Bielefeld that studying so much at night takes a lot of energy and the nerves suffer. It leads to chronic exhaustion.

Lahr is a great disappointment for me. I understood from Tante Schneider's letters that an apprenticeship was at least secure for 1957. When I arrived here, I realized that all this was fictitious. I am beginning to think that the invitation to come here was motivated by my providing cheap help rather than their wish to help me with my career.

Tante Schneider praises my versatility and talents, and she has rather great expectations. In spite of all the praise, I realize now that there is nothing in this for me. Did I work so hard to get my Abitur for all this? You will understand that for all those reasons I decided to help myself and not to rely on the help of others.

The Schneiders were in München where they met Heidi Grussendorf *[the daughter of family friends in Frankfurt]*, who thought she knew of an apprenticeship in Tübingen. They suggested that I go to Tübingen. I am very skeptical but will take this opportunity to hitchhike to Tübingen and talk things over with the Köberles. I will try my luck there and will go for studying chemistry at the university. What do you think? I miss someone who understands me and can advise me in such important things.

Meanwhile I started to work in the boutique and I like it. You would love all the beautiful things, particularly the textiles. I feel like buying everything in the store. The young owner is from Dresden and is very nice and friendly. Tomorrow will be my first day alone in the store. We redecorated the store windows today. The only problem is that I cannot communicate too well with the French customers who shop here frequently *[Lahr was in the French occupied zone of Germany]*. I don't understand a word of French, not having had any in high school. I wish Gisla were here to help. But instead of learning French, I have to study Latin now.

The chocolates, which I started to eat while writing the letter, are finished, and the letter is finished as well.
Much love,
Hadwig

Lahr, May 8, 1956

Dear Mother, Gisla, and Ute,

Here is a report about my trip to Tübingen. Our neighbors took me on Sunday from here to Karlsruhe with their car. From there I hitchhiked to Stuttgart and on to Tübingen. I never had problems getting rides with friendly people. I arrived at the Köberles' late Sunday afternoon. They put me up at a Lutheran hostel and gave me a concert ticket for the evening. They were very sweet to me. They are much more giving people than the Schneiders. I felt at home with them.

I went to the university on Monday morning and informed myself about how I can finance my studies. I also went to the Chemistry Department where I met a research associate who studied with people I worked for at the Research Institute in Gatersleben. What a small world.

I met a very nice student from Halle *[East Germany]*. He is here since December and was the student of a famous chemist in Chemnitz. He accompanied me on my errands and helped me to find my way around. He gave me a tour of the castle. We went rowing on the Neckar and to a movie at night.

The Köberles had me for lunch and the Grußendorfs for dinner. I liked Grussendorfs' daughter Heidi very much. She is a year younger than I am and is learning to be a seamstress. We liked each other.

I loved the days in Tübingen and was enchanted by the old town with many students rushing about. I decided to start studying chemistry in the fall. I hope to prove that women can also be successful in the sciences. At the beginning, the professors tried to get rid of me, just like they did in Göttingen. After a few interviews, they realized that I am serious about it. I will have to study eight or ten semesters for the diploma *[master's degree]*. The curriculum contains all the subjects that interest me.

You must wonder why I changed my plans from pharmacology to chemistry so quickly. In order to serve my years of apprenticeship for pharmacology, I would get no more than forty Marks per month, on which I cannot live. I wanted to study chemistry in the first place. Now the problem is to find a place to stay, but I am in the process of solving that. Until then, I have to save every penny I make.

I hitchhiked back to Lahr today with a heavy heart. I liked Tübingen so much that I would have liked to stay there. As far as rides go, I had no problems coming back. I found a ride, which could have taken me all the way to Italy. Alas, I could not go there. The whole trip did not cost me a penny, and I had so much fun. The police almost chased me off the Autobahn, but out of compassion they let me go. *[It was illegal to hitchhike on the Autobahn, but many poor students did it anyway.]*

I will also go this week to the University of Freiburg to inquire about the possibility of studying there. I am told that it is very difficult to be accepted in chemistry because of the shortage of lab spaces there. It is also more expensive there.

I better go to sleep now. Tante Schneider yelled at me for having my light still on.

Please cross your fingers for me!

Lots of love,

Hadwig

Lahr, May 22, 1956

Dear Mother,

Thank you for your letter. I am happy that you approve of my plans. I hope to be able to leave here as early as June 15.

I would like to ask you for a few things. I am in debt and have no money whatsoever. Sometimes I don't know how I will survive. Can you please send me notebooks, folders, plain writing paper, and chemistry textbooks? I would like very much the chemistry textbook by Langenbeck, perhaps you can find a used one. I will be able to use Peter's textbook at the beginning since he offered to help. He is the chemistry student from Halle whom I met on my first trip to Tübingen.

The Grußendorfs' son studies business management here in Tübingen. His name is Ott-Heinrich, do you remember? When we were children in Frankfurt/Oder we used to tease him with the following song *[which loses in translation]*:

> Heinerle, Zigeunerle,
> Was macht denn deine Frau?
> Sie wäscht sich nicht, sie kämmt sich nicht,
> So ist sie eine Sau.

> Heinerle, little gypsy
> Do you know what your wife does?
> She does not wash herself, she does not comb her hair,
> She is a pig.

I wonder why he took this from us little kids who were at least eight years younger than he is. Now he is the perfect gentleman.

We carry beautiful things in the store where I work. Some things we sell only by order, but we have beautiful jackets, sweaters, and blouses by Bogner, pottery, handmade jewelry, baskets, brass, handwoven blankets and pillows, lamps, handblown glass, scarves, and batik articles.

The owner's baby was born a week ago. The mother and child were well when I visited them in the hospital. I will be able to leave Lahr as soon as the mother recovers and can tend her store again.

Love,

Hadwig

Lahr, June 1, 1956

My dear mother,

Thank you for your long letter. I now have all mail sent to the store. Tante Schneider used to keep my mail, so that I would work and not read my letters. It is worse than in prison here.

I will answer all your questions. I found a place to stay in Tübingen. Prof. Stelzenberger, another theologian and colleague of Professor Köberle, will let me stay in their attic room. It is furnished with a bed, a closet, and a chair. It is enough for me until I find a proper room.

I was planning to go to Tübingen on October 6, but I will not be able to leave here until the 16th. I often feel like crying. I am so homesick and very tired of Lahr. The fall semester starts on November 1. Perhaps I could stay until then in München. Ute Schneider has offered her place until then. It would be a good opportunity to discover München, which is an exciting city. I could also use the change of place and pace.

I still don't have a confirmation of my scholarship. I would like to come home for Christmas when I will be on vacation. We would have so much to talk about.

I count every day until I can leave here. I am very unhappy in this house. They took me to the movies yesterday. They let me sit on the cheapest seats, while their "majesties" sat on the most expensive seats. At the table they eat butter while they give me margarine. Tante Schneider fears constantly that I eat too much of their food and that I may spend five minutes **not working** for her. I am not so much put out by the work but by their attitude toward me. The only person who has compassion for me is the housekeeper. She cried when I told her that I will leave. I want my freedom very badly, even if it means having no money and starving. I don't want to dry up in this godforsaken place.

Tante Schneider's praise irritates me more than when she screams at me, which happens quite often. All this is called charity. The most annoying part is that I have to be grateful for it all.

You wanted to know about the party here in the house while Ute was home with a bunch of friends. Most young men did not even show basic politeness to me. I suppose they assumed that I was the maid. I went to bed very early on that night. I had a much better time on the few days that I spent in Tübingen than I had during the six weeks in Lahr. I liked working in the store. I am not a second-class citizen there and I don't feel like a prisoner. When there are no customers, I can knit or read your letters. Please write again soon, I miss you all.

Love,

Hadwig

I cannot believe today that these people, so-called "friends of the family," were so cheap. In contrast, how generous Schimmel's family was toward me. They had five children of their own and were probably poor in comparison to the Schneiders. I had fallen into a trap. Tante Schneider made it sound as if there was a place for me in a pharmacy, which was not true at all. She sounded so friendly, promised to make me feel like one of the family, but all she wanted was a maid whom she did not have to pay. I realized that very soon and tried everything to leave there as soon as I possibly could. I stayed there for six weeks only and would have stayed even less, had I not felt obligated to take care of the store until the proprietor was able to take it over again. The first time I hitchhiked to Tübingen, I had a few pennies in my pocket and managed to come back without spending any of the money, but I had accomplished a lot. I think that Tante Schneider underestimated me. I had a lot of energy and determination and could rely on my own resources. All this I learned during my life in East Germany.

Lahr, June 6, 1956

My dear ones at home,

The nice mailman brought your letter to the store today. The business here is not terribly good. I made seventy five Marks for the store today, which is "booming business." I received the watch and the candy. Thank you so much. Now I am able to tell the time of day again without carrying an alarm clock. In the past I did not know when it was time to close the store. From the pictures of Gisla, I gather that she gained weight, but I get thinner by the day. It is not attractive to be so tall and so thin.

Please send me a textbook of electronics from my things. Are there still textbooks of chemistry or physics among them? I wrote a letter to father for his birthday. I tried very hard to write a nice letter. Will he read it or will he throw it in the wastebasket?

My father had not written me or asked about me since I left home. I think that he was very upset about my leaving. He knew that I had no chance for a university education in East Germany. I thought that he would understand, particularly since he was an academic himself. Later he was proud of my accomplishments, but at the time he acted very coldly toward me.

Their "majesties" drove down to Lindau. I stayed here with Frau Jans, the housekeeper, who is like a mother to me. We are spending a last quiet weekend together in Lahr.

I was happy to read that you now ride a bike. That is just great. I am convinced that you will become an athlete yet, who knows maybe even a bike racer.

Love,
Hadwig

Hard Times and Good Times

✦

Letters Home from Tübingen

The Eberhardt-Karls-Universität in Tübingen was founded in 1477 and is one of the oldest universities in Germany. It is famous for departments in medicine, theology, law, philosophy, and science. A Protestant seminary, the *Evangelische Stift*, was founded in 1536.

Johannes Kepler studied here in 1587. Other famous Germans associated with the university are the philosophers Hegel and Schelling and the poets Hauff, Hölderlin, and Mörike.

The student body has grown steadily since World War II. Today there are twenty-five thousand students at the university. The academic year begins at the end of October. The fall/winter semester runs from October to mid-February, the spring semester from mid-April to mid-July.

The town of Tübingen lies about forty kilometers south of Stuttgart. It has retained its old-world charm into modern times. It has crooked little streets and alleys, half-timbered houses, wine cellars, and many student pubs. Historical landmarks of the town are the city hall and the marketplace, the fifteenth-century *Stiftskirche*, the old Bursa, the Hölderlin Tower, and the castle *Hohentübingen*. The river Neckar flows through the town and is the same river that flows through Heidelberg. Students punt on the river for relaxation. The boats are moved along by planting long poles into the ground of the shallow river. Every summer various student groups and fraternities compete in a race.

The cultural life in Tübingen has always been very rich. There are concerts, theater, exhibitions, and lectures. Many famous groups such as I Musici and the Amadeus Quartet were performing regularly in Tübingen.

Very soon I would be able to move to Tübingen. I had registered at the university on one of my earlier trips. I borrowed the registration fee from some of my mother's friends. I had also saved a little money from my job in the boutique. I applied for a scholarship, which should start any time. The West German government provided scholarships for people like me who came from East Germany and whose families were still left in the East. Such a scholarship was created in Bad Honnef, a suburb of Bonn, and was called the *Honnef Model*. I qualified for this scholarship, which would cover most of my living expenses. I had another scholarship for the tuition. For this I had to take a special exam each semester for each course I had taken. My grades had to be at least a "B" for the scholarship to continue. Therefore, I had to take exams constantly and had to work for the courses. Every vacation (we had many more vacations than students have in the United States) I usually worked a temporary job in order to increase my income. I lived on a subsistence level, but I was so happy to be a student and did not care about the rest.

It took a little time in the first semester to get set up, but that was no problem either, as my mother's friends were very helpful to me, and soon I was on my own.

Tübingen, May 14, 1956

My dear Mother,

I made it! After much paperwork, I am now officially a student of chemistry. I love Tübingen. Great numbers of students are rushing about to go to their lectures, and I am one of them. My studies have not started yet and I am still in the process of getting settled. My scholarships, my curriculum, and a place to stay have all been arranged. All the hardships were worth the goal to be independent and to be a student. The Köberles are wonderful to me, also the Grussendorfs.

Tübingen, view of the castle and the Neckar.

There will be more difficulties, but no matter, I am on my way. It all happened very fast, and a week ago I could not have imagined any of this. This is how it all happened so fast: An express letter came from Peter, the student who had helped me and shown me around in Tübingen. He advised me to register immediately for the summer semester. I would have to do it this week to make the deadline. At first I thought that I should not rush into anything and that it would be better to earn some more money.

Last Thursday I went with the Schneiders to Freiburg, where I supposedly could find work in a clinic, but I was too young for this position. On the way home in the car, I decided to go to Tübingen the next day and register for the summer semester. The Schneiders arranged a place for me to stay in Tübingen. I think they want to get rid of me by now. They must have understood that I will not be exploited.

Tante Schneider's daughter came home for vacation. She is nice enough, but she plays the lady and is very pretentious. She is constantly concerned with the social correctness of her actions. I get along much better with Heidi Grussendorf. She is down-to-earth.

Peter was very helpful again. He had all the forms for me to fill out and gave me so much advice that my head was spinning. We met every day while I was here. He invited me to dinner several times and we hiked on Sunday across the Osterberg. His Vordiplom *[BS]* examinations will be in six weeks.

I will receive a transitional scholarship for the first three semesters. After that, I will receive my regular Honnef scholarship. I will not be able to move permanently to Tübingen before the middle of June. I cannot leave the store right now and still need to make some money. I will not miss much at the university. I registered for only 13 hours of lectures per week. In the winter semester, I will add botany and start my first lab course. I will have to find a job for the summer vacations. I was never as poor as I am right now. I have become so frugal that it borders on stinginess. I did not have thirty Marks for the registration fee. I had to borrow it. However, I think that better times will come.

Never in my life did I have to fill out so many forms. This is mostly because of the scholarships. My mood is so great, I feel myself soaring into the sky. Hopefully it will stay that way. I will be so happy to leave Lahr, where people took advantage of me.

Love to all of you,

Hadwig

Tübingen, June 16, 1956

My dear Mother,

Thank you for the lovely letter and the good wishes for the new beginnings. I arrived here last night and am very happy. When I left the train station in Tübingen, I felt as if I had come home. In the train I met a young man who treated me with cigarettes and drinks and helped me carry my heavy suitcases. I always meet nice people on the road, which is something that did not happen back in Gatersleben.

You can imagine that it was not very difficult to say good-bye to Lahr. The only person who will miss me is Frau Jans, the housekeeper, who accompanied me to the train. Tante Schneider, who constantly plans theatrical productions, wanted me to come back in July to play Helena in "A Midsummer Night's Dream." I am sure she was upset because I do not want to do this. I worked up to the last minute and went directly from the store to the train.

My college life begins on Monday. On Tuesday I have lectures from 7 AM to 12 PM. Wednesday, Thursday, and Friday the lectures start at 7 AM. Thank God, there are no lectures on Saturday. It seems that there is much time available, but I have to use it to study. I would also like to get involved in some kind of sport again.

I visited the Köberles and brought them a little present. All my things are now unpacked and hung up in the closet. Later I will go to the Grussendorfs, and tomorrow I will explore the neighborhood.

I will gladly accept your offer to send you my laundry. It will be much cheaper for me to send it to you than to have it done here.

It would be perfect if you could take your vacations here. If it could work out, it would be wonderful. I am looking forward to seeing you again soon. It has already been a whole year since I left home.
Love from your very happy Hadwig.

Tübingen, castle entrance.

Tübingen, June 19, 1956

My dear Mother,

I just finished updating my lecture notes and don't really feel like writing letters. However, I would like you to know how I survived my first day of lectures. It was a piece of cake.

There was not much new material in chemistry, physics, and math, but I will have to review these subjects because I forgot quite a bit since high school. The only difficulty I have is with stoichiometry *[math applied to chemistry]*. The professor teaching this subject has already offered his help. This will get me going soon.

My very first lecture was quite an experience. There was standing room only, and for two hours I stood alternately on one foot at a time because the lecture hall was so crowded. Students sat on stairs, on windowsills, and in the aisles. The University of Tübingen has 6212 students and has room for only 3000. But none of this will dampen my spirits.

Here is some good news: My first three semesters are financially secure. The transitional scholarship will pay 150 Marks per month but not during vacation time. I hope my good luck will continue.

I explored the library and the cafeteria today. The food in the cafeteria is not bad, but it is crowded there as well. This is why I am grateful that the Grussendorfs invite me often for dinner. I need many textbooks for which I don't have the money. Can you help me and send me the following? I need a physics textbook covering electricity and wave theory, also a book by H. Fiedler "Math for Chemists." Please send them soon.

This was the only help my parents could give me: sending me textbooks, clothing, towels, and writing material; doing my laundry; and sending occasionally a home-baked cake.

I just finished reading a great book, an autobiography by Sauerbruch, "This Is My Life" *[Sauerbruch was a legendary German surgeon]*. Father sent me a very nice letter.
Love,
Hadwig

Tübingen, June 28, 1956

Dear Mother,

Thank you very much for your offer to help. I know how difficult it is with the crazy exchange rate *[one West Mark for every ten East Marks]*. I think that I can make it for this semester. I will compile a list of books I need, and if you can order them for me, that would be great. I have not seen Peter for a long time since he is cramming for his exams, otherwise he could have suggested some important books. Dr. Brodinger *[one of my professors]* already lent me a textbook for the subject he teaches and told me to come and see him anytime I need help. As you see, I always find helpful people.

I hitchhiked yesterday to Stuttgart to look for a room for the duration of my vacation job there. I found a young man who offered his help and took me around. I found a room for twenty Marks per month, which is only five minutes away from Bosch where I will be working. The room is terribly old-fashioned, but rooms in Stuttgart usually go for between sixty and one hundred twenty Marks. I have an interview at Bosch on July 7. I hope that they will let me work in the laboratory. I love Stuttgart. It is a real city, very elegant and growing rapidly. Perhaps I will spend three happy months during the summer there.

I will now go to a rally, where we will complain about the overcrowded lecture halls, and afterward I will play volleyball. As you can see, the free time I have when I am not going to lectures has already been filled.

When will you come? I will be free between the end of July and August 6. How long could you stay?

Love,

Hadwig

Tübingen, July 8, 1956

Dear Mother,

Thank you for the great package. The lab coat fits well and the cake is so light and delicious. The Köberles invited me to dinner. While I was there, I met their daughter Irene, who is an accomplished singer. They asked me when you would come for a visit. What are your plans and when will you move into the new house?

The Research Institute of the Academy of Science, where my parents worked, was supplying houses for their employees, and my parents were about to move into a newly constructed single-family house.

I biked to the castle Lichtenstein yesterday. Two Hohenzoller princesses still live there. They look like two ordinary old spinsters. I took the route via Reutlingen and Honau to the castle and back via Gönningen and Gomaringen. My face is now as red as a tomato from the heat and the effort.

I am still looking for a place to stay for the winter semester. I can stay here only during the summer. It is very difficult to find rooms. Most of them go from hand to hand, which makes it very tough for people like me with no connections and not yet many friends. I had much better luck in Stuttgart.

Many thanks and lots of love,

Hadwig

Tübingen, city hall.

Tübingen, July 13, 1956

Dear Gisla,

It is 5 AM and I just returned from a ball. I have a lecture at 7 AM and it is not worth going to bed. I write you this letter instead. A student invited me to the ball and picked me up with his motorcycle. It was quite a sight with me sitting on the back of the bike in a dress and with a pillow under my bottom.

The directory of youth hostels, which I sent to you, came back today. The East German authorities would not let it through. I am sorry that I cannot help you with this. I have to study for my scholarship exams in chemistry and physics. Starting in August, I will work in Stuttgart. I hope to work in a lab at Bosch. This kind of work would pay better than an office job.

Have you moved to the new house yet? Please, draw me a plan of the house and your room.

Love,

Hadwig

Stuttgart, August 5, 1956

My dear Mother,

I wish you a very happy birthday. Your present will come late and I hope you don't mind very much. It has only been a few hours since I arrived here. Gisla *[who had visited me in Tübingen, all the way from the East by bicycle]* helped me to carry my very heavy suitcase to the train station. I had two students helping me here when I arrived. I would never have managed by myself with all that weight.

My landlady is extremely nice. I believe that I will be comfortable here. Gisla will stay in my room in Tübingen until she continues her trip. We had a good time together. We took several trips, including a hitchhiking trip to Stuttgart. Her boyfriend Wilfried came on Saturday. We went punting on the Neckar and then ended up in a milk bar, like good little children, no alcohol. On Sunday we visited the Tübingen castle and the chapel at Wurmlingen. Wilfried *[Gisla's boyfriend]* and I left at about the same time on Monday.

I talked to Gisla as you had asked me to do. I think that it was not really necessary. She is still quite innocent and also very reasonable. Your daughters are not promiscuous thanks to our upbringing. You can trust us. I thought of Wilfried as a little boy, although I am only a few months older.

My job at Bosch starts tomorrow, and I wonder how it will go. You will probably spend your birthday in the middle of the moving chaos. All your daughters are gone and you have no help. We will make up for it some day in the future.

Lots of love,

Hadwig

We had extended vacations between semesters in Germany (from September to November and during April and May). It was probably designed to give students a chance to earn money. Many companies hired a certain number of students during those vacations. It was more or less charity on the part of the companies. I don't think our work was all that important, and we did whatever was required from us just to make some money for the next semester. My work in the office at Bosch was very dull. One day they did not have anything for me to do and they gave me boxes and boxes of paper, which had been used on one side. I had to cross out those pages so that the other side of the papers could be used again. This is German frugality!

My coworkers were a very friendly bunch. They all liked me. One of them was a basketball coach for a local ball club. They had a women's team, and when he saw how tall I was, he recruited me immediately. I had never even heard of basketball, and he spent many evenings teaching me the fundamentals and got me ready to play games very soon. Often we were allowed to use the basketball court at the American base. Since the Americans were so much better than we were, they coached us also. During training sessions, we played with the men, but we played our own games against other women teams. Even when I had to be back in Tübingen, I hitchhiked once a week to Stuttgart to practice with my team or for a game. I could always stay with the same landlady from whom I rented the room while I was working at Bosch. She became a good friend, and I could stay with her whenever I liked.

Stuttgart, August 19, 1956

My dear Mother,

Please excuse this terrible paper, but I left my stationery behind in Tübingen. Gisla surprised me with her visit on Wednesday night. I was already in bed and received her in my nightgown. I was very happy to see her.

We spent a last day filled with fun. She picked me up after work. We bought her train ticket and had dinner at the youth hostel. She paid for the dinner because I was again totally broke. We went window-shopping and particularly enjoyed the beautiful furniture, which would look so great in your new house. On Friday I took Gisla to her train. By now she will be back home with you. How did she survive the trip?

Right now I suffer from reading mania, which means that I read about three books per week. It compensates for the fact that my brains are absolutely unnecessary at my job.

I went back to Tübingen for the weekend and brought back my sports gear. I will join a basketball team here in Stuttgart. They are regional champions.

While I was in Tübingen, I went to see the Grussendorfs. They will soon leave for Italy. Heidi "lost" her appendix but is already recovered. Ott-Heinrich had just returned from Paris and had many interesting stories to tell.

I will go back to my mindless job tomorrow. I work nine hours a day in an office at Bosch. The food in the company cafeteria is cheap and good. I am working in the sales department, where we are now preparing for inventory. My coworkers are mostly older men. They are very nice to me and give me goodies like fruits, cake, or eggs for breakfast. They tell me that they know that students never have enough to eat and they don't want me to collapse. However, I am in great shape.

Imagine, I read in a local newspaper that Irene Stechemesser [a classmate from high school in East Germany] established a new shot-put record in a competition in Leipzig. How about that?

I send you lots of love,
Hadwig

Stuttgart, September 25, 1956

Dear Mother,

I have not written for a long time because I was very busy. We have a lot of basketball practice. I love it and have made much progress and will play at the first regional championship game.

I managed to get a cheap ticket for Bach's Mass in B-minor, which will be performed tomorrow in the new concert hall about a block from where I live here.

I remember the performance very well. The new hall had amazing acoustics, and when I heard the chorus at the beginning of the mass, it gave me goose bumps all over. The B-minor Mass has been one of my favorite Bach pieces since that experience.

There are many wonderful concerts and performances in Stuttgart, which I would like to attend, but the tickets are so terribly expensive. Father sent me a nice card from Hamburg. When did he get back?

I visited our friend Wiltraud yesterday. *[I knew her from Erfurt. She was a onetime fiancée of my Gofferjè cousin who died in World War II.]* She lives in a nice apartment not far from here and has been married for four years. Her son Klaus is ten months old and very cute. During the time when I was there, he was a very good baby. She is a wonderful mother and is very happy in Stuttgart.

She showed me her new washing machine and she let me try her electric sewing machine *[at home, we were still using an old-fashioned treadle machine]*. They asked me to visit them again soon, which I will do.

Love,
Hadwig

Stuttgart, October 20, 1956

Dear Mother,

When I came back from basketball practice, I found your letter and the package with the textbook. Thank you so much for both.

> After having read your letter, I had a good cry, but what can we change?

The letter must have contained news about one of my father's affairs, which were still going on. I often wondered why my mother never asked for a divorce.

> Since father has written to me more often recently, I somehow assumed that things were going better between you. Now I feel like I got a cold shower and it makes me very sad. I wish I could tell you to leave everything behind, pack your things, and come over here. However, Ute's disease makes it very complicated, and I am not yet established here. I hope that the doctors in Würzburg will be able to help Ute.

Ute got permission to go to Würzburg, West Germany, to be treated by the specialists there. My mother and sisters did eventually leave East Germany and moved to Würzburg so that Ute would have access to the MS specialist and the medical facilities there.

> Did you receive my package, or perhaps I did not get one of your letters. I did not hear from you for a long time.

The East German authorities censored the mail, and frequently letters did not reach their destination. Some letters were probably kept and never forwarded again.

> Well, the "interlude at Bosch" will soon be behind me. The work was not very interesting, but the fact that my coworkers liked me made it more bearable. One of my colleagues has invited me to his house to meet his family. I liked it in Stuttgart and made many new friends. I have to be back in Tübingen by November 5, in order to take care of finances and other things. I also don't have any coals yet to heat my room during the winter semester.
> Much love,
> Hadwig

Tübingen, November 4, 1956

My dear Mother,

I arrived here this afternoon loaded with all my things, and I have begun to get somewhat organized. While I write this letter, I am warming my hands on a hot plate from time to time so that my hands are warm enough to write. I have no coals yet and therefore no heat. The blouse you made for me arrived too and fits very well. You are also working on my jacket and I feel that I am much in your debt for all the things you do for me.

We won a game in October, 76:13, of which I made 13 points. Our coach called me the basketball miracle, and it made me very proud. We played and won three games on that day. I was so excited that I could not sleep that night but went anyway the next day to Augsburg to visit the Zwislers *[the family of my mother's sister]*. They were very good to me, but I did not get the sleep I needed. Cousin Herbert *[a relative on my father's side, who lived in Augsburg and whom I had not seen in many years]* took me out to dinner. We talked much over wine and caught up on all the things that happened while we had not seen each other. Cousin Uli had a week of vacation and was home, but the weather was so bad that we could not do much. I knitted and sewed and helped Aunt Irma.

Uli and I went on All Souls' Day to the cemetery to visit the family grave in Augsburg. Later I had dinner with Herbert again, and afterward he showed me all his wonderful photographs. My silly snapshots are terrible in comparison.

Herbert Gofferjé was a professional photographer. His father, Paul Gofferjé, owned a photography store in Erfurt, but Herbert left East Germany like I did and lived now in Augsburg.

Uli and I visited yesterday yet another cousin *[from my mother's side]*, Ulli Timm, whose wife was gone, and we had to get his place back in order. Afterwards we sat with coffee and cigarettes and listened to his latest records. He is a very nice chap. Cousin Walter Kroder *[the son of my mother's other sister, Klara, also a chemistry student]* came in the evening and we had much fun drinking punch and playing cards. It was my farewell party because I had to leave the next day. Uncle Heinz gave me the train fare for the trip home. They want me to visit them again soon.

At noon I stopped in Stuttgart and visited my landlady Ms. Welch, who had baked a cake for me. I took the train back to Tübingen and tomorrow it is back to studying. Is Ute still in Würzburg for treatment? When do you think she will be able to come home? Please, write me her address so that I can send her a letter.

Is it true that "the old man" will leave? Is it for real this time, or will things go on the way they have been? I think it is a good idea for you to separate. We have not had anything from our father for a long time either materially, intellectually, or otherwise. If I can come home for Christmas this year, it would be nice not to have a sulking father sitting in the other room.

It is late and I must go to bed. Thank you again for everything.

Love,

Hadwig

Tübingen, November 18, 1956

Dear Mother,

We had a game on Friday, which we lost by ten points. We embarrassed ourselves terribly. I stayed with my friend Margit over the weekend and came back to Tübingen today. I bought fabric for a winter coat. I will send it to you and would be very grateful if you could start sewing it for me.

It is very cozy in my "pad." Around me lay old clothes, lots of papers, books, and writing utensils. Amongst all this I drink my tea, which I enjoy often these days. Unfortunately it is almost finished.

Last week I heard a concert in the "Amerikahaus" *[U.S. cultural center]*. The black baritone sang so beautifully, he brought the house down. I am so hungry for culture right now that I will treat myself to a ticket for the Berlin Ballet, which will be here next week.

How is Gisla? She has not written to me for a long time. Is she studying so hard that she has no time for writing letters? I will be with you again in only four weeks. Time passes fast for me here. Tübingen has a lot of things going on, but often it is also exhausting.

I study in the new student union rather than in my unheated room. It has nice warm study rooms for people like me. There is even a perfectly furnished kitchen where students can prepare meals. Everything is provided from the pots and dishes to the silverware. One can cook a complete gourmet meal there.

I need the textbook by Gehrtsen. I have already spent fifty Marks for books, which is not enough since they are so terribly expensive. Although I get a 15% discount, it is like a drop in the bucket. Thank you for helping me out with this.

Love,

Hadwig

My mother managed to get a permit from the East German authorities for me so that I could come home for Christmas vacations. I was very much looking forward to seeing my family again, but at the same time I was worried about my return. Would they let me come back to the West again?

At the time my father was director of the scientific library at the Research Institute in Gatersleben where I had also worked, and my mother was working there also. They had access to West German publishing companies, and they were able to order most of my textbooks, even though they were published in the West. When they received the books, they would send them to me. The arrangement was of great financial benefit to me. My parents helped me, not directly with cash, but in all other possible indirect ways. Getting the textbooks for me was one such way.

My mother was at the time considering a divorce. My father had a mistress again, and mother was tired of his unfaithfulness. He has had mistresses all along, as long as I can remember, and I did wonder why my mother had not left him earlier. She stayed mostly for us children and did not like to see the family breaking up. She seems to have been ready for a separation now. We three daughters were always supportive of her in this matter.

Tübingen, November 20, 1956

My dear Mother,

I am concentrating on my studies, and I have little time for much else. I am also taking French now, outside the university, but have too little time to study for it as hard as I would like. I am making good progress in my lab course in physics. I have already finished five experiments, while most of the students have only done two. I will advance to the next level after Christmas.

I had lectures until 8 PM today and came back very tired. I had five letters in the mail, yours among them. I read it immediately and want you to know that if you decided to separate from father and ask for a divorce, I will always be on your side. It is sad, of course, but you must make the best of the situation and help yourself. Don't worry about us three girls, we are mature enough to understand and are independent now. I have learned here that it is always best to help oneself, rather than be unhappy.

I am very happy here. The only thing I miss is my family, but soon I will see all of you for Christmas. I cannot wait until then. The pictures of your new house made me even more homesick. Schimmel's family invited me for Christmas, but I will let them know that I will be going home.

Tell Gisla that I thank her for her long letter. I will try to get her the presents she wants. My room is not heated and my fingers are now too cold and stiff to write more and I will have to end this letter.

With thousands of good wishes,

I will always be your Hadwig.

Tübingen, December 13, 1956

Dear Mother,

The travel permit arrived, thank you very much. I am very much looking forward to spending Christmas with you, but I am scared of the trip itself. Will it all go without complications? Will the Communists let me come back here again? On my way to you, I will stop in Würzburg and visit Ute *[she was still in a clinic there to be treated for her MS]*. I am not sure when I will continue my trip, Saturday night or Sunday morning. I will send you a telegram as soon as I know my arrival time. It would be nice if you or Gisla could pick me up at the train station because my suitcase is very heavy.

I hope very much to find father in a good mood.

Are there still some of my old clothes at home, which I could wear around the house? If you already have the textbook, I could even study a bit while I am home.

I am all excited about coming home. I missed you all very much.

Love,

Hadwig

My trip home was more or less uneventful. I was allowed to come back to West Germany. On the way back, we were asked to leave the train at the border station. We were locked with our luggage into a large room and could not leave until everybody's luggage was checked (I don't know what for, it was probably just harassment). The train was scheduled to leave at a certain time, no matter what, and we were very nervous about getting back on the train in time. We just barely made it, and it was a mad scramble with all the people and their luggage. As usual, the East German government managed to create war conditions, even though it was peacetime.

I had some of my friends visiting while I was at home. It seemed that I had not been gone for very long, but there was already a difference in the way I was thinking. My friends who stayed back kept muddling on. Eventually the more I got involved with new friends and my life in the West, the more I lost track of my friends in the East. I did not see them again until 1998 when we had a partial class reunion in Dresden.

Tübingen, January 7, 1957

Dear Mother, Father, and Gisla,

I am alone again and sit in my "pad." I don't feel much like studying and I will write you a letter instead. I arrived back here last night shortly before midnight in a rather exhausted state. The train crossing the border was terribly crowded. It reminded me of the conditions in 1945, and I was surprised that everybody managed to get back on the train. Somehow I ended up in first class, where I traveled sitting on my suitcase. At the border we were all chased out with our luggage, and after having been checked by the armed border patrol, we barely managed to get back on the train. I was so confused from the experience that I got off the train at 4 AM and was stranded at some godforsaken train station. From there I took the next slow regional train to Würzburg. Aunt Edith Schmidt expected me in Würzburg. I asked the conductor to announce my later arrival in Würzburg on the public address system. After the terrible train ride, I finally landed safely at the home of the Schmidts *[they were distant relatives on my mother's side]*.

I was filthy like never before, took a shower, and went to sleep. The Schmidts are very likable. Their son also studies in Tübingen. I went to the hospital in the afternoon to visit Ute. She was in the same shape as I found her when I saw her the last time. Not much has changed with her health. On the trip back to Tübingen, I was again traveling in an overcrowded train with no place to sit down.

I am glad to be in Tübingen again, but I had a wonderful time staying with you and hope to be able to come home for a visit again soon. My skis, which traveled with me, arrived as well as I did. I hope that I will get to use them soon.

Love to all of you,

Hadwig

Tübingen, January 13, 1957

My dear Mother,

I thank you for your letter. I am sure that you received mine in the meantime and you heard about the tribulations of my return trip. It feels very strange to be by myself again, but I will get used to it since I have not much time to think about it.

I heard a wonderful concert on Wednesday. Music by Bach, Mozart, and Benjamin Britten were on the program. Later in the week the author Albrecht Goes was reading from his work, and I was lucky enough to get a ticket for it. I was very much looking forward to this. Although I was bothered at the beginning by the pathos in his voice, reminding me of a sermon in church, I liked it very much. He fascinated the audience by reading from his "Genesis" and "Brandopfer" and from his poems. The last reading was so vivid that one could experience it directly. You asked me about his other works, but I don't recall now what else he wrote.

The university had a center for contemporary German literature, and many authors held readings and discussions, which were open to all students. I took advantage of as many of these as I could. Thus I got educated in German literature as well as in sciences.

I have already done three experiments in the physics lab course, and I am using the slide rule that you gave me. It makes the calculations so much easier.

At the moment, I have a small, temporary job. I type letters for a second-rate lawyer. I am not very good in typing as you know, but he is even worse and appreciates my help. The winter semester will be finished in six weeks. It is a pity that the semesters are so short. I prefer studying to working at some unexciting job.

Do you have snow already? I am still waiting for my ski boots, which are still in Schimmel's house. As soon as I have them, I will be ready for the slopes.

Much love,

Hadwig

Tübingen, January 21, 1957

Dear Mother,

Thank you very much for the package. It arrived today together with your letter. We had a game on Friday against Backnang and won it 47:14. I will work again at Bosch in April and will stay again with my landlady Ms. Welch, who is looking forward to having me there.

We went skiing with a group of friends. I fell and hurt myself on rocks, which were not covered because of insufficient snow. I hope that I will recover for my next game on Wednesday. We will play against our most serious rivals. Our team has been invited to come to Versailles in June. We will drive there. It should be fun.

Can you please get me a paper for proof of citizenship? I want to apply for a passport as soon as possible, just in case it takes a few months.

A math student invited me to a dance at his fraternity. Imagine me, who never liked fraternities, and now going to a dance there. We will see how I will like it.

We played a game on Wednesday against Prag-Stuttgart and won 40:32. We lost the first game against them, and our regional title depends on only one more game. I managed to achieve the decisive basket. It was a hard fight and we were utterly exhausted after the game. Our men's team played against Tübingen here, and I was there for moral support. They won against all expectations. They thanked me profusely for my presence and support. I am still hoarse today from all that yelling. We are so happy when we win a game that we hug each other afterwards. This is enough about basketball.

The Köberles had me for dinner yesterday. I brought them a bouquet of flowers, which frankly were much too expensive for me. However, they gave me some money when I left to buy myself some fruit, but I ended up in a bookstore and bought a paperback by Kierkegaard. My fellow students and I are crazy about the existentialist philosopher.

I had some friends who were philosophy students, and we spent a lot of time discussing philosophy. Since I was a chemistry student and did not know much about philosophy, I learned much from them.

My friends, who are mostly medical students, want to go skiing tomorrow. We will meet at noon and make plans.

I am glad that Ute is doing better. I have to leave now to go to my typing job. Let it be enough for today.

Love,

Hadwig

Tübingen, February 2, 1957

Dear Mother,

Thank you for the package. The cookies arrived in crumbs, but they were delicious nonetheless. I have also eaten all the apples. When I have something to eat, I eat it all at once, as you know.

I am at present very unproductive. I sometimes procrastinate all day, which is terrible. I need a rest every once in a while. Did I tell you already about the fraternity dance? It was very nice, very intimate in a beautiful fraternity house. We danced until two in the morning and then somehow were driven home in a Mercedes. Some members must be rich, I suppose. Unfortunately I had a very bad cold on this weekend. I would have stayed in bed if I did not live alone. I am feeling better now.

Love,

Hadwig

Tübingen, February 11, 1957

My dear Mother,

There is not much time, but I want to write this letter anyway. I passed my exam in physics a few hours ago and got an "A." You can imagine how happy I am. There was even a question about quantum theory. As usual, nobody asked me the material for which I had prepared.

I will move in with my friend Tutte on March 1. I have just spoken with the landlady. I will have to pay only thirty Marks per month and only half during vacation, imagine the savings for me, even if the place is further out of town. It is a forty-minute walk to the university. There is also a bus we can take, and when the weather is good, we will take our bikes.

I was in Stuttgart last weekend and went to Bosch to talk to my old boss to make sure that I can work again in the same department. It is all arranged for me to start on March 4, even though another student was supposed to work there. They would like me back. I also have my place to stay with Ms. Welch. Like last time, I am sorry that the semester will be over soon. There is another exam for me to take, which I will pass, and a lab space for me for the next semester is already secure. I hope I will have that much luck in the future. Perhaps I may be able to pass my Vordiplom *[BS]* examinations with "A"s. If my cousin Ossi in München can do it, I can do it too.

Schimmel wrote me that her father had a stroke. He is as sick as he was last winter. As you know, her father spent many years in a Russian prison camp, and he came back in very bad health.

We are going to a jazz concert tonight and I will have to close. I will write you again soon and will send you everything that could be washed so that I will not have the stuff hanging around during my move.

Love to you, father, and Gisla,

Hadwig

Tübingen, February 20, 1957

My dear Mother,

Thank you so much for the textbook. I looked through it immediately. I will write a separate letter to father and thank him for getting it for me.

The exam for the lab space is tomorrow. I had to submit all my transcripts and letters of recommendation. My friend Brigitte saw the letters, and after having read them said that I should have absolutely no problem getting a space with those glowing reports. However, I cannot rely on those things alone. I have studied much chemistry since my last exam in physics. When I woke at night, I saw the formulas of Nicotine and Pyramidon in my mind. I think and breathe nothing but organic chemistry. I want so much to do well. I feel assured that I am better than some of my fellow students and am confident that I will succeed, in spite of the horror stories that I hear from fellow chemists. I have no fear.

My friends Brigitte and Tutte (who will be my new roommate) will come for dinner to celebrate the end of the semester. Soon I will have to get organized for my move. I will go early to Stuttgart, since I will be here alone and all my friends are getting ready to go home.

Here is some bad news: We lost the championship game against Prag-Stuttgart. We played so badly that we would have lost playing against the worst team. We did not understand why we lost so badly and I was very upset. The winners were honored with flowers, and the next day the radio reported an undisputed victory for them. There is not much one can do except to study some more chemistry.
Love,
Hadwig

Studying chemistry in Germany involved a lot of experimentation in the laboratory. The universities were already lacking space for lectures. Lab space for the experimental courses was even scarcer. There was a fierce competition for the few spaces available, and we had to pass an evaluation and an exam before we were granted a laboratory space. We spent many hours doing required experiments and taking tests after each section of completed experiments. We actually spent many more hours in the laboratory than in the lectures. German-trained chemists were well known for their laboratory skills. When I was working on my PhD thesis at MIT, which involved a lot of experimentation, my German chemistry background was a great advantage for me.

Tübingen, February 26, 1957

Dear Mother,

I returned exhausted from visiting many offices and government agencies to get a West German passport. I will have to go again tomorrow, since I have not finished yet.

I had an interview this morning at the Chemistry Department in regard to my lab space. I don't have a final decision yet, but the professor told me that I would get one. Although I passed the exams with good grades, he tried again to talk me out of studying chemistry. He told me to talk to Prof. Berger in Stuttgart and consider studying food chemistry instead, which is a much shorter and simpler education. Perhaps I should at least look into it. I feel that by now I have proven that I am at least (if not more) as capable as my male fellow students. I will let you know what I will decide.

My professors have repeatedly tried to talk me out of studying chemistry, although my grades were as good or better as those of my male fellow students. This continued through graduate school. When I was only one of three students in my class at MIT, who got a test question right, the professor had to give me a good grade, but he could not help to write the following comment on the margins of my paper: "female intuition."

My move to the new place is imminent. I will move further outside Tübingen. It is country-like and beautiful there in the summer, and the woods are very close by. The room is cheap and the landlady is friendly.

For the application of a passport, I need from you a form of consent, please send me one soon. I also need the original letter of the refusal from the University of Jena. I think father has it *[the West German government needed a reason why I left East Germany]*.

I had to have passport photos made, and they came out well. I will send you one. I will be in Stuttgart the day after tomorrow, you will hear from me from there.

Love,

Hadwig

Stuttgart, March 5, 1957

Dear Mother and Ute,

Two working days at Bosch are already behind me. I do the same work as before and know my way around. The last days in Tübingen were very hectic with many errands to do and the move into the new place. All that is now behind me.

The Köberles invited me again and gave me an envelope, which when I opened it at home contained fifty Marks. This will help me very much since I had very little money left for the month of March. I was very pleased. They are such good friends of yours.

I received a letter from the Chemistry Department stating that at the beginning of the next semester I will have a lab space for the required chemistry experiments, which will take several semesters. I am very happy about this and feel I should study some analytical chemistry during vacations, but I will not have much time because of my job.

I saw an exhibition of Danish crafts. I loved all the beautiful things, and you would have liked them too. My landlady and her companions are always very nice to me. I feel very much at home here.

I need towels. Can you please send me several?

How is Ute's health? I hope she is better. I thank her for the two cards she sent me.

Your

Hadwig

Stuttgart, March 19, 1957

My dear Mother,

Thank you for your two letters and the package with the clean laundry. I also enjoyed very much the chocolate candies. They did not last very long.

I am at present very much undecided if I should study food chemistry or go for chemistry in general, which will take sixteen semesters to get a PhD. Considering my financial situation, this is a long time. How much of one's youth should one spend trying to make it and spending most of the time over books?

My job at Bosch is very boring again. When I come home, I study French and chemistry or knit or write letters. This is not an exciting life. Sitting around like that will make me into a real "nerd." I don't have the money to do something exciting, and I am very lucky that I don't mind to be alone.

I will have some free time between Easter and the beginning of the new semester and plan to hitchhike through Bavaria. I will first go to München, and after that I will play it by ear. I am not able to enjoy the beautiful spring weather here since I sit all day long in the "monkey cage" at Bosch, and it always rains on weekends.

My friend Margit left without saying good-bye, which upset me very much (she went to Austria to get married).

The other night I was waiting at 11 PM for a streetcar in the center of Stuttgart, when my friend Helga and her brother Detleff, who were also waiting, recognized me. It was late and we did not have much time to talk then, but we arranged to meet the next day and catch up. She is working in a bank, and Detleff is an apprentice at Daimler Benz. She has not done much with herself since our high school graduation in Erfurt.

Helga is a childhood friend from Erfurt. We had known each other since we were six years old. This was the beginning of a renewed friendship with her and her family. We had not seen each other or heard from each other for many years. Helga lived now with her mother, sister, and two brothers in Stuttgart. I started to spend many a weekend with them, and later she studied also in Tübingen, where we spent much time with each other.

Tutte, who is going to be my roommate starting the next semester, sent me a food package from home. What a great thing to do! My relatives would never do this, because they cannot imagine that I am a starving student. The money from the Köberles is already used up for food.

How is Ute? You have not told me anything about her since she has come home from the clinic in Würzburg. Did her stay there actually help?

I wish I could come home at the spur of the moment and see for myself how you all are. Tell Gisla to write a letter to me and tell me what she wants for her birthday.

My landlady Ms. Welch sends her regards.

Love to all of you and the pet hedgehog *[it seems that they had a little hedgehog for a pet]*,

Hadwig

Stuttgart, March 30, 1957

My dear Mother,

Thank you for your letter and the packet with all the goodies. "Je te remercie beaucoup." I am sending you a package with dirty laundry and some useful things. The goodies are from Ms. Welch. She sends her greetings again.

I received my tax return and treated myself to a new black anorak. Too bad that you cannot admire it. I will visit Helga tomorrow. We will just "hang out" since the weather is not very enticing to do anything else. "Il fait mauvais temps" every time I don't have to work. I make great progress in French and study with a tutor who is a student at the Technical University.

Please tell father that Herr Siegele *[my father's friend, they knew each other from the youth movement in Germany in the twenties]* came to see me a few days ago and invited me to their place in Cannstatt for next week. He is very nice and has a daughter and a son who also study in Tübingen. I will report to you after my visit.

I still play basketball. At present we train for our games in April against the Bavarian champions. I missed yesterday's game, and it may have been good to see how much they need me. I have my new passport now, and I am ready to travel the world. Watch out, here I come.

I have almost decided to study food chemistry. I will go to the university in München after my Vordiplom *[BS]* and see if I would like to continue my studies there.

Last week I babysat for Waltraud's child, she sends her greetings. How I would like to help you in your garden, but it is not possible. I wish I could fly home, perhaps by helicopter, and land in your cucumber patch.

"Je t'embrasse et reste toujour ta fille,"
Hadwig

Stuttgart, April 6, 1957

My dear Mother,

I will write quickly a few lines to you. I am very busy with basketball. We will go today to Göppingen for the deciding games for the South German championship.

My visit at the Siegeles was very pleasant. I will tell you more about it later.

Please send the textbooks for physical chemistry to Tübingen, not here. I have serious financial worries. I have to pay out of my own pocket for lab equipment and for all the chemicals that I need. I don't know how I will manage that. It will take a lot of money, which I don't have.

Greetings to all of you at home and to the little hedgehog.
Love,
Hadwig

Stuttgart, April 17, 1957

My dear Mother,

Thank you for the letter and the package with the laundry. Please, send everything to Tübingen, where I will be soon. I could use both dictionaries (French and English). Please send them with my lab coats.

Tell Gisla not to be sad that I cannot buy any fabric for her now. I just got the bill for all my lab equipment, and it is a lot of money and will take everything I saved.

I will take two weeks of vacation now. I will have to work immediately when the summer vacations begin. Here is my plan for the trip through Bavaria:

April 4, beginning of my hitchhiking trip:

I will spend Easter at Mochental with Dietlinde. On April 23, I will continue to München, where your friends the Schultes invited me. I will return to Stuttgart on May 3. We have games on May 4 and 5 when I have to be back, and the semester begins in Tübingen on May 6.

I will write you postcards so that you will know where I will be and when.

I hope you all have a very happy Easter.

Lots of Love,

Hadwig

Tübingen, May 8, 1957

My dear ones at home,

I thank you for all your letters. I will answer only with one collective letter to all of you. The "medal" that Ute sent me hangs here above me on the wall. I have worked so hard that I think I truly deserved it.

I will have my lab space next week. Before I can start with the experiments, I will have to pass an exam in inorganic chemistry. This is in preparation for the work I will be doing in the lab. I will continue my French lessons at the "Centre d'Etudes," a center for French Culture funded by the French government *[like the French Library in Boston]*. Unfortunately it is at the same time as my basketball practice with the Tübingen team. During the semester, I train with the Tübingen team, since going to Stuttgart every week would be too much.

Is it as cold there as it is here? It is still necessary to heat my room, and it is already May. I'll be hearing the Brandenburg Concerti in a concert tomorrow and am looking very much forward to it.

This is not a very long letter, but I am terribly busy and wanted to answer your letter soon. I will write more at some later time, when things have quieted down a little bit.

Thank you all,

Hadwig

Tübingen, May 27, 1957

My dear Mother,

I just returned from the Chemistry Department where they told me that I have to wait longer for my lab space. I did not expect this at all. I thank you for the lab coats you sent and hope that I will soon be able to use them.

I returned last night from a weekend visit to Dietlinde. Parents of a student have given me a ride on Saturday and brought me back again on Sunday. As always, I had a great time in Mochental *[Dietlinde and her husband taught at a boarding school, which was in an old abbey]*. The Blaseys live in a large room with brand-new furniture. It was done with great taste and is very comfortable. The children are very attached to Hans and Dietlinde, who are like surrogate parents, and I would not mind to be one of their students there. We ate so well all weekend that my stomach complained. I am not used to so much rich food. The weather, however, did not cooperate with our good time. We had a terrible storm and had to stay indoors, or we would have been blown away.

My friends and I saw a good play in a student production. It was much better than the county theater company, which plays here often but is unbearably bad.

Next Thursday will be our yearly department picnic. I think I will go in order to meet some people. It would be good to increase my little circle of friends. My friends and I are planning to spend spring break in Innsbruck, Austria.

All my love,

Hadwig

Dietlinde's mother and my mother were classmates in school and best friends. Dietlinde is twelve years older than I am. She tutored me in Russian and was my great idol when I was still in high school, and she was already a student in Jena and Leipzig. I found her very smart, accomplished, and sophisticated, and I wanted to be just like her when I grew up. I was one of her bridesmaids when she got married and caught the bouquet when she tossed it. Even though it took many more years, I was indeed the next one to get married. She had left East Germany with her husband shortly before I did. They both were teachers at a boarding school in Mochental, situated in an old abbey in the middle of the countryside in a beautiful setting. They were wonderful to me when I was a struggling poor student in Tübingen, and they are still my closest friends in Germany.

Tübingen, June 5, 1957

Dear Edith, Mother,

This is how you signed your last letter and I had to laugh. Where was your mind when you wrote the letter?

I am very excited about your visit. I am sure that you can stay with Ms. Welch if you write her early enough. I will come to Stuttgart and we can meet there. I would prefer a weekend when I don't have lectures to attend, but I will come any day of the week if it does not work out for a weekend. I will also come to Mergenthau where you will be visiting your school friend Sophie. It is a great idea to take a vacation and rest on Aunt Sophie's farm rather than travel around. It would be even better if we could go together to the Ammer See *[a lake in Bavaria]*.

I visited the Köberles for lunch. Uncle Adolf thinks that he can find a summer job for me in a hotel in Switzerland. I will have to start by August 1, since it is the vacation season.

I make good progress in my lab work and have not yet made any mistakes. Let's see how it will go when it gets more complicated. I am having great fun.

I heard the Amadeus Quartet perform last night. It was exceptional.

Love,

Hadwig

Tübingen, June 19, 1957

Dear Mother,

I want to send you a report of our trip to Austria, so that you may get an idea where we were. Tutte and I hitchhiked to München, where we met our friend Brigitte. It was very hot and we swam in the Isar *[river in Munich]* on Sunday and started our trip together on Monday. We went via Garmisch and Mittenwald to Innsbruck, Austria. We had a ride with a very nice man who treated us to ice cream in Mittenwald. Innsbruck is pretty, but I only like the inner city. The outskirts are dirty and neglected, perhaps because the Austrians are a lot more relaxed about these things than we Germans are.

The great event was our four-day hiking trip through the Karwendel Mountains. Four Innsbruck students were looking for two girls to go on the tour, and Brigitte and I joined them. That made six of us: three boys and three girls. Tutte stayed with her friend in Innsbruck.

We were a very compatible group. Two students were from Freiburg, Germany. One of them had studied already for 17 semesters. He had such a wonderful sense of humor that our laughter alone tired us on the trip. Brigitte and I had no hiking gear with us, so we borrowed things. I wore boots that belonged to the late husband of one of the students' landlady. They were much too big for me and I had to wear extra socks. At the end of the trip when everybody had blisters on their feet, I was okay and comfortable. Our group looked like a bunch of defeated soldiers. We actually took a photo of our footgear because we looked so unbelievably ugly.

We took the train to Scharnitz, bought food supplies there, and climbed to the "Karwendelhaus" *[a cabin in the mountains]*, where we stayed overnight. It rained on the second day, but we had rain gear and continued. The mountains in rain have their attraction. There was a lot of fog, and suddenly a peak showed through the fog in front of us. We stayed for the next night at the "Falkenhütte"*[another cabin]*. We arrived late and there was not much room left for sleeping. It was already dark, because the generator had been turned off. We groped in the dark to find room between two feet of sleeping people. If there was enough space, we crawled in to sleep. We never found out who our sleeping partners were, particularly since some of the serious mountain climbers got up before the light of day.

The weather was good on the third day and we hiked in shorts, taking breaks with snowball fights. We heard stone avalanches grumble in the distance and sometimes we saw them. We climbed up to the "Lamserjoch Hütte," and before we retired in our primitive sleeping quarters, we climbed another peak nearby. We were now 2100 meters high.

On the last day, we hiked down in glorious sunshine. If there was snow, we skied down the hill in our boots only, which was fun and much faster than trotting through the snow. We took a break at an "Alm" [*a cabin on a mountain meadow with cows and their caretaker*]. We drank some fresh milk and went on down to the "Achensee," a mountain lake famous for being terribly cold. We tried to swim, but nobody had the courage to enter the icy water.

We took the train in Jenbach and rode back to Innsbruck. We spent another weekend in Innsbruck where we met many students. We hitchhiked back on Monday and dropped Brigitte off in München. We arrived in Tübingen and were treated to coffee and cakes by our "chauffeur," an architect. He even drove us right to our front door. A terrible thunderstorm had started, and we were glad not to get soaked at the last minute of our wonderful trip.

I drew you a map and send you a few dried Alpine flowers, which were very pretty when they were fresh. Perhaps you will recognize some of them from your trips into the Alps. Please, write soon and tell me when you will come. It is time for me now to get back to my work in the laboratory.

"Karwendel-Heil,"

Hadwig

"Skiing" on rocks.

Footwear.

My Beloved Mountains

✦

Summer Jobs in Switzerland

Tübingen, July 21, 1957

My dear Mother,

I thank you for your card. We had a wonderful time together during your visit here. I hope that you got home without any problems.

I have suddenly turned into a workaholic in order to alleviate my fear of the next exam. I couldn't sleep at night, I was just too nervous. I passed but did not "ace" it. To study physics feels like a rest in comparison to the chemistry I had to cover. My physics exam is on July 29, the last day of the semester. This interferes with my plan to tour the Black Forest by bike.

I was talking about the exams that I had to take at the end of each semester in the subjects I had taken. I had to pass with at least a "B" in order to get a scholarship for the tuition.

There is a new scholarship for which I will apply on Monday. I would get 200 Marks month, also during vacation time. This would be super and I will try to get it.

Please, arrange for me to get a student train ticket in case I can come home in October. I will enclose a list of textbooks that I need for the winter semester.

Lots of love,

Hadwig

Tübingen, July 29, 1957

Dear Mother,

Our bike tour was canceled. I did not have enough time and my old bike would not have lasted through the trip. It falls apart about once a week. I am in the process of packing my suitcases, because I will go to Switzerland on July 31.

The physics exam is behind me and my last analysis in the lab was ruined. Oh well, it is time to move on. I will hear soon about the new scholarship. Whether I can come home in October will depend on whether I will get the scholarship or not.

I was going to wait for my roommate, Tutte, to come home, but I will go to bed now, I am tired. I will write you from Switzerland.
Love to all of you,
Hadwig

Friends of the Köberles ran a hotel in Reuti, Switzerland, belonging to the Methodists. I was offered a vacation job, which included room and board. Since life was more expensive in Switzerland, my pay was higher than it would have been in Germany. With room and board free, I could save all my money for the next semester. Financially it was a better deal than other vacation jobs.

Reuti-Hasliberg, August 3, 1957

My dear Mother,

The train trip was wonderful. The Swiss trains are very comfortable and the scenery is breathtakingly beautiful. We took the route: Schaffenhausen-Zürich-Luzern-Brünig-Hasliberg. I had the company of a nice teacher from Stuttgart in my compartment. I helped her with her suitcase since she was handicapped. I could not understand the first Swiss who addressed me in the train. What an embarrassing situation. I called the Hotel Victoria [my workplace] from Luzern and took the bus from there to the Hasliberg, where the manager of the hotel and a foot-man awaited me.

I have already been here for three days but have not yet written to you. I have no idea how long the mail will take to get from here to you, that is why I will write you now for your birthday. I wish you a very happy birthday and lots of good luck. I am sorry to tell you this only on paper and not in person. I hope you will like the little present, which is on the way to you.

You are probably waiting eagerly to find out how I found things here. The landscape is singularly beautiful. I have a simple room in the attic, and from the window I see the mountaintops of Eiger, Mönch, Wetterhorn, Wellhorn, and Engelhörner. Even though it is August, all mountains are still covered with snow. I have not yet been able to go out and explore. My work hours are very long, 13 hours a day. After such a day, I fall half dead into my bed as you can imagine. It is a much work to take care of so many guests in this hotel. I should have been serving in the dining room, but I don't have the appropriate outfit: black clothes and white aprons. As of now I am the girl for all the jobs that need to be done. I am part-time in the kitchen, and part-time I am in room service. The work is simple, but I have fun, particularly in the kitchen. I wonder though how soon I will get tired of this.

The staff is very nice. People come from all different places: there is a footman from the Elsass, a local minister's widow works in the kitchen, a hotel intern is from Germany, a crazy woman washes dishes, there is a refugee from Hungary, and there are other strange but also nice people. The boss and his wife are friendly and do a lot of work themselves.

The guests are mostly elderly people. They are either bourgeois Germans or righteous Swiss. That is all I know about them since I don't have much to do with them. They are pampered here. They have comfortable rooms and great food, and everything is done to spoil them. There is also an annex, a simple wooden structure where youth groups often stay. I would prefer to stay there, simple but comfortable.

There is another side to this place: Every room has a religious quotation on the wall, including my room. Every sentence has "God" in it and every day begins with a morning service, because this is a private hotel under religious (Methodist) management. I am getting used to it and it does not bother me.

My first day here, the first of August, is a national holiday. They celebrated 667 years of the existence of the "Schweizer Eidgenossenschaft" *[Swiss Federation]*. There were parades, fireworks at night, and bonfires on the mountaintops. Our boss gave a rousing speech for the fatherland. The best thing about it all was the food. I am such a materialist and eat here like a pig.

On my next day off, I will go hiking, no matter what the weather will do. I have trouble understanding the local dialect that is spoken here. They use many French words, which I understand best. They try to speak "Hochdeutsch" *[high German]* when they realize that I don't understand them. There are also people who speak only dialect, and with them I definitely need a translator.

I am very tired and would like to go to bed. Please write again soon. Lots of love and "grüezi" *[Swiss greeting]*,
Hadwig

Hasliberg, August 17, 1957

My dear ones at home,

Two weeks I have been here so far and I like it more and more. I got quickly used to long working hours. I want to describe a typical day for you. From 6:30 in the morning until breakfast, I work in the kitchen, and after that I have to make up the rooms. To make up the Swiss feather beds is an art. They have to be shaken and pushed into a sculpture, which took me a few days to learn. After making the beds and cleaning rooms, which are not dirty, I go back to the kitchen, where I like it best. Since there are not enough personnel, I get to do everything. The meat course is the only thing that is done by the cook only.

I am allowed to make the dessert, sometimes special diet food, the vegetable course and often the salads, and the cold cuts and cheese platters. By doing and observing, I am learning how to cook. The guests do not order their individual food. They eat the general menu, which changes every day.

The greatest benefit about this job is that I am at the source of the food and can eat as much as I want. I have eaten already two lunches today and this happens often. The Swiss cuisine is different from ours. It is rich and very labor-intensive. We have an hour off every afternoon. I mostly sleep then or read a book. We have to be rested to work again until 9 PM. I have befriended a young intern, and we do things together when we have time off. We have two afternoons per week free and went on such occasion to the beautiful Lake Brienz, where we took a steamship trip to Interlaken. This is a nearby town full of luxury hotels with international guests. This is a new world for me, but I prefer to go back to our hotel on the "Hasliberg."

I went again to Interlaken. The occasion was the Tell festival. The local citizens perform every summer the story of Wilhelm Tell [*a Swiss folk hero*] on an open-air stage. I found it very exciting that the stage was filled with ordinary people (not only actors), live horses, and cows. I finally learned how to understand the Swiss dialect.

Mother suggested I should go on a hiking tour before I return to Tübingen. Erika (the intern) and I have already planned such a trip for October. At that time we will not work here anymore, but we can stay in nearby Goldern with the widow, who helps out in the kitchen during the season. Many years ago she ran her own "pension" and school for home economics.

I am free this afternoon. I went out and up the hills in order to take some photographs. I celebrated mother's birthday on the "Gummenalp" with fresh milk in the cabin of an old cow farmer. I go up a mountain in my free time whenever the weather is good.

I am sending you a postcard so that you can admire the impressive mountains. Just looking at them often helps me when I get discouraged. All I have to do is look out of my attic window.

Two Italian and two German mountain climbers had an accident at the north face of the Eiger. One Italian could be saved, the other one was found dead in his ropes. The German climbers cannot be found and have probably fallen off the mountain. The north face of the Eiger is notoriously dangerous and has bad weather very often. The first climbers made it up there only recently. I can watch this overwhelming and scary mountain from my window.

I hope to be back home in October, in time for Ute's birthday. I will write you the details later.

Greetings to all of you,

Hadwig

An "Alp" or "Alm" is a mountain pasture. The cattle are driven up the mountain to spend the summer and to graze on the luscious mountain grass. There is usually an "Alpbauer", a farmer with them who lives in a log cabin and milks the cows. The milk is made into cheese right there on the mountain. This way, the cows can stay there all summer long. When the weather gets cool in the fall, the cows are led down the mountain. This is always a great event. The cows are decorated with flowers and beautiful ceremonial bells around their necks. I have watched the spectacle of a parade of cows reentering their village, where they are stabled for the winter. Letting the cows graze the mountain meadows in the summer is general practice in all the alpine regions of Germany, Austria, Switzerland, Northern Italy, and France. It is this healthy grazing that produces the rich and tasty milk and makes the best chocolate.

Hasliberg, August 27, 1957

My dear Mother,

I thank you for your letter. I receive little mail here, and a letter from you is very much appreciated. Nothing much has changed here, except that I work exclusively in the kitchen from now on. I am glad not to play the chambermaid anymore. The hours of work have not diminished, but I was free yesterday afternoon and climbed up the "Mägisalp." The Swiss cows are simply beautiful. They have such soulful eyes that cannot be described. You have to see them. I am planning a hiking trip to the "Giebel" with Erika, and we talk often about our hiking tour in October. Can you please send me my warm-up suit, which I will need then?

I am terribly tired and have to go to sleep and will not write anything more today. I hope that Ute will be home from the hospital for her birthday.

My love to Father, Ute, Gisla, and especially to you,
Hadwig

The view from my window.

Hasliberg, September 10, 1957

My dear Mother,

I just reread your very nice birthday letter and must admit that I will never be able to write such beautiful letters as you write. My letters to you must seem very cool and factual. I write often even though I am not always in a writing mood, but I don't want you to wait a long time for my news.

My birthday passed like every other day. I had to work and nobody knew that it was my birthday. I got your greetings and a little package from Schimmel. There were at least those things that reminded me that I had become 20 years old, so horribly old.

You asked me about my hiking plans. We don't yet have final plans. We may start on September 23 or on October 1 and go for ten days. We plan to go first to the "Engstlenalp" and to the "Jochpass" and then on into the area of the "Jungfrau": "Rosenlauigletscher" *[a glacier]*, "Grindelwald," "Schynige Platte," and "Rothorn." There may be changes. It will depend on the weather.

There is a lot of work in the kitchen at the moment. We have a conference of Methodist preachers from Switzerland. I suffer presently from the "Föhn," other than that I am well. I have already gained ten kilos. This extra weight should last me through the meager times in the next semester.

The "Föhn" is a warm, dry wind that blows down the valleys on the north side of the Alps. Many people get affected by this wind and get tired or feel generally unwell.

Since the food was free and I never got enough to eat when I lived alone in Tübingen, I stuffed myself in order to have resources for later. I would lose all the extra weight in the next semesters.

You will have received the card from Interlaken. When I was there, I was almost hurt in a car accident. I had the afternoon free and the hotel manager offered to give me a ride to Interlaken in his new Opel *[German car]*. He is a very careful driver, but the streets are extremely narrow and curvy. Suddenly a very wide car came toward us. We either would have crashed or we needed to go to the extreme right, which is what the manager did. He scraped his car against the rock wall and demolished the side of his car. It was a question of centimeters. Thank God we were not hurt. It was quite scary.

We had a beautiful full moon the day before yesterday, and a group of young people working at the hotel wanted to hike up the "Plauplatte" during the night and watch the sunrise from the top. Unfortunately the weather spoiled our plans. On the next full-moon night, we did climb the "Plauplatte." It was a bit eerie but also very beautiful. It is a different world up on a mountain above the tree line with the moon shining down on us. We could not stay long because we had to go back down to be ready for work in the hotel in the morning. As we walked back down and got just into the tree line, we heard a very strange moaning noise, which startled us. It could not have been a human being at this hour in this place and it must have been an animal. Because the noise was so unexpected, we were all a little bit scared and started running down the mountain. At 7:00 AM we all reported back to work and nobody knew about our night's adventure.

Many years later, I was watching a nature show on television and found out that a deer or an elk makes this kind of moaning sound. I heard it again during rutting season in the woods of New Hampshire in a similar situation.

We have a young farmer's wife for extra help in the kitchen. Her brother is a mountain guide. He could perhaps take us up the "Wetterhorn" in October. That is the great big mountain in the front of my panorama from the window. I am going crazy with excitement when I think of the possibility. I hope that it will really happen. When I look up at the mountains, I feel this longing and want nothing more than to be up there. I assume that the mountain climbers feel that way and even risk their lives just to get up there, above the world, so to speak. I can understand the irresistible attraction while I am here and look every morning at those amazing mountains.

Could we have a combined birthday party for Ute and me when I come home in October? Perhaps we could invite a few friends? Please, send my train ticket to Tübingen. If I don't get to go up the "Wetterhorn," I will be home by October 11 or 12, otherwise a few days later. The new semester does not begin until November 4.

Let it be enough for today.

Lots of love,

Hadwig

Hasliberg, September 9, 1957

My dear Mother,

Thank you for your letter and please thank Ute from me also for her letter. Please, don't worry about our hiking trips. We are not foolhardy. We will start our trip tomorrow. Everything is ready. I inherited a pair of good, sturdy hiking boots. We are wearing pants and wool socks. I have a heavy ski parka, wool mittens, a heavy sweater, and your Alpine hat, which you wore on your mountain tours. We will look like a pair of bums, but we will have everything we need. We are responsible about the climb up the Wetterhorn and will have a professional guide, who will not take us if we are not prepared. We are not even sure yet if we can really go. The weather is great at the moment, although it snowed quite a bit last week. We hope that sunshine will finally prevail.

I have almost decided not to come home. I am terribly afraid that I will not be able to leave again, if they find out that I left illegally. I read in your last two letters how much you are looking forward to seeing me again, but will the trip be without danger? I do want very much to come, but should the authorities retain me, I would be beside myself. I don't know what to do, to dare to come or to stay in Tübingen. At any rate, send the permission for my trip to Tübingen. Please, write again soon.

Love,

Hadwig

Hasliberg, October 7, 1957

Dear Mother,

After receiving your letter, I decided to come home, no matter what. I am leaving here in three days. I will go on to Stuttgart on October 11 and may leave from there on the same evening or early the next morning. I will send you a telegram and let you know my exact arrival. I am so much looking forward to seeing all of you again. I have so much to tell, it may take up the whole time that I am there.

I will tell you about my trip when I am there. I can tell you more details than I could do in a letter. I will also bring pictures. You know already that I was in Lugano, Locarno, and at the Lago Maggiore, which was not planned. You must have received my postcards.

I am a "perfect" cook now. I made another cake, which came out well, but it does not succeed when others bake it. I did not learn how to cook meat because only the master cook does that. Last week when the cook was on vacation we managed to cook without her. There were three of us, all amateurs, and we had the help of the crazy dishwasher.

Presently we have 110 guests. They are here for a course for youth group leaders. I took leave of the mountains yesterday on my free afternoon. I will miss the mountains very much when I have to go back to Tübingen, but I have to leave and need to study before the beginning of the new semester.

I am looking forward to my trip home.

Lots of Love to all of you,

Hadwig

The hiking trip was very short. We had good weather the first day and arrived at our cabin, where we wanted to stay overnight. There were no overnight accommodations, which we did not know, and we had to hike another two hours to get to another cabin. We arrived there dead tired. The next morning was dark, rainy, and foggy. We decided to go back down and hitchhike back to the hotel. We wondered what to do now with our vacations. The weather is usually good on the south side of the Alps, and we decided to hitchhike to the Italian-Swiss area, south of where we were. Thus we had wonderful unplanned days in Lugano and Locarno. We stayed in a youth hostel, which was full of mice. We could hear them scurry around all night. It was a wonder that they did not crawl into our sleeping bags. The weather was great and we were glad to have come this way. I also got hooked on the delicious cappuccinos that are brewed there.

Tübingen, November 7, 1957

My dear Mother,

It is already a whole week since I have returned from my visit with you. I am back "in the groove" again.

I am struggling with a very difficult analysis in the lab. I also heard that I have to take exams so that I may get my scholarship this summer. You can imagine that I am pleased about it. I have spent hours waiting in front of the professors' offices so that they may give me a date for the exams. This means that I must study hard and be frugal until the money is granted.

My visit with Dietlinde and Hans was very nice, as always. If I cannot come home for Christmas, I can visit them. I will, however, have to fill the "empty spaces in my brain" with chemistry and physics during my Christmas vacation. I will go to Stuttgart to play basketball tomorrow. I cannot really afford the time, but I have to balance my activities. I cannot study all the time.

My bicycle is literally falling apart. The front wheel rolled away from it the other day. Someday there will only be the bell left over, which is not working anyway. Let it be enough for today. Don't forget to watch Sputnik II and see if you can identify the race of the dog that is on board.

Love,

Hadwig

Tübingen, November 14, 1957

My dear Mother,

I was very pleased to have received your letter. I have not heard from you for a while and wondered why. My financial situation is precarious at present. I spent all my savings and I am waiting for my scholarship. I also have debts, which I cannot pay back. The first part of the scholarship exam in physics is behind me, but I am still waiting for a date for the chemistry exam. I goofed my last lab analysis and have to start over again. All subjects are more difficult now. It is not as easy as it was in the beginning semesters. When I get home from the university, it is already 8:30 PM and I am usually dead tired so that studying more at night is not very productive. I don't have time for a private life, just study and work.

I continued with my French course today. We speak only French and often I don't understand a word and I must study for this also. I hope that my landlady and her family will go to bed soon. The stupid music they play bothers me, and there is constant talking in the background. I need my peace for studying or sleeping. Ute will have to wait with the oranges, since even bread and margarine are a luxury for me these days.

All my love to you,

Hadwig

While I was waiting for my scholarship to get approved, I was without money and food. I was so hungry that I could not walk in the street and pass stores with their windows full of foods, the bakeries with breads and pastries, and the butcher shops with meats and sausages. My stomach would twist when I saw such food and could not have it. I had no means to eat in the student cafeterias. I don't know how I survived those times. Although I was lonely, cold, and hungry, my idealism kept me going. My great idol was Marie Curie. I remember reading in her biography that as a student at the Sorbonne she was cold at night in bed for lack of heat in the room. She piled heavy objects, such as drawers, on herself, believing that the weight gave her a sense of warmth. I had the ingenious idea to iron my bed at night before I got in. This took out the chill. My mother sent me a heating pad as a Christmas present. With that, it was luxury. The money that I got sometimes from my mother's friends became my "emergency fund" for such times.

Tübingen, November 24, 1957

Dear Mother,

My latest news is that beginning tomorrow I will work in a factory in the afternoons. I will do my lectures and the lab work in the mornings and will work from 2:00 to 11:00 PM in a factory, which makes transformers. It will take away precious time for studying, but I cannot live without money. I study on the weekends, but there are so many subjects to be studied that the time is not enough. My landlady has been recently very nice. Occasionally she even feeds me.

A fellow female chemistry student invited me yesterday. That was unusual. For some strange reason, I have not much contact with the few female students in my class.

In case I can come home for Christmas, if I can even afford the time, I will not have enough money to bring presents. Please tell Gisla not to have illusions about expensive presents. There are simply no funds for presents. Could you also please inform father about my predicament? But don't push him for money. If he does not part with some willingly, I don't want it. Please do not worry about me. Somehow I will get through this. It always worked out until now. I just have to hang in there.

Love,

Hadwig

Tübingen, November 27, 1957

Dear mother,

You may wonder why I am writing so soon again. Your package arrived yesterday and I want to thank you. I have also received a "life-saving" package from the Richters, your friends. Did you write to them about my difficulties? Your friends always come through, but the relatives don't care. I can make it without their help.

The remaining exam is behind me now and I passed, although I did not do extremely well it. I must have been good in physics, the professor told me so himself. This is strange because I don't really feel very secure in physics, but I always do well.

Are you going to apply soon for my permit to come home for Christmas? I have to know as soon as possible whether or not you will get one. I have to quit my job in time and plan accordingly.

I just found out that I need a minor for getting a PhD. How can I possibly find the time to study for another field? My workload is getting bigger and bigger. Students taking their exams for a degree study day and night. Peter just told me that he postponed his "Diplom" exam *[for a master's degree]* until May because he is so pressed for time. This is all for today. I have to get back to my studies.

Love,

Hadwig

Tübingen, December 9, 1957

My dear Mother,

It is already 10:00 PM and I am sitting in an unheated room, but I will write you anyway today. Who knows when I will have the time again to write you a letter? Thank you for your long letter and the Christmas package. I found both after my return from Dietlinde's. Again I loved my visit with them, and if I cannot come home, I will have a wonderful Christmas with them.

My work in the factory has become routine by now. The trouble is that I have to stay up later at night in order to study. I am so looking forward to a vacation. For once I would like to get enough sleep and take it easy. I am beginning to go a little nutty from the chronic overwork. The factory has extended work hours before Christmas, and I am now working also on Saturdays from 7:00 AM to 12:00 noon. You can imagine that there is not much time left for studying, which I have to do at night, and I have to give up some of my sleep for it.

Dietlinde gave me weight-loss pills for you. I will send them as soon as I can. I need pills for gaining weight. My Swiss fat reserves are used up.

Unfortunately my wristwatch broke down and I am running around again with my alarm clock in the pocket. You still have one of my watches at home. Can you please send it to me soon? I hope it will arrive safely, considering that it has to cross the border.

I will not be able to bring Christmas presents. I am saving up for my train ticket home. Other than that, I am doing all right and hope that the scholarship will come through soon. Manfred Hausmann is reading tonight, and I am looking very much forward to a pleasant evening.

Love to all of you,

Hadwig

P.S.: My landlady is turning into a whining dragon. She complains so much that she can barely catch her breath: "Ja, wissest se, wenn me koi Maa meh het" *[Swabian dialect for "You don't know how it is without a husband"]*.

Tübingen, December 12, 1957

My dear Mother,

Here is good news: I did get my scholarship. I had to go to the student offices and complain about the delay. Unfortunately I do not get any money during vacations, as I had hoped. In order to get paid during vacations, I would have to apply for every semester separately and possibly wait two and a half months for the money to be paid. What a nuisance! I am relieved and can sleep again without having to worry where the next money will come from. The uncertainty was much harder to bear than being hungry all the time.

My job will continue until the beginning of the Christmas vacations. I have been paid ahead of time and must now work to earn whatever money I have already received. Otherwise I would have to bring money back to the factory.

Tomorrow is another exam at the end of a lab course. I studied until 2:30 AM last night. Oh, how much I need a vacation! The winter semester starts on January 2, which does not give me much time to come home and to rest. I am waiting every day for the arrival of the travel permit. I will take the night train to you as soon as I have the permit. In case a permit is refused, I will visit Dietlinde on December 21. I wish I knew what is going to happen. Father has sent "pills" via Hamburg. Is it a present or a loan?

"Pills" was a code for money. Transfer of money between East and West Germany was illegal. Communist authorities checked the mail often, and we used code to be safe.

Life looks good again. I will send you a package with very small presents just in case I cannot come home.
Lots of love,
Hadwig

Mochental, December 22, 1957

My dear ones,

Life is very good here with Dietlinde and Hans. It is so restful, although I study a few hours every day.

I wish you all a wonderful Christmas, as far as it is possible to have a happy Christmas in East Germany. I was thinking again about all the abundance of foods and things we have here, even though it is often hard earned, but we have it. I hope to get a permit for next year. The stupid regulations will perhaps get better with time.

I thank you, mother, for the package, and I thank father for the pills from Hamburg. They alleviated the worst pain. I will write him separately. I wish for Ute that she would get better, now that she is home with you. Gisla should help you, since I cannot do it now. I will write you more in the future.

Lots of love to all of you,

Hadwig

Mochental, December 26, 1957

My dear Mother,

Thank you for the lovely Christmas letter, which I received here, and thank you for the good cookies. We started eating them immediately. We telephoned Tante Mariele *[Dietlinde's mother in East Germany]* today. It took us two whole days for the call to go through. We had a very cozy Christmas here. It was very sumptuous for former East Germans as far as our culinary welfare was concerned. It is cold here, but we have not yet had any snow.

Did you receive my package in time? I have gotten very nice presents. I now have a fountain pen again. I am writing this letter with it. In case you find my old one at home, you can throw it out. I also got a pair of Chinese slippers and two little books. I brought for them Corelli's Christmas concert on an LP.

I wish you could be in Mochental and could relax as I can. The students are gone and it is very quiet here. Dietlinde pampers me. I have a little problem sleeping, because I am not as exhausted as I was before. My life is too relaxing now. I am knitting on my sweater and make good progress.

Dietlinde and Hans loved your book and will write you separately. Cousin Herbert sent me a pious book and thirty Marks, which was sweet of him and surprised me.

We are about to go for a long walk. The weather is great and we want to take advantage of it. I must stop writing now.

Many thanks and lots of love,

Hadwig

Tübingen, January 9, 1958

My dear Mother,

I am sitting in the chemistry library and have a little time, so that I can write you this letter. Parents of students gave me a ride back from Mochental, and I arrived here on Tuesday night.

Upon my arrival I found your package and thank you very much. You don't have to send me food anymore. My "larder" is now full again. I have a bad conscience when I think how much money you spent for all this food.

Everything is back to normal here. I have to catch up with the material that I missed while I was working and not studying, but I am making progress. Soon I will be caught up.

How is Ute? Does her health still improve? I almost forgot to thank you for the seventy pills. They will help much like always.

Thank you and much love,

Hadwig

Tübingen, January 19, 1958

Dear Mother,

Please thank Ute from me for her letter. I am very slowly getting my work done but have to stay up until midnight almost every evening. There is no chance of getting enough sleep. I am also behind with my French lessons. I hope that I don't have to give it up altogether. It would be a pity.

There are two concerts this week that I want to hear: Mozart's Requiem, the Eroica, Bach's second violin concerto and music by Max Reger. I heard such good music in Mochental that I miss very much their collection of recordings.

I was in Stuttgart last weekend and visited Helga. She and her family live in one room, just like in 1945, but they are all together again *[they had recently left East Germany]*. My visit was very pleasant. Helga even forgot to show off, instead she admitted that she has no friends and feels very lonely. I am in a similar situation, but I have no time for friends and no time to worry about it either. I usually see Tutte *[my roommate]* only late at night. We both come back from town with the last bus at 11:00 PM.

Love,

Hadwig

Tübingen, January 24, 1958

My dear Mother,

It is a pity that you have no occasion to hear concerts where you are. Regardless of my finances, I am going to every concert possible. A young and very good violinist from Vienna recently played Bach's violin concerto in A-minor and a sonata for solo violin. It was outstanding and the public showed their appreciation. We can get inexpensive student tickets for these concerts, or if we are clever, we sometimes cheat and get in without a ticket.

I partied last Sunday with my room neighbor, with the son and daughter of our landlady, and with "Moscht" *[the local fermented apple cider]*. When I had to go back to the lab on Monday, I was thoroughly hung over. We had a basketball game last Friday. We won against Tübingen. We play against Degerloch on Saturday, and I hope we will win this game also.

Love,

Hadwig

Tübingen, February 22, 1958

My dear Mother,

I got nothing done in the last days because I have a terrible cold. I tried to go to the lab but came home with a bottle of red wine and made a hot punch. I drank most of it and crawled to bed quite "smashed." As a result, I am feeling much better today.

The St. John's Passion will be given tomorrow, and I am looking forward to hearing it. March is approaching, and I will have to work somewhere. I am glad that I can work in the Hotel Victoria on the

Hasliberg again. They want me very much for the kitchen since I am familiar with that work now and the cook is going for a vacation during that time. Let's see if I can replace the boss in the kitchen, haha.

Tutte came over today and I shared a jam sandwich and my last money with her. Someone stole her last five Marks and her wristwatch. She was very upset. A little red wine helped to calm her down.

Nothing terribly exciting is happening here. I refused an admirer recently, and a fellow student suggested that I make a notch in my heel for every shunned admirer. That sounds like a good idea but could weaken my heels dangerously. I have really no time for admirers.
Good night for now, it is already midnight again.
Love,
Hadwig

Hasliberg, March 5, 1958

My dear Mother,

After having taken care of my finances for the next semester so that I don't have to wait for my money again, I considered leaving Tübingen today. I wondered if I would get to Reuti before the evening since I am hitchhiking this time. I left at noon and was lucky. I arrived in Luzern *[Lucerne]* at 7:00 PM. From there I took the train to Brünig and called the hotel manager to pick me up from the train station. I was at the hotel at 10:00 PM, and the whole trip cost me only 4.60 Swiss Francs. Nobody here knows that I hitched rides to Luzern. If they found out, they would be appalled that I live such a "dangerous" life. There is still a lot of snow here, and it reflects the sun so much that I cannot go outside without sunglasses. Snow or no snow, it is so beautiful up here, and I am glad to be back in my beloved mountains.

I visited Frau Burckhardt on my free afternoon. She was very ill, but she is healthy again and her spirits are not at all diminished. I borrowed a few books from her so that I have something to read in my free time.

I also have to write a letter to Erika, who is now in Brussels. She has invited me to visit her there. I have an offer to hitch a ride with a fellow chemistry student. If it works out, I will visit her.

I am glad that you like the wool I sent you. Fortunately we have the same taste in such things, which makes it easy for me to find what you like. Don't worry about the money. I have spent much during the last month anyway, and while I am here, I need only a little pocket money.

Love to you, Ute, and Gisla,
Hadwig

Frau Burckhardt, a widow living in a nearby village, was originally from Germany and helped out in the kitchen during the vacation season. She was a very educated woman. She had become my friend during the last summer when I was working here. It was a relief to have some intellectual company among the people working in this hotel. She also supplied us with mountain gear when Erika and I embarked on our hiking trip.

Hasliberg, March 20, 1959

My dear Mother,

Thank you so very much for your letter. You asked me so many questions that I want to answer them right away. I will stay here until April 2. I plan to hitchhike back to Tübingen. I have to take care of some things there and will start a bike tour on April 5. I am going with a young man from Augsburg whom I met on one of my hitchhiking tours. I told you about him. He is a pleasant and dependable friend. Our destinations are: Freudenstadt, Strassburg, Basel, Zürich, and Freiburg.

Financially I am in good shape now. I assume that I have to wait for my scholarship again next semester. I have not touched the retroactive pay from last semester. This means that I have some reserves now. In addition, I am paid for the months of March and April while I am working here. I think that I can afford the bike trip. I am planning to get my "Vordiplom" *[bachelor's degree]* in the winter semester. I would like to be free during the summer vacations to study for it. I am therefore saving like mad. It would be even better if I could come home and study there.

Will Ute be home for Easter? We don't have spring here, but lots of snow. We went sledding, and my bottom has huge black-and-blue spots from it. When I sit down and yell from the pain, everybody is startled.

My work here is pretty much as usual. The only difference is that we are not as busy as we are in the summer (when it is high season). I am done in two more weeks. Time flies when we are busy. The capacity of my stomach has decreased much since last summer. If I eat a lot of rich food, I get sick because I am not used to it. Swiss food is traditionally very rich. I felt terrible recently, and I wanted some strong alcohol to help me digest the fat. This is an alcohol-free hotel, and there is no alcohol to be found anywhere, not even for cooking. Someone remembered that the pig, who is fed with the leftovers, was sick and that he was treated with brandy. What is good for the pig is good for me, and we looked for it and found it. Anyhow, the pig's leftover brandy cured me.

Love,

Hadwig

Tübingen, April 3, 1958,

My dear Mother,

You must have received my postcard from the Hasliberg, and you will know that I am now again in Tübingen. I arrived here last night. I had good luck again with getting rides. By the time I got here, I had been riding in many different cars.

It was much warmer on the Hasliberg, where the sun is much stronger than it is here. How is your Easter weather?

"Jacky," my buddy for the bike tour, will arrive on Saturday. I am excited about our trip. It always makes me very happy when I can travel and see many places. I wish you could do that too, but you are stuck with the Communists who don't let you travel.

I just noticed that my boss from the Hasliberg hotel has given me an extra 20 Swiss Francs. A little extra always helps. I will buy a new bike today. The old one needs to be retired. The expense is worthwhile since I will use the new bike for my daily trips to the university. I will also look for a pair of shoes for Gisla.

Love,

Hadwig

Tübingen, April 16, 1958

My dear Mother,

I came back today from the bike tour. I had to take the train for the last stretch. We rode for 36 km in constant rain and were soaked through. Our clothes were so wet that we literally had to wring them out. I took the train in Sigmaringen, but poor Jacky continued on his bike to Memmingen. The wind was also against us, as if the rain was not bad enough. This was a lousy end of our trip.

We started out on Easter Sunday and rode 60 km to Freudenstadt. The youth hostel there was terrible and we continued the next day to Strassburg. Here was the actual beginning of our sightseeing. I loved the old city with its narrow streets and old houses. We tried their good and inexpensive wine. The cathedral is overwhelmingly beautiful. The youth hostel was a place with a lot of character, very relaxed and French. We continued on Tuesday along the French side of the Rhine and the Rhine-Rhône Canal until Basel. This was a distance of 133 km. We managed it because it was all flat terrain and we had the wind in the back. It was, however, the longest stretch I ever biked in one day. I was overcome by a hunger attack just before Basel. Fortunately we had baguettes on the back of our bikes, and I devoured one of them right then and there.

Basel is a very attractive town. I feel at home now in Switzerland since I have been working during vacations there. They also have a great cathedral, which we visited. We spent some time in the zoo and then went to the Rhine harbor. We rummaged around everywhere and ended up in the corn silos. We also stood at the famous corner where the three countries Germany, France, and Switzerland touch.

We rode the next day to Zürich. We visited an amazing crafts exhibition. Walking around the streets of Zürich, one can see that the Swiss never lost a war. There is much wealth in this country, which manifests itself for instance in the many fancy cars the Swiss drive. The people are very friendly everywhere. We did not stay in Zürich, because the youth hostel was very crowded. We rode on to Schaffhausen. We had a nasty wind against us, but the beauty of Schaffhausen made up for the unpleasant trip. The city has many old fortifications. The youth hostel was in an old manor. We visited the Rhine falls and took it easy, just wandering around.

On our way back, we came through beautiful landscapes in the Black Forest. The weather was good and we did not rush through this area: Schluchsee and Titisee. Occasionally we had to push our bikes through snow. It was much colder here than in Switzerland, probably because of the elevation. We continued downhill along the Danube, riding through Donaueschingen, Tuttlingen, and Beuron where the youth hostel was in an old castle. It was very romantic. The upper

Danube valley is very picturesque, and we were sorry that we did not have more time. It is the perfect place for hiking. We visited the castle Wildenstein, which was built in 940. We poked around in every corner. It felt as if it were our castle and we were knight and maiden of the castle. We shared some soup from a banged-up old pot and felt very much at home. The real "soup" came the next morning when it rained and rained all the way to Sigmaringen where I gave up and took the train. My new bike withstood the hardships better than I did. We were as tanned as we were dirty when we returned from our three-country tour.

Much love,

Hadwig

Tübingen, April 25, 1958

My dear Mother,

For all of last week I was terribly sick with the flu. This must have been the result of having been drenched and cold on our last day of the bike tour. I went to bed with a fever and felt miserable, particularly since I lay there all alone and had nobody to do anything for me. I could not sleep at night. My landlady was not visible through all this. I would have been so much better to be sick at home, but I am better now.

Jacky, my trip companion, is a great biker. He carried most of our luggage already and pushed my bike up the mountain and sometimes even me, when it was necessary. I think that at the end he had a crush on me. He is really still a kid, although a very nice kid. Others of his age would be smoking, drinking, and flirting with girls. He is very serious and loves nature and the mountains.

I have many good intentions for the new semester. Even though I will not have many lectures, I have much lab work to do. I plan to be in the lab every day at 8 AM, and there will be no more "fooling around" with my fellow students. I finally had to chase the guys away from my workplace, or I would get no work done. Now I have the reputation of being unfriendly.

"Fooling around" needs to be explained: We sometimes made explosives just for the hell of it. We also blew paper bags full of air and smashed them with a loud noise so that the lab assistants came running to see whose experiment had blown up.

Things are a little uncertain in matters of scholarship. I never know exactly when I get money and have to have a reserve for the lean times. I finally managed to have a little spare money, which I will not touch unless absolutely necessary.

Did Gisla receive the shoes and does she like them? What did you do on Gisla's birthday while I was sick in bed?

Lots of love,

Hadwig

Tübingen, May 7, 1958

Dear Mother,

I just finished my final exam for a section of lab work. I have studied much and knew much but could not use any of it in the exam. Instead I messed up the obvious, but it is now behind me and I can start with the next group of analyses. I have a great relationship with the lab assistants and wish it would help. Of course, they will not tell me the results of my experiments. With that, I am on my own.

There is a conference of Nobel Prize winners in Lindau. I would be terribly interested to go to something like that. Even though we have student discounts, I cannot afford to spend the money or to be away from my work for five days.

I could use Kortüm's textbook of electrochemistry. The course is getting very difficult. The subjects are getting more difficult every day. Peter has his Vordiplom exams next week and fears to flunk them.

How is Ute, can she work again? It would be great if she has recovered so much that she can work. I miss your garden this time of year. I would like to sit outside and study. Instead I am here working in a stinky lab.

Tübingen is beautiful again in the spring, just as it was when I started to study here.

Lots of love,

Hadwig

Tübingen, May 28, 1958

Dear Mother,

Since I can use Ms. Welsch's sewing machine, I bought fabric and made myself a new dress in two hours. It is one of those new short shift dresses and looks very good on me. I lost weight and my old clothes don't fit anymore.

There is an opportunity for me to go to Berlin for a week. It is a conference for students organized by the SPD *[Socialist Party of West Germany]* and very inexpensive. I am politically neutral, but I signed up for the trip. I will be in Berlin starting June 19, and it would be great if I could meet any of you while I am there. *[It was still possible to take the subway from East to West Berlin.]* I suggest we meet at the Weidendammbrücke, you can take the train to Friedrichstrasse. Please telegraph me and tell me if and when you can come. Perhaps you want to meet in a different place? I will be busy with lectures during the day, but I am free after 5 PM and on Sunday. I very much hope that it will work out and am looking forward to see you again.

Much love,

Hadwig

Tübingen, June 10, 1958

My dear Mother,

Please, don't worry about me. I have enough to eat but lose weight anyhow. It must be my very busy life that does it. I am actually eating a lot.

I was in München last weekend. I was very lucky to hitch a ride with a Mercedes 190 SL and we "whooshed" at 160 km per hour all the way from Stuttgart to München. My friends and I had a great time at the Hofbräuhaus and in Schwabing. We spent most of the night in a club there and then went for breakfast at the "Donisl." This is a meeting point for everyone who had been out all night. You can find the mayor of the city and very simple folk sitting democratically next to each other.

Standing constantly in the lab causes me pain in my feet. I walked home barefoot from a concert the other day. My companion had to carry my shoes but did not take his own shoes off to show his solidarity. This same admirer thought to have seen my bicycle standing in town a few days ago and attached a letter to it. It turned out, however, that it was not my bike at all. I wonder what the owner of the bike did with a love letter. It is a pity for the letter writer that he is much too short for me.

Love,

Hadwig

Tübingen, June 20, 1958

My dear Mother,

My return to Tübingen still feels strange. I feel so far away from all of you after having had a chance to meet you, Ute, and Gisla in Berlin. Our trip back was uneventful. We were all very tired. The bus left there at 3:30 AM and we had not slept much the night before. We went to the theater in East Berlin and saw Brecht's "Die Mutter." Helene Weigel *[Brecht's wife, a famous actress]* played in it. After that, I went dancing with a bunch of law students from our group. We hardly had time to get detoxified before we got onto the bus on Thursday morning. The whole trip was a great success.

There is no news about my scholarship. I am stuck again on one of my experiments, and the progress is very slow. But I am not the only one among my fellow chemistry students who complains that we get on very slowly with our lab work.

I am also quite unhappy that I had to postpone my Vordiplom examinations into the seventh semester. Thank you for sending the delicious cake. It did not last very long.

Lots of Love,

Hadwig

Tübingen, June 26, 1958

My dear Mother,

Occasionally I need a restful weekend. This weekend is one of those. I have to be fit for "cooking" the last analysis for the lab in analytical chemistry on Monday. After all that, I will have to start with quantitative chemical analysis. Not only do we have to find out what is in the mystery mixture, but also how much.

For relaxation I am painting and drawing again. A fellow student saw one of my drawings hanging in my room and liked it very much. He told me to do more. This motivated me to buy paper and paints and produce something very primitive almost every day. But I am having fun. Somewhere at home should still be my watercolors, which I left behind. Perhaps you can send them to me. Ask Gisla, she may know where they are.

There will be a poetry reading with works by Busch, Roth, Morgenstern, and Ringelnatz. Tübingen offers a diverse cultural program during the semester and I want to take advantage of as much as I can.

Great news: the scholarship money for May and June has finally arrived. It was about time. My friends and I will celebrate with an outdoor punch party.

Be well and lots of love,

Hadwig

Tübingen, July 1, 1958

Dear Mother,

Thank you for your wonderful letter. Your letters are always beautiful. A few typos make no difference.

It is unbearably hot here. I would like to go to the pool, but it will be too crowded in this heat. I had a little crisis last week. I was so sick and tired of all that lab work that I could not concentrate on anything anymore. I wish I could have come home. Instead I took time off and went to Stuttgart. Today I "talked to myself" and I am back at my work. It just gets very tedious at times and I need a break.

I was invited to a concert in the castle of Bebenhausen. The atmosphere of the surroundings was very nice, but the music was played poorly. On the program were string quartets by Beethoven and Haydn as well as Mozart's Quartet with oboe. We went for some wine afterwards in order to recover from the bad experience.

Another semester is finished and all my friends are leaving and going home. I have had invitations from my fellow students, but I don't want to visit. I would like to go home if I could or else I will stay here. My friend and neighbor, a medical student, came over to tell me about his financial problems. We usually console each other. Not only is he from East Germany, but he is also an orphan. He was evicted from his room, and when he finally found a place to stay, he, Tutte, and I sat on the wall along the Neckar and celebrated the end of the semester and the end of some of our problems with a bottle of Schnapps. Afterwards we went to an apple orchard not far from where we live and we stole enough apples to last us for months. There happened to be a NATO maneuver in the area. We found American soldiers in the orchard and asked them to protect us with their machine guns from the owner, should he show up. We also practiced our English with them. We felt very secure picking our apples, and they enjoyed the diversion.

I am sorry to hear that Ute got so suddenly sick. I hope it is not anything serious. Please give her my love and tell her to get well soon.
Love,
Hadwig

Tübingen, August 4, 1958

My dear Mother,

A very happy birthday to you! This is not a very happy time for you. It is sad that Ute is back in the hospital *[she was diagnosed with typhoid]* and you cannot go for your vacation. I hope that Ute will recover. Is there anything that she wants and I can send her? Where is Gisla when all this is happening?

I have made a new friend here. She plays basketball with the Tübingen team and is 5 cm taller than I am, can you imagine that? She lives in her parents' house where I visit often and sometimes I can even use her sewing machine.

Peter, my neighbor and medical student, came with me last Sunday on a bike trip into the Alb *[the hilly countryside around Tübingen]*. We climbed the "Achalm" near Reutlingen. I painted up on top while Peter chased the flies, which tried to interfere with my work. We live in a beautiful area, and trips like ours are very pleasant. I wish we had more time for such diversions.

My landlady keeps bugging me about gas and electrical bills and will soon again increase my rent. I am tired of it and will look for another place closer to town and closer to the Chemistry Department.

I hope that this letter will find you in a better mood than when you wrote to me. You are right when you say that all we can do is bear the unfairness of life. It would be so much better if we could be together and support each other. I am glad to have found a comrade in Peter. He has had his own problems in life, and it helps us both when we talk things over. In spite of all the unpleasantness, there are always moments filled with beauty and we can take courage from those moments.

Much love,
Hadwig

Tübingen, September 1, 1958

Dear Mother,

A package is on the way to you. Please take fruits, honey, and the cookies to the hospital for Ute. I also included some coffee for you. I hope that it will arrive in good condition and the fruits will still be fresh.

I returned yesterday from Mochental. It was as always very nice there. Hans and Linde bought a new VW and we did much driving around. "Metternich" *[nickname of their colleague]* was always with us. He had just returned from a year in France, which did not do anything for his "nerdiness." We went to Blaubeuren and visited the "Blautopf" *[a very deep blue pond]* but did not see the mermaid. She must have had her day off. We also saw a beautiful 15th century altar in the abbey church. We rummaged a little in a potter's shop but did not find what we were looking for. We visited Frau von Arand *[painter and art teacher at the school in Mochental]* in her studio on Saturday. I took my water-colors to her. She liked many of them. We spent almost three hours looking at her artwork. I love her work, and she gave me four of her watercolors and gave me many pointers, which I will use in my next painting session. I also read two books and listened to good music on records. I felt sorry that I had to leave yesterday.

Love,
Hadwig

Tübingen, September 16, 1958

Dear Mother,

I should have written a letter to you a long time ago. I am cleaning out my closets. I am giving clothes away, because I need the room. Most of the time I wear only blue jeans and a sweater. I don't need most of the clothes in my wardrobe. I received the letter and some "pills" from Leipzig, thank you very much.

We had our first game of the season yesterday, which we played against Tübingen. We won 35:7. That is not bad for the first game.

I am so glad that the new semester is starting soon. You asked me if I wanted a permit to come and see you. I have too much work now, and it would be better if you apply for a permit for the Christmas vacations. I always prefer to spend Christmas at home, rather than be a guest in some friend's house.

I am glad that Ute is getting better. I thank her for her letter and will write to her soon. My life is not exciting at the present time, because I study, study, and study.

Love,

Hadwig

Tübingen, October 3, 1958

My dear Mother,

Thank you for the letter and the package. The Communists let everything in the package come through. Nothing was confiscated.

I wanted to stay another week in Stuttgart but came back to Tübingen, since I plan to be in München on Saturday and Sunday. I want to meet with "Ibicus" *[my cousin Walter, a chemistry student in München]* and investigate if I could continue my studies there. I also considered Göttingen, but the laboratory facilities are ancient there. I wonder if I can switch easily from living in provincial Tübingen to living in a big city like München.

I am worried about the set of weights. You may not be able to get them, and I will have to find a used set. A new set costs seventy Marks, which I cannot possibly spend for it. *[We needed very accurate weights for quantitative analysis. Every student owned his own set.]* I also have to buy coals for the winter soon, although we have wonderful warm weather still and I don't have to heat my room yet.

You don't have to send me apples. I have plenty because we helped ourselves in the orchard, do you remember? The Stelzenbergers gave me a whole basket of apples, and I can even help myself in the garden of my landlady.

Is there ever good news about father? I am glad that I am not financially dependent on him. Ute is getting better and that is good news. Please, give her my love.

The pharmacy congress is over, and I spent all day waiting to meet the people from Gatersleben. I was quite angry that I had to waste a whole day. I finally spoke with Mrs. M. this evening before she was driven to the train station. She gave me the books and the goodies that you sent with her. I had neither lunch nor dinner for fear that I would miss them. I was frozen blue, but now it is behind me. I ate the whole cake you sent, since you can imagine how hungry I was and I have only a piece of bread in the house, which has to be enough for tomorrow's breakfast. I have not heard anything about you from the congress participants. Nobody took time to talk to me for a few minutes. All I could do was send greetings home to you with them.

I want to thank you for all the things you do for me, considering how difficult it often is for you. I hope that I can be with you on Christmas.

Love,

Hadwig

Tübingen, October 20, 1958

Dear Mother,

You must be very busy since I have not had a letter from you for a long time. Please tell Gisla to write me again. I am waiting for Peter to come by. We want to "forage" for some more apples. We will look for the best apple trees on a walk by daylight and then go back at night to get what we need.

Peter studies physiology at present and carried a brain in a jar the other day. He finds these things fascinating. When it is not our studies, we discuss contemporary music. I want to be able to understand and enjoy the modern music. Peter plays the piano and understands contemporary music much better than I do.

Do you think there is a chance that I will get a permit to come home for Christmas *[the issuance of permits often depended on the political situation]*?

Much love,

Hadwig

Tübingen, October 24, 1958

My dear Mother,

I have been waiting for days for mail from you. It would be so nice to have a letter and some distraction when I am sitting from morning until night over my books. I hope that everything is in order and that the reason why you don't write is only lack of time.

We have cold weather now, and I had to start lighting my coal stove. We played five basketball games recently. We won four of those, and one game was undecided. There is a good chance for us to make the championship for Württemberg *[a "land" of the Federal Republic of Germany]*.

Many students have come back to town. A sure sign that the new semester is starting soon. I participated in another seminar in Bergneustadt. I came back yesterday. We stayed in a beautiful house in a hilly landscape and enjoyed the luxuries. We were about 50 participants, ten students, and the others came from all kinds of professions. We had to listen to many lectures. There was one married woman and I, the only young woman among all these men. I had to hold my own in the discussions at which I was very successful. It was very interesting and motivating. I traveled back on Saturday and took a break in Köln *[Cologne]*. Two students from Köln, who were at the seminar, wanted to show me their city. They showed me churches, interesting excavations from Roman times, the new modern theater, and a Kandinsky exhibition. Köln has much modern art and sculpture, some by Barlach, my favorite. Then there is the famous stained glass window by Marc Chagall in the cathedral. I am so lucky that I can expand my cultural horizons on these occasions, and I think very often that you are locked up in East Germany where you have no access to this world. I understand very well that you are "starving" for culture.

Did the ballpoint pen for Ute finally arrive? I hope that it was not confiscated at the border check. Please, let me know when she gets it. Lots of love,
Hadwig

Tübingen, November 16, 1958

My dear Mother,

Thank you for the present. I will buy warm pajamas. I am always cold at night sleeping in an unheated room. I usually study in the warm university library and don't get home until 11:00 PM. I heat my room only on Sundays, and when I get home, my bed is very cold. I have used my electric iron to warm up my bed by ironing the sheets before I get in. This works well.

I am sending you a few photographs, which Peter took on one of our bike trips. The awful jacket I am wearing is Peter's jacket. He lent it to me because I was cold. He is forever the gentleman.

I hope everything goes well with the fleas on the pug. Although I don't know how to take care of pugs, I will follow your instructions *[this was code again for some money transactions]*. It is time to go to bed. I am starting an electron microscope workshop with practical applications tomorrow. It will be very interesting.

Much love,

Hadwig

Tübingen, November 28, 1958

My dear ones at home,

Thank you all for your long collective letter. You seem to have to deal with difficulties again *[I don't remember what the difficulties were]*. I am also at a low point. I have problems with health, chemistry, and money. My work in the lab does not progress anymore. If my fellow students did not complain about the same things, I would take it personally when the experiments don't work out. My scholarship is again uncertain, but I hope it will get approved like it was before. I would love to come home for a weekend, but I will have to wait until Christmas. If I could, I would come home and help you with your housework, which would be like a vacation for me. I am studying too much again.

There is a concert tonight with music by Corelli, Boccherini, Vivaldi, and Stravinsky played by the Musici di Roma. This will be my relaxation.

I will send another pen to Ute. Too bad that it never arrived. I wonder who is using it now, some Communist censor? Can you please send me "Electronenmikroskopie" by Mahl & Golz? It is published in Leipzig and I cannot find it here.

Yes, you may send a package to Peter. He will love it. He allows me to listen to his piano practice, which he does in the student center. He plays very well. He played from Schubert's "Kinderszenen" the other day. That is all for today. Please, let me know about the travel permit, as soon as you know.

Love,

Hadwig

Tübingen, December 3, 1958

My dear Mother,

The pug from Köln had thirty fleas, and the textbook came also. Do I have to send it back in four weeks or can I keep it? I need it all semester long. Thanks for sending it so promptly.

Tutte and a friend came visiting and we had a knitting session. It is getting really cold here and I go to bed with my bathrobe and socks on. I have a terrible cold and stayed in bed today.

Your express letter came with the travel permit. I am all excited that I can come home for Christmas. I will leave here on December 18 and let you know my exact time of arrival. Unfortunately I have to send the permit back. The birth date is wrong and I don't want to have any problems on the border. Please, send it back again via express mail. I will do a little Christmas shopping next weekend in Stuttgart.

Peter and three other medical students surprised me with a visit. They wanted to have a Christmas party, and I shared with them your cookies, which they loved, and was asked to send you their compliments. Could father have my violin repaired and send it to me, or I could take it with me when I come? I could investigate about taking lessons, if I can possibly afford them.

Love,

Hadwig

Falling in Love with Paris

◆

Internship in France

Tübingen, January 11, 1959

My dear Mother,

Meanwhile I arrived back in Tübingen and think about the wonderful time I had with all of you over Christmas vacation. My luggage was not inspected at all this time. Our train was one hour late and I missed my connection in Stuttgart. After I got back, I visited Tutte, because I needed company. It is hard to get used to being alone again.

A large package came in the mail from your friends. When I unpacked all the goodies, I began to sing. The best foods were in the package, coffee, chocolate, sausages, and more. I will have enough to eat for a while now. Many people gave me presents. The Köberles had me for dinner and gave me money. Ms. Welch gave me a book, jams, and more food.

I visited Helga. Her family lives now in a new apartment outside Stuttgart. She told me much about our classmates and teachers in Erfurt [*she must have been visiting East Germany*]. I love the beautiful ring you gave me. Everybody admires it.

We are a group of four students who have a date for our Vordiplom oral examination. It will be on July 2, 1959. We have study sessions together and plan to have a "dress rehearsal." Yesterday I was from 8:00 AM to 4:00 PM in the library, where I could study with minimal interruptions. When my brain started to smoke, I took a walk with Peter and afterwards we stuffed ourselves with all the good food that I now have. I will finish soon my last lab course. It was often very frustrating, but it was also fun.

Please, give my greetings to Ute and Gisla.
Love,
Hadwig

Tübingen, February 20, 1959

Dear Mother,

Would you like to hear about my summer plans? Helga, who is now also studying in Tübingen, asked me if I would go to Paris for one week in June. The trip is organized by a student organization. I am also applying for a job in the laboratory of the gas company in Paris. I would work there from September 1 to October 15 and get paid 4500 francs per month. This means that I have to work on my French.

It is a pity that you cannot spend your vacations in Bulgaria as planned. You could come instead and visit me here, but after my examinations, which would be the middle of July.

Wolters, an "old" classmate from high school in Greussen, visited me. Back then I did not like him. I don't like him much better now. He has not changed. He is still showing off and is the same boisterous loudmouth. However, it was fun to hear about my classmates and find out where they all landed. Wolters is taking a course in an old castle near here and invited me to visit him there. I can use a break from studying and will go on the weekend.

Love,
Hadwig

Tübingen, February 28, 1959

Dear Mother,

We finished the electron microscope course on Monday and I got an "A" on the final exam. This will also count for my tuition scholarship exam. Tuesday was such a beautiful day that my exam partner, Hans, and I left in the middle of the physical chemistry lab course. We annoyed the lab assistant by writing on the blackboard: "Have fun with work, greetings from Schwärzloch." We went to Schwärzloch, a traditional student pub outside town. They serve the famous "Moschtbowle," a punch made with hard cider. We found a group of students there who were already quite happy from drinking this "stuff." One of them claimed to be a "purebred" Erfurter [citizen of Erfurt]. He invited us to eat a traditional Erfurter meal with him, but we will see if he remembers any of that when he is sober again. An artistic medical student gave me one of his drawings with the inscription: "To the most charming and alcohol-resilient lady of the evening." I hung it up on the wall of my room. It was hard to go back to the physical chemistry lab at noon the next day, but we could not avoid it, the experiments had to be done.

While Tutte and I walked home from the library the next evening, our stomachs were growling from hunger. Neither one of us had any money to buy food. We looked in vain for a piece of bread in our bags. Luckily we ran into a fellow student, Eric, who lives close to us and invited us to a chicken feast. I had not talked to Eric for weeks and avoided him. After an evening of drinking, he came to the house where I rent a room and locked my landlady into her living room downstairs. He then came upstairs and almost broke down my door with banging and shouting. Between his ranting, he whispered through the keyhole that he wanted to give me a kiss on my ear. The door of my room was fortunately locked and I did not react. The next day all hell broke loose and my landlady was furious about the disturbance in the middle of the night. I expected Eric to apologize, which he did not do, and as a result I did not talk to him anymore, but now that he was sharing his chicken with us, I forgave him.

The next day I was plagued by hunger again and visited the Stelzenbergers. They filled me with so much food and made me so round and fat that I could have rolled down the hill on my way home.

I received from uncle Bahn thirty pills *[code]*, which helped kill the pain that always hits me at the end of a semester. We have the most beautiful spring weather here. Good weather always lifts my spirits, even if there is not enough food around and the examinations are looming in July.

Much love,

Hadwig

Tübingen, March 3, 1959

My dear Mother,

Thank you for your postcard from Leipzig. Your French is still very good. I wish I could speak it like you.

We had an important basketball game on Saturday. We played against München and embarrassed ourselves. We lost 69:39. I had five fouls in the second half and was taken out of the game. Those München women are tough and hard. I still am black-and-blue from crashing into them. We drove four hours to München, played our game as soon as we arrived, and returned the same night to Stuttgart. We got back by 4:00 AM. It was very stressful, but I am recovered now.

The other day a Mercedes pulled up in front of my house. The occupants asked for me, but I had no idea who they were. It turned out that they were the Rohrbachs *[friends of my mother who had immigrated years ago to the U.S. and lived in Andover, Massachusetts]*. I don't know how they found me or recognized me. We never saw each other before this day. They were on their way to the Black Forest and took me out to dinner. We talked much about you and our relatives. Tante Martha *["aunt" Martha Rohrbach]* does not understand why my actual relatives in Augsburg *[my mother's sisters]* do not do more for me. The Rohrbachs are still very much German, not at all like Americans, although they have lived in the USA since the thirties. Tante Martha suggested that I should apply for a Fulbright scholarship to go to America for a year. Their son went to Germany on such a scholarship. I hope that I made a good impression on your friends. I tried my best for your sake.
Lots of love,
Hadwig

Tübingen, March 26, 1959

Dear Mother,

It is better that you have sent the Easter package here. I am looking forward to it. I don't know yet where I will be for Easter. Linde said she would send me a telegram and pick me up, but I don't know if that is before or after Easter. Meanwhile I have an invitation from a fellow student to spend Easter with his family in Ulm. What can I do but wait? I console myself with going to the movies.

Peter rowed me up and down the Neckar for two hours yesterday. The poor guy must have very sore muscles today. Sometimes I have to take off a day or two since I usually work for eight to ten hours a day. I hope to finish most of my studies by the end of April. I will then have two months for reviewing the material.

I received unexpectedly forty "pills" and will use them to buy fabric for a black dress, which I need for the examinations *[traditionally students took their oral exams in formal dress—dark suits or dark dresses]*.

Peter and I came upon Wolters in town, but we snuck away and hoped he did not see us. I did not want him to visit me again. He was not at all nice to me in high school.

Happy Easter to all of you!

Love,

Hadwig

Tübingen, March 31, 1959

Dear Mother,

By Good Friday I had not yet heard anything from Linde and called them. They could not have me for Easter. I packed my things and went to Ulm to visit with Hans' *[my exam partner's]* family. This was his second invitation, the first time I did not dare to go. We just got back from Ulm and will continue to study tomorrow. Hans' family is from Berlin and they are great people. He has a younger brother and a sister. They are all very close to each other. We lived like kings over the holidays and had much fun. On Saturday we saw "A Masked Ball" by Verdi in the theater, on Sunday we went sightseeing. Except for the old part of the town and the cathedral, Ulm is not a very pretty town. We went to the theater again on Sunday but stayed home on Monday. The weather was bad and we read and listened to recordings. The weekend was a good opportunity to get to know Hans. We knew each other from the first semesters, but we usually just kidded around and talked much while we took all our lab courses together. We can have serious conversations now, and I hope that we will be good company for each other and that we will pass our exams. We drank often enough to our success.

Many kisses,

Hadwig

Tübingen, April 14, 1959

My dear Mother,

I thank you for your postcard. I am always looking forward to mail from you. I am very nervous about the upcoming examinations. The relationship with Hans is unfortunately in trouble. We fell in love since Ulm and that interferes much with our working together. I wish we could still be the buddies who constantly joked with each other and took nothing seriously. Instead we see each other daily, and when one of us is down, the other one gets upset. It is hard to concentrate on our studies. We had a good talk, and for the moment the distraction is under control. I hope you don't mind me telling you about all this nonsense, because nonsense it is.

I am so absentminded that I embarrassed myself recently in the student union. I stood talking to another woman student and was loaded with papers and heavy books under my arm. Along came a very handsome guy who stared at me. With a loud crash, I dropped all my books and papers at his feet. He picked up everything for me, and his friends made great fun of him. I was so embarrassed that I wanted to become invisible. I am such a silly goose!

Our examination date was to be fourteen days earlier, but we managed to have it postponed again to July 1. The whole deal will take fourteen days anyway. I think it would be safest if you plan to come the middle of August, just in case of delays. We can then celebrate your birthday together.

I owed money to a fellow student and went to repay my debts. He is a philosophy major, and soon we were involved in a philosophical discussion about Sartre. I must be a good listener since he likes to present me with his outlandish and revolutionary theories. Our arguments are always fun and I learn much about philosophy from him.

Peter is in the middle of his premedical examinations and will probably pass them with an "A." I will be very happy for him. He deserves good grades. He not only works hard, but he is also very enthusiastic about medicine. I am sure that he will make a very good doctor.
Much Love,
Hadwig

Tübingen, April 24, 1959

My dear Mother,

Thank you very much for your very nice letter. It relieved some of my loneliness, which overcomes me occasionally. You can imagine that the last weeks were very distressing. It was a constant battle between reason and feelings. Hans and I have come to a quiet understanding that we will not see each other as often. It just interfered with our concentration on what we need to study.

I have passed the final exam for a lab course and have to do only one more experiment in physical chemistry. Soon I will have finished that course also. Jacky came to visit me on the weekend of May 1, but I sent him home again. He was upset, but I need my nerves to get ready for the exams. I have no time to play until I have passed my Vordiplom exams. After that, I would like to continue to study elsewhere, perhaps in München if I can get lab space in their chemistry department. I need a change of scene. I have been here for too long.

We will be going to Paris from June 13 to June 19. I wrote you that the bus tour is organized by the ASTA *[a student organization]*. Helga is going also.

Peter has lent me several important books. He is always helpful and one of the most genuine friends I have.

Much love,

Hadwig

Tübingen, May 14, 1959

My Dear Mother,

Thank you for the package and the cake, which I took over to Peter. He sends his thanks also.

It is very hot here and I had to adjust my study schedule. During the day, I take the books outside and sit on the banks of the Steinlach *[a stream nearby]*, where it is much cooler than in my room. Most of the work gets done at night when it has cooled down. I study until 1:00 AM and then sleep late the next morning.

When my brains need a little rest, I write you a letter as I do now, then I can continue studying. I have covered a great amount of material and hope that I will be asked something that relates to what I studied.

Next week I will go to a concert with music by Händel and Haydn, that way I will have a little break. I see Tutte often. She has passed her "Physicum" *[premedical exams]* and real medicine is starting now. She has to examine patients and does not feel very comfortable about it, particularly in gynecology. I wonder if she would make a good doctor. Peter, on the other hand, is very excited about it all and demonstrates to us all the new things they have been taught.

I have to get back to studying. Chemical formulas fill my dreams every night and I am constantly thinking about the upcoming exams.

Lots of Love,

Hadwig

Tübingen, May 24, 1959

Dear Mother,

My black dress for the exam is finished. I sewed it yesterday and today. It is very elegant and makes me look very slim. I will send you the rest of the fabric and ask you to make me a jacket to match. I will send the pattern also but you need to find some buttons for it.

Your letter came as I was studying thermodynamics and I needed an interruption very badly. Your trip to the Black Sea sounds wonderful. I am glad for you.

I passed my oral exam for the last lab course today. There are usually about twenty students in the audience, which makes it a little bit more nerve-racking. Hans did not do well and he should have flunked, but he made it by the "skin of his teeth." I was the only woman student and had to uphold the honor of my sex, which I did.

I have a great tan and you would not believe that I study most of the time. I am in a great mood these days and hope it will stay this way. I see the end of this last effort and cannot wait until I am done with the exam.

I have attended only one single lecture this semester and that was a medical lecture. We often audit lectures that are not in our field. If one of our friends has an exciting professor in his class, we get together and audit just for fun. This is what we did at the medical lecture where students were called to examine patients. We sat in the last row to be inconspicuous, but one of us, a philosophy major, was called up front to examine a patient and make a diagnosis. Of course, he could not do this, and the professor told him that he knew immediately that he is a theology student. We were afraid that we would all be called up front, but we got away with it. This was the first and last lecture of this professor that we audited. We are going to other lectures where we do not look like we don't belong there.

Love,

Hadwig

Tübingen, June 6, 1959

Dear Mother,

The day before yesterday, a young woman stood at my door and claimed that I am her aunt. It was the daughter of Brigith *[my stepsister]*. Ursel is only two years younger than I am and happens to study in

Tübingen. She just started her first semester. She found my address from the student directory and came to find me. We liked each other immediately and made a date for some time later. We decided to get together as often as we can. When you come visiting, you will get to know her also.

It is still very hot here and I sleep in the morning, go out in the afternoon, and study at night. My room is directly under the roof, and when the sun is on it all day long, my room becomes boiling hot.

My finances are out of equilibrium again, but my mind is calm. I only miss being at home. I wish I could be there and study in your beautiful garden. Tutte, Peter, and I are going to a concert with contemporary music: Fortner, Stravinsky, Boulez, and Bartok. I will now go back to my studies until I am ready for bed (which will be very late again).

Much love,

Hadwig

Tübingen, June 10, 1959

My dear Mother,

The package with the jacket arrived this morning. It looks great, and I am surprised that you could make it so fast. I will finish the last stitches on it soon. Helga was here and liked it also very much.

I ran into one of my "old" teachers from Greussen in town today. He is actually still very young and was our physics teacher in high school. When I asked him what he does in Tübingen, he said that now he studies physics because he had studied German literature before. No wonder he did not know beans about physics when he taught us and he was at most one lecture ahead of us. He could not explain anything and we could not understand. It was a disaster. Other than that, he is a nice guy. We had other teachers back then who did not know what they were teaching, including our chemistry teacher and Russian teacher. Good thing we survived this inadequacy of teachers.

I wish you wonderful vacations and hope you get a well-deserved rest.

Love,

Hadwig

Tübingen, June 21, 1959

Dear Gisla,

This letter is addressed to you, but it is also a report about my trip to Paris for all of you. I have been back for two days now but I am still very tired, the trip was exhausting.

Paris is an unbelievably beautiful city and just like I had imagined it. Everywhere is an atmosphere that reflects the generosity and "laissez-faire" attitude of the French. It made me very aware of our German stodginess. The French immediately recognized us as Germans. They spoke German to us, although we had not spoken and they could not have found out from the language. It must have been just the way we looked and conducted ourselves. American tourists, of which there are plenty, are also recognizable. It seems there are more foreigners than French in Paris. Our hotel was in the area of the opera. Helga and I tried the metro and found that it is very easy to find one's way around, as long as one knows what "sortie" and "correspondence" mean and what the name of the end station is. My French was just barely enough to ask for a street, to shop, or to deal with the garcon in a restaurant.

The "Place de la Concorde" is the most beautiful and grandiose square in Paris. From there we walked up the "Champs Elysées, where we admired the good taste and imagination in the decorations of the shop windows. Everything has French flair. We sat down in one of the attractive cafés and ordered "citronade avec glace" after having secretly checked with the dictionary. We climbed on the "Arc de Triomphe" and took a sightseeing trip around the city.

We met a girl from Stuttgart who did not speak a word of French. She joined us and in no time three Frenchmen "made the move" on us. One of them spoke a little German and we managed a conversation, but there was no hope to get rid of them again. They invited us to go dancing; we said we could not dance. Then they invited us to the movies, but we said we were half blind; they invited us to see Nôtre Dame, which we said we had already seen. Finally we managed to get rid of the three Frenchmen and the girl from Stuttgart, but we had to outrun them to the next metro station. The trouble with Paris is that the men are indefatigable in pursuing women. When we were at the café, someone threw little paper balls at me in order to get my attention. They are very resourceful and never give up.

I loved "Montmartre," which is very romantic, and painters are everywhere and want to paint your portrait. We were not allowed to go into "Sacrè Coeur" because our dresses were too low cut. The Eiffel Tower is a rusty monstrosity and spoils the whole image of Paris. In the evening we went to the "Quartier Latin," to the Sorbonne and the "Boulemiche" [*Boulevard St. Michel*]. On Tuesday we went to Chartres. The cathedral there is even more beautiful than Nôtre Dame. We spent the afternoon in Versailles, which was disappointing, since it looked very run-down and I expected more opulence. The "Petit Trianon," once Marie Antoinette's playground, on the other hand, was very romantic.

Despite our tiredness and so many new impressions, we had enough wine in the "Quartier Latin" so that we were fit enough to go to a "bal musette" behind the Bastille. Even though we had enough men in our group, the Frenchmen almost "attacked" us and wanted to dance with us. We continued on to a jazz club where we listened to Bill Coleman and Mezz Mezzrow. Finally we ended up in "Les Halles," the large market with its merchants and clochards. A butcher ran after me and gave me a pig's tail calling: "un souvenir." We were back at the hotel at 5:00 AM.

The next morning we went to the Louvre but did not have enough time to see everything that should be seen. In addition we were very tired and it was difficult to concentrate on the great art. At least I can say that I have seen the Mona Lisa and the Venus of Milo. We checked out the "Bouquinistes" [*bookstalls along the river*] at midday and took a boat trip on the Seine in the afternoon. We tasted wine in a wine cellar near the Eiffel Tower, and at night we went to the theater "Ambigu," where we saw Marcel Marceau. Our poor knowledge of French was no handicap with the pantomime. We also saw the "Place Pigalle" and "Moulin Rouge" and never saw such a rich assortment of prostitutes. We could almost not get our male students back to the hotel.

On Thursday we went shopping in the department store "Galeries Lafayette" and in the afternoon visited the "Jeu de Paume" [*museum of Impressionists*]. This is my favorite museum and I will have to go back, should I be in Paris again. The artists exhibited there are Monet, Manet, Sisley, Seurat, van Gogh, Toulouse-Lautrec, and others. I could spend hours there. We wandered along the "Champs Elysées" in the evening until it was time to get into our bus. We started out at midnight and arrived in Tübingen the next day utterly exhausted. It took me two days to recover.

These few days were not nearly enough time to see all of Paris, although we performed a regular marathon and saw as much as anybody possibly could in such a short time. It was an orientation for me, and if I get the internship at "Gaz de France," I will find my way around the city. My French is sufficient to communicate, and I will learn the rest very fast, once I am there and have to speak only French. Lots of love to you, Gisla, and to all of you,
Hadwig

Tübingen, July 5, 1959

Dear Mother,

This is a report about my exams. The oral exams in three subjects, inorganic chemistry, analytical chemistry, and physical chemistry, are behind me. I was very relaxed and able to concentrate. Whatever I did not know immediately I could figure out. I will find out my grades only after I have had the exam in organic chemistry, which will be on July 10. After that, there is still physics for which I don't have a date yet.

Hans did not do very well and I had to answer many of the questions given to him.

It was very hot here in the last weeks, which made studying indoors very difficult. Sometimes I went with my books into the garage where it was nice and cool. You will hear more from me soon.
Love,
Hadwig

Tübingen, July 13, 1959

Dear Mother,

Nobody can blame you for being very angry at the East German authorities that you could not get a travel permit and cannot come and visit me. These are the drawbacks of living in the Communist part of our country. But don't fret, perhaps I can come and see you if they give me a travel permit. We can still be together and I can get some needed rest.

I have been very sick with the flu and a very sore throat. I dragged myself from bed to desk and back to bed again. This is not a good time to be sick, and the heat here does not help.

I also have good news. I passed my exams with a "B" in all subjects. I am finished now, hurrah. I had the physics exam last Tuesday. I went there with much dread but was told that I had done well also. I am so glad to have it all behind me. I lost weight from all the stress, but it feels wonderful to think what I have accomplished since I started here in my first semester.

It is not so wonderful that I am alone now and cannot share my bliss with someone. None of my friends are around. I am flirting at the moment with a chemist, Hubert, who will take his "Diplom" exams in winter. He was nice enough to pick me up after the exam, but he went home for today and I will not see him until tomorrow when we have a date. Hans did not do well at all and is very quiet and depressed since he probably flunked. He has hardly spoken to me and will leave tomorrow for his internship in Norway. It must have been hard for his male ego that I passed and he did not.

Brigith visited me last week. We got along famously and enjoyed gossiping about our father. Perhaps we should visit him together in Gatersleben, what would he say to that? Brigith is charming, with lots of spunk and very open-minded. She is about to marry for the third time, which amuses me somewhat. I have gone swimming with Ursel a few times. She seems to have a hard time making friends here.

I will go to München with Tutte on Monday to see if I can continue my studies at the Technical University in München. We plan to be roommates again. I need a job badly because I am very broke. I am not even sure if I can afford to come home. Life in München will be much more expensive than it is here.
I know you are happy with me that I have done it, sometimes against all odds.
Much love,
Hadwig

Tübingen, July 23, 1959

My dear Mother,

Tutte and I have been for three days in München. I must apply first to the Technical University, and they will tell me in September whether I will have a lab space or not. It does not make any sense to change universities without getting a lab space. I will have to take mostly lab courses, and without the facilities for experiments, it makes no sense to go there. It has nothing to do with grades. The available spaces are usually reserved for their own students, not for anybody coming from another university. It makes also no sense to look for a room in München. I will stay in Tübingen for the present time.

My two cousins, Ossi and "Ibicus," are also studying chemistry in München and were the best hosts. We met them every morning and raised hell for three days *[they let liquid air into the dorm, which filled it with a white fog]*. I am sure they had fun entertaining two young girls. As you know, Ossi is very charming and I get along really well with Ibicus. They told us they wished that all their female cousins were like us. They said their sisters were terribly boring. We had a great time, even if our trip was not successful for a transfer to the Technical University.

I am so happy that you could get a travel permit for me and I can come home. I don't know what to do with myself just now. I will arrive with a large suitcase full of dirty laundry. I will leave here on August 3 and I will be free for the whole month of August. I am still waiting for an answer from "Gaz de France." I will be finally able to enjoy your garden too.
Love,
Hadwig

Paris, September 2, 1959

My dear Mother,

"A dead body sees Paris," was that not the title of a thriller? I am the dead body now. As always, I have had help with all my problems for this adventure. I was lucky that Hubert checked my mail while I was home. He read the letters from France and sent me a telegram. He came back with his family from the "Bodensee" *[Lake Constance]* and came by on Sunday evening. He is so attentive, although I sometimes ignore him. He forgave me that I stood him up before I left for home. We went dancing and got home very late. I drank only coffee or I would not have lasted. He gave me good advice and helped me to take care of a lot of formalities. He had to leave on Monday, but another friend helped me to take my heavy suitcase to the train station. I left

Tübingen on Monday night. I have a few nights without sleep behind me and I arrived very tired in the morning of September 1 in Paris.

The first thing I did was to buy a map of the city. I then asked to find the Rue Cambon, but got lost. Nobody had told me where I needed to be. I finally took a taxi to the headquarters of the "Gaz de France." They knew about me, thank God. I am working in the "laboratoire d'essay" in "Gennevilliers." My boss is friendly and I can communicate with him, because he speaks very clearly. My fellow workers are very helpful. A young lab assistant took me immediately under her wing. Luckily another German student is working in the same lab. He lives in the same dormitory in the Sorbonne where I was supposed to stay. He told me that it was for men only, and I began to suspect that something was wrong. My mail from them had come to Mr. Gofferje and they had arranged for me to stay in a men's dorm. I could not stay there, of course. I don't know what I would have done without the help of the German student who knew his way around and spoke better French than I did. The "Cité Universitaire" has many dormitories for foreigners and we walked from dorm to dorm trying to find a place for me to stay. We had no luck. Meanwhile it was 9:30 PM and I had not slept for three nights and had no roof over my head. I ended up in a hotel close to the "Gare L'Est." I will stay here for two nights. The place is small and not too expensive.

I will not appear before noon at work tomorrow and will ask them to help me find a place, if possible not too far from the company. The working atmosphere is great. Nobody works too hard and everybody is very relaxed. The canteen has great French food. We work until 6 PM, which is a bit late if one has plans in the city. The company is in a suburb of Paris, and it takes some time to get back into the city.

My French is still minimal. It is harder to understand than to talk, but I will learn it in no time. I am having a lot of fun and will write you as soon as I have permanent accommodations.

Please cross your fingers that all is going to be well.

Love,

Hadwig

Paris, September 6, 1959

Dear Mother,

Since my last letter to you, I have gotten settled in and my French has already much improved. Understanding is still a bit harder, but that will come in time. I have no inhibitions whatsoever with the language and dove right in. My coworkers claim that I have already improved and that I have a very good pronunciation. That may perhaps be the politeness of the French rather than the truth.

The company has put me up in a hotel, where several employees live. I get a reduced room rate and it is not expensive at all. The hotel is on the end station of the metro, "Porte de Clinancourt." Every morning I take from there the company bus. Each person who gets on the bus shakes everybody's hand and says "bon jour." The ritual is repeated in the evening with "bon soir" when we ride back. It takes a long time to do that every day, but that is the tradition, the French are very polite.

I have not done any work yet. Nobody can explain to me what to do. I will start on Monday with gas chromatography and will do daily analyses of the gas that is produced here. Since nobody is working very hard around here, I will have plenty of time on the side to work on my French. I am free on Saturdays and Sundays. On Saturday I saw the Marc Chagall exhibition, which was in München, but I could not see it there. In the afternoon I went to the "Museé Rodin." I loved his sculptures and will have to go back there. Today, on Sunday I went back to my favorite Impressionists in the "Jeu de Paume." Monet is the best of them all.

While I was in the Louvre and admired the Venus de Milo, a French lady approached me and told me that I had the exact same profile of all the Greek statues around us. All I could say was: "Vous trouvez?" How about my Greek profile?

Later I got stuck with another French admirer and I could not get rid of him (déjà vu) I used him to practice my French and then told him tall stories. I said I was in Paris with my parents and I have to meet them. He wanted to meet me the next day at a metro station, but he will have to wait a long time. I will go to the "Comédie Francaise" tomorrow with a bunch of German students. We will see "Le Misanthrope." As I was getting the tickets, I met the manager of our hotel, who invited me to an apéritif and I practiced my French conversing with him. I take every opportunity to speak French and I am making great progress. Every evening I learn a new lesson in my book and I read the daily newspapers. All Parisians stand around reading newspapers in the street. I am now one of them.

The food in the company cafeteria is very good and I drink with my lunch the obligatory vin rouge, like all the others. I will leave the letter and continue it some other time.

It is a few days later and I will continue. I received your letter and thank you. Nothing happened on my birthday because nobody knew about it. My stay here in Paris is a continuous birthday for me. The first letter that I received here was from Hubert. It was a lovely letter in French. He already misses me. I am worried about his upcoming exam. He writes that he is unproductive and cannot concentrate. This makes me feel guilty, but he is very smart and he will succeed.

You write in your letter that I might be lonely, but I don't even think of loneliness. I get along famously with my coworkers, because I constantly talk to them (remember nobody works hard). I am not like other interns before me who kept to themselves. They have taught me card games and "Boule," which they play during lunch hour. Nobody can pronounce my name here. Unfortunately it begins with an "h," which the French don't pronounce. They call me "Geneviève" and have much fun with my new name. They also make me say words in French that I don't yet understand and as a result I say some terrible things, which makes them laugh. For instance, they ask me to conjugate the verb "embrasser," which means something else when used without an object. I don't mind and have fun with them as well.

I went with René, the other German intern in the company, to an event, where we met another German student who is very tall. As we wandered through the Quartier Latin, everybody talked English to us assuming that we were Americans since we were so tall. The tall German was such a typical tight-mouthed North German who, although nice enough, does not at all fit into the Parisian atmosphere.

Last night René and I went to the opera, where we saw Gounod's Faust and enjoyed it immensely. This time we had no problems understanding like we did when we saw Molière. At least we can boast that we were also in the Comédie Francaise.

While I was standing in line in front of the box office to get tickets for the opera, some Frenchman had his hands on my behind. This was really annoying. They never leave me alone. I hit him with my purse. Another time the same thing happened to me in a crowded metro. I was with my friend F. and told him, but instead of protecting me, he just laughed it off. This is typical for a Frenchman.

Until today we have not yet had one single day of rain. It is still very warm and the sun shines every day. The money I make will be spent for hotel and food and the rest for going to theaters, operas, sightseeing, etc. I am here primarily in order to experience Paris and not to make money. I hardly work at my job anyway and mostly kid around with my coworkers. I have not heard anything from the Technical University in München about my transfer. The next letter will tell you about my future adventures here.

Until then, lots of love,

Geneviève

Paris, September 21, 1959

My dear Mother,

You should have received my six-pages-long letter. It would be a shame if it had been lost. I am in great form. My French gets better every day and I am having so much fun. The other intern, René, went back to Germany and I speak only French now. My colleagues say that my progress with the language is sensational. I also understand everything now. I talked with my manager about sailing and music and fought with others about modern art. I still make mistakes, but they always kindly correct me, which helps me speak better. In the evenings I also study French and read newspapers and magazines. I will buy the latest book by Francoise Sagan and see if I can read it in French. I am here for three weeks only and I feel as secure as I feel in Germany.

Last Saturday I went shopping in the "Galeries Lafayette" and "Printemps" and had to spend Sunday in the museums because all my money was gone. All museums are free on Sundays. I was in the opera again and saw "Don Giovanni" but did not like what the French did with Mozart.

The only bad thing here is that the company grounds are very dirty. The gas is manufactured from coke and there is a lot of coal dust around. I am very grimy when I get back to my hotel. Soon I will run out of clean clothes.

I have had no news from München. If I cannot go next semester, I will console myself that I will have another semester in Tübingen when I can be together with H. He is a very serious and motivated young man, who is also very smart and has a brilliant career in his future. Please, write if you received my long letter meanwhile.

Love,

Hadwig

Paris, October 3, 1959

Dear Mother,

My stay here is going to be over soon. I wish I could stay longer. I asked if I could come back next year and was told that it may be possible. I have met a charming Frenchman, F., who is somewhat useful to protect me from the advances of other men. He took me with his scooter into the surroundings of Paris including Versailles last weekend. We had a little fight and I have not heard from him, but he may still show up.

From München came bad news. They don't have a lab space for me, only for their own students. I will continue to study in Tübingen and will have to find a place to stay as soon as I get back. H. sent a strange letter. I will not answer and wait until he "normalizes" of his own accord. You will hear more from me soon.

Love,

Hadwig

Paris, October 16, 1959

My dear Mother,

This is my last letter from Paris. My stay here is coming to an end. I have my train ticket home but leave with a heavy heart. I will have to come back at least once more in my life.

I spent the last weekend visiting the "Salon de l'Auto," an international car exhibition, with F. Not that anybody is going to buy a car, we went just looking and daydreaming. Afterwards we went to the "Quartier" and ate the traditional "Choucroute," an Alsatian specialty. I also went to the movies and understand films now very well. How is work in the library in Gatersleben? Soon you will hear from me again from Tübingen.

Je t'embrasse,
Hadwig

Tübingen, October 20, 1959

My dear Mother,

Tübingen is a sad place after Paris. I find it even more provincial than ever before. I went to the hairdresser and asked them for a Parisian hairdo so that I will feel better, but I came out with the usual local, boring hairdo. I was upset. People have no imagination here.

Finding a room is very difficult. In desperation I took a room that I cannot afford. It will cost ninety Marks per month and I have only two hundred Marks to spend per month. The room is in a new student dormitory and is very comfortable and bright. Heat is included in the rent, which helps, and the dorm has showers, kitchens, and a laundry and ironing room. In spite of the luxury, I have a strange feeling in my stomach when I think about the rent. I plan to stay here only until spring. They usually take students only for the whole year. I hope they let me move out again, or I will have to stage a scandal so that they will throw me out.

The last two days in Paris were beautiful. I was invited for dinner in my friend's house and thus saw a French private home. They told me that they don't like Germans because of what Hitler did, but once they got this out of their system, they liked me anyhow. They recorded my speech on a tape recorder. We had a good laugh about my French. It sounds weird to hear oneself in a foreign language.

The trip back was uneventful. A young Austrian traveled with me in the same compartment. He had brought along a liter of French red wine and handed me the bottle from time to time with the result that I was a bit unsteady when I disembarked the Balkan-Express. I had nothing in my stomach and had to order a Schnitzel immediately. I felt like crying when the train left Paris, but the presence of the Austrian forced me to control myself. Linde invited me for the first weekend after my return. It was a good buffer and helped to ease myself back into German bourgeois conformism.

Hubert borrowed his father's car and wanted to pick me up, but I was already in Mochental. The poor guy missed me again. I found him on Monday buried among his books. We were both equally happy to see each other again. We have fallen a little in love, but unfortunately he is very busy preparing for his exam. We met today for lunch at the student cafeteria. We sat there very properly and talked, which is not like it would be in Paris, where you can kiss each other between bites of food and nobody would find that remarkable.

I will be able to move into my "palatial" room by November 1.

I am still in my old room and have to endure my landlady's cleaning mania. I prefer the French dirt.

I revel in my Parisian memories by looking at the pictures of my beloved Impressionists. Even a short stay in a foreign country widens one's horizon by kilometers.

Much love,

Hadwig

Time to Move On

✦

Applying for a Fulbright Fellowship

Tübingen, November 1, 1959

My dear Mother,

Thanks for your last letter. I moved into my new place yesterday.

It is too bad that you cannot see it. It has all new furniture. Visiting hours are from 10 AM to 10 PM (not that I ever really observed it). The house parents are very relaxed. It feels so good to have no landlady who pokes her nose into all my private affairs. Her son helped me move and she has invited herself for coffee, but even that will pass. I did not sleep well in the first night. I don't know if it was the new place and the new bed or if it was sleeping in a heated room, which I am not used to doing. I spent much of the time before the move in the student union and I am glad to have my own place finally.

Hubert has his exams on November 12, but we spend as much time with each other as we possibly can. He is very sweet to me, but he is a typical Swabian and I often miss a certain generousness and liberality.

The Swabians are the population living around Stuttgart. They are well-known for their hard work, honesty, and uprightness but also for their bourgeois attitude.

Meanwhile F. wrote me a lovely letter in French. Who knows, perhaps we will see each other again someday. I would love to go back to Paris in the spring.

Tutte will come to see me on her way to München. I will miss her in the future. She was a good friend and a great roommate. She and I played matchmakers and got Helga and Peter together. They are now inseparable. Helga has problems with men, and when there is trouble she comes to me. I know Peter very well and she should be happy that he is interested in her.

I had a date with a fellow student yesterday and forgot it completely. I only remembered at night, when I was already in bed. He is a good photographer and will take my pictures, which I can then divide among my other admirers.

I will send a package tomorrow with all the things that you requested. Please excuse the delay. My move complicated everything.
Love to you, Ute, and Gisla,
Hadwig

Tübingen, November 11, 1959

My dear Mother,

The first week of the new semester is already behind me. I will take your gentle reprimands to heart and start concentrating on my work again. You are right, I cannot go on and enjoy life the way I presently do. I have already started to work in organic chemistry. My colleagues have been very helpful with the organic experimentation and showed me how to use the reference library. It feels like I have to study a new field, but it is still chemistry, just different. An "old" friend from the first semester came back from München for a visit. Of course, we had to celebrate this reunion with a "Viertele" *[local wine]*. Hubert came to my new "pad" and liked it so much that I had to throw him out by 10 PM. Remember, we have house rules. We are not allowed to cook, iron, or wash laundry in the room. I have done all that already and Tutte stayed with me overnight. Tutte, her new roommate, Helga, and I celebrated my luxurious place with French champagne. Later we took Tutte and her friend to the train.

H.'s exam is on Thursday and he wants to take me to München with his father's car when it is all behind him. Perhaps I can visit Ute M. when I am there.

It is Sunday today and I was in church. You will wonder why I suddenly go to church. Uncle Köberle was giving the service and I wanted to hear him. His sermon was very good. His son-in-law recently died in an accident and a second child is on the way. I don't know any details, but it must be a terrible thing to have a sudden death in the family.

I have signed up for an advanced French course and wanted to take English also. I need to brush up my English for reading literature in organic chemistry, but the course coincides with the French course. It will have to wait.

Love,

Hadwig

Tübingen, November 18, 1959

Dear Mother,

A very tricky experiment kept me in the lab all day. I did not have time to go for lunch. I also passed my first exam for the organic lab course. That is nothing in comparison to H.'s achievement. He passed his Diplom exam with an "A."

We celebrated with a good dinner and a bottle of wine. He went home today for a few days of rest *[his parents lived not too far from Tübingen]*. This will give me also some time to work. We are becoming dependent on each other, which worries us a little. Neither one of us has had such a close relationship before. I don't know if it is love. You wrote me that I should not waste my love on people who do not deserve it. He deserves it because he is a wonderful human being, and perhaps we need to get to know each other more. We have not really known each other for all that long. Helga thinks the world of him. Don't worry, I will not get distracted from chemistry. I decided to take botany as a minor, which will use up more time. I will discuss my future with Ute M., who is several semesters ahead of me and has more experience.

Meanwhile it is 11 PM and I have to get up early to continue with my experiments tomorrow. The last exam was at 8 AM and I got up at 5 AM and learned basically everything in three hours.

Much love,

Hadwig

Tübingen, December 3, 1959

My dear Mother,

I have had my old landlady and her daughter for coffee. Since my room was very neat and clean, she must have approved. I am glad this is behind me and I don't have to deal with her anymore.

I have celebrated the Advent season with Helga by cooking a dinner. H. came later and ate the leftovers. I am very angry with him. We went to the movies last night and met other chemistry students. When we are alone, he is very sweet to me, but as soon as somebody he knows appears, he behaves as if nobody should have any inkling that we are an "item." This went so far last night that he let me go home alone. I cursed his Swabian bourgeois conformism. He just cannot let go and be natural, damn him! When I ran into him today I pretended not to see him, but he came towards me with a large grin. What can I do? I will not be available for some time. Perhaps he will change his ways, although I doubt it, since he does not even know that he hurts me by his manner. I bought some yarn and went home and started knitting, which is good therapy.

Please excuse me for bothering you with my silly problems. On the other hand, it is wonderful that I can write you everything and come to you when I have a problem. You have not even met H. and know him only from my letters. Our relationship is usually very harmonious except for his stupid conventionalism. I should send him packing, I am so mad. Please, don't mind me.

Much love,

Hadwig

My mother was a wonderful letter writer. She always knew just what to write. Here is her response to my letter of December 3. Her letter was written in German, and I hope that my translation will do her justice.

Gatersleben, December 12, 1959

My dear Hadwig,

Your letter from December 3 arrived yesterday. I thank you. It is wonderful that you all write *[meaning my sisters and I]*. Reading your letters helps me through the day and provides things to think about in all those sleepless nights. I am happy to hear that you have a comfortable room in the dorm. You now have a place where you can retire, rest, and feel cozy.

Helga has become a trusted friend, you being a companion more for her than she for you. You tell me that you have a knitting project, which will bring you pleasure during the Christmas time. I am glad about that. Where might you be for Christmas this year? I am sending you a book about artists and their art. I liked it and hope that you will like it also. You have insight into artistic lives and into the lives of brilliant painters. The package is filled with something very small. I could not bake anything, please forgive me.

I have been thinking about your problems. It is difficult to advise you because everybody has her own heart in these matters and often we don't even understand our own feelings. Otherwise we would not always come upon problems obstructing our path. I can understand your anger. You talk about Swabian, bourgeois conformism, which certainly exists, but mostly among simple people. Greatness and generosity among Swabians is rare, but when it manifests itself, the brilliance of such a Swabian makes him very lovable. One example is Theodor Heuss. It appears that H. has had a bourgeois, but solid and respectable, upbringing. You must consider if he can change or grow beyond it, which is seldom possible. This stands in such contrast to his intellectual abilities. People can grow together if love does not make them blind. I certainly grew intellectually in the company of your father, and the rest was done by suffering. We learn how to distinguish the important things from the unimportant ones in our lives, and only the soul is important in the end. I don't know if I expressed myself well enough.

I can very well imagine that his integrity, conscientiousness, and ambition aggravate you. You did not feel these things so intensely in your youth. You came from an artistically oriented family. A compromise is probably best, a solid foundation with a good dose of flair. We have had many friends like that before 1945.

You are right to be proud. Why is he so strange? Should nobody know that you are friends? Could he be jealous, or does he want to find out how you react when another man approaches you? Did you not tell him that he should not leave you alone like that? I would make myself rare. If you had been able to study in München, it would have given you a certain distance in which to think it through. The only thing to do is to talk about it. Honesty is very important.

If H. loves you, he must not make such mistakes and suddenly act strangely. You don't go on a date with him so that he leaves you standing by yourself. You don't have to be embarrassed, on the contrary. A man does not have to be extravagant, but he must be generous to a woman and spoil her a little. If he does not know how to be generous in the beginning, he will never be generous. Be aware of egoists, they become worse with age.

Oh, Hawi, there is still so much to discuss, but it is so difficult to write only. Would you like to talk to Köberle, he is great for such matters. He has looked deep into human souls and has been constantly there for his five children. He would take the time to talk to you about your problem, think about it.

I will have to close. Please send me a map of your dorm and your way to the chemistry department, so that I can imagine where you live. Draw me also a picture of your table, perhaps I will have a tablecloth for you.

Be well, I am always with you in my thoughts,

Your Mother

Tübingen, December 10, 1959

My dear Mother,

You must have received my complaining letter. All is better. H. and I had a good talk and besides I made him jealous. Now we are even. We forgave each other and life can go on.

Unfortunately I cannot buy shoes for Gisla. If I did, it would mean that there is no money left for Christmas presents for the rest of you. That would not be fair. She has finally written me a letter and complains about a dull life and the fact that she has to "serve" father while you are gone. Ask her if she could live on 110 Marks per month. I eat margarine instead of butter and don't go to movies or concerts unless somebody pays for me. You know that I would fulfill all your wishes and more if I had the money. Please forgive the whining. I know that I have a better life than you have behind the iron curtain, but I am still living on a shoestring.

Lets us change the subject. I want to write about my plan to go to the USA. I am applying for a half-time assistantship at Wellesley College, which is near Boston. It would start in September 1960 and would last for one year (or two if I wanted to stay longer). They will pay me 1800 dollars, of which I have to pay for room and board and would be left with 60 dollars per month. I have no idea how expensive life is in the USA but hope that I can make it.

H. was in America and is very supportive of my plan. I could take a full-time assistantship with double the pay, but I would have no time for my own studies. I don't want to lose too much time of my education. I will also apply for a travel scholarship. What do you think about the whole plan? I will have to come to a certain point in my studies here so that an interruption does not interfere with the requirements. We will have to see what happens to my application. I wanted you to know about this and tell me what you think.

Thank you for being so understanding in matters of H. He and I are getting along well again. I did what you suggested and was not available, until he finally came to see me and we had a talk. He truly loves me and I can depend on him, he just needs to loosen up a bit. Smart men are complicated and he is not an egoist, I am the egoist.

He invited me to a ball at his fraternity. I have not accepted yet. I don't have a dress for such an occasion. We can always just go dancing if we want to, we will see. But don't think that worrying about H. is all I do. I work an eight-hour day in the lab during the week and study the theory during the weekends. I am making slow progress.

With lots of love,
Hadwig

Tübingen, December 23, 1959

Dear Mother,

I am well but feel lonesome. Most students in the dorm left and we are only three students now. I am the only person on my floor. Everybody went home for Christmas. I spent the time reading and painting but will go to the Nierentzes' in Stuttgart *[Helga's family]* tomorrow because I don't want to spend the holidays alone. H. went home for the vacations and I thought I would not miss him, but I do. We had a pre-Christmas last night and cooked ourselves a great meal in our fancy kitchen in the dorm. He brought me very nice presents, a book with Rilke's poems among others things. As it became 10 PM I had to send him away *[dorm rules]* and he had the brilliant idea to climb on the tower of his fraternity and see the night view from there. As we came back down, we met a friend of his who invited us to a drink in his room. His friend was busy painting. His whole room was hung with his artwork. I think that he is very talented, and when he heard that I paint a little, he wanted to see my things. My attempts at painting cannot be compared with what he does, but someday he will come and will want to see my stuff. H. is naturally very jealous when he realized how well his friend and I get along.

One of my "neighbors" in the lab brought me a Christmas present today. I was very touched. "Ibicus" *[my cousin in München]* wrote me a very nice letter. Tutte has become his "honorary female cousin." He is dating her and writes that he is happy to have at least one of his cousins living in München. It looks like I should take up matchmaking.

I hope that you have received the present from me. I wish you all a very merry Christmas and I will think of you.

With lots of love,

Hadwig

Tübingen, December 29, 1959

My dear Mother,

Without any money but in a great mood I have returned from Stuttgart. I found a mountain of mail, which needs to be answered. I thank you for the package with all your presents. Please thank Gisla for me for the perfume. Brigith sent me cookies and H. sent some delicious pastries. You don't need to apologize that you did not bake anything for me. I have enough baked stuff here.

Brigith wrote me a letter. She had visited father and found him somewhat strange, but well and mentally alert. He was working when she came.

Life with Helga's family was very unconventional. We never got to bed before 3 AM, breakfasted at noon, had lunch in the afternoon, and instead of dinner we had "high tea." We did nothing, and finally I fixed a skirt for Helga so that I had something to do. They gave me my bus fare in return. Peter came and stayed over. He brought me some marzipan. We joked around a lot, and as I played chess with Lothar, one of Helga's brothers, he got mad because of one of my moves against him and as retaliation he started to make variations of my last name. "Schlonnerhey" stuck and everybody calls me that now.

All sorts of papers for the America project surround me. There are many forms to fill out, which I don't really understand. I hope I will win this war with those papers. H. will help me with this. He is starting to be sad about my leaving for USA, sounds like he is really in love with me. On the other hand, he very much supported my decision to go. I am now learning (reviewing) my English.

How is Ute? I will write her a letter. Just this minute the calendar arrived from you. I have seen it before and wished I had it and now here it is. You know how much I love Barlach's sculptures. Thank you very much. Have a very happy New Year all of you. I will probably stay here by myself.

Thanks for everything.

Love,

Hadwig

Tübingen, January 2, 1960

My dear Mother,

I am glad you received the package with my Christmas presents. I am always worried that the mail does not get by the Communists. I am well but totally broke. I own four copper pennies.

I am waiting for H. this weekend and want to talk with him about the USA project. I don't understand most of the forms that I will have to fill out. They want me to take some silly test. I have no idea what this test is [it was the SATs]. Tante Martha wrote me from Andover, MA, and told me that Wellesley College is one of the best colleges in the East and I should accept if I get the assistantship. Their neighbor's daughter goes to Wellesley and I can probably get rides with them. Tante Martha invited me to stay with them. She said they would be happy to have me. What do Ute and Gisla think about all this? I hope they will not be jealous. A new language and a different land sound very attractive to me. What does father say? Probably not a word.

Because I review so much English, my French got stashed away in the last crevices of my brain. French is a much more beautiful language, but I have to know English now. I tried to study on New Year's Eve, but the Mozart music on the radio was too good to be missed. I decided to listen to music and go through my love letters and throw out those, which are no masterpieces. As I read them, I was so amused that I sorted them and put them all nicely back in their box. When I am an old lady, I will have something to laugh about, or cry. Who knows?

You wrote not very flattering things about our stepsister and said that she is very much like father. You may be right. I thought so too when I first met her. For all I know, I may be just like him also, but I would never get married three times. I appreciate my personal freedom, and this affair with H. is getting too close. It is just as well that I will go away. When I come back, we will see if we like each other still as much as before.

I am reading American literature now. I read Eugene O'Neill, which must be great on the stage, and also Hemingway. You asked for Peter's address. I will send it to you as soon as I get it from Helga. Could you send me a good English-German dictionary? I hope they are not too expensive.

Don't fret about your letters. They are always beautiful. I am not such a good letter writer. I had Christmas mail also from Paris. Oh, how I miss that wonderful city.

Je t'embrasse ma chère Maman,

Hadwig

Tübingen, January 23, 1960

Dear Mother,

It seems a long time since I wrote you. Please, excuse me. I am extremely busy studying chemistry, French, English, and American history. The little free time I have I spend with H. We have great snow and went skiing last weekend. We took the special ski train. H. brought along a friend and his girlfriend. The men were good skiers but we women were pitiful. H. showed much patience and taught me the new style. He did that in Swabian dialect: "hang nunterzus," which means "face downhill." It was hilarious. I have learned how to make a left turn, but I cannot turn right without falling. At the end of the day, I was demoralized. Back in Tübingen we made a stiff punch to recover. On our way home we took ski curves around the street corners and looked like we were drunk, but we were only crazy about skiing "hang nunterzus."

I broke a very expensive apparatus in chemistry, after that I ruined a water pump. Disgusted, I left the lab and went to see "Research Associate" H., who also left his work behind, and we went first into a café, then shopping, and then for dinner. H. is getting much better and more relaxed. He is not so overzealous anymore about his work. He also finally acknowledges my existence publicly. This is great progress.

Occasionally there are still problems. He invited me to go with him to the Mardi Gras party of the Chemistry Department. Yesterday he told me that he had invited two more women, since there were never enough women at these parties. I was raving mad and did not accept. I don't want to be 1/3 of a date. If the other chemists cannot find women, he does not have to provide them. That is not my problem. We finally got to an agreement that he will take the women to the dance and find them partners, after which he can come and pick me up as his official date. Do you have an idea for a costume that will cost me nothing? Helga suggested I should go as a siren with only a net over me, funny.

My application for USA is accomplished. An American student lives in my dorm in the room across from me. I asked her to help me. We worked on it for two evenings and it is ready now. The SATs are given in English. It will be a wonder if I pass them, or how I pass them.

My French course is conducted in French only and I am learning more and more. H. says that he will place a French ban on me. He is thoroughly annoyed about my enthusiasm for anything French, the language, the country, and the people.

Wellesley College sent me a course catalog. If I have enough time, I will continue with French there. I need a job before I go across the ocean. I have debts here and must pay them before I leave. I hate this constant penny-pinching.

Father wrote me and asked me to tell him what I want for my birthday and for Christmas. That is for last year! Where has he been all this time?

Much love,

Hadwig

Tübingen, February 7, 1960

Dear Mother,

I was very scared to hear that you were ill. It is scary when you are sick because you hold the family together and without you we are in great trouble. Please take as much rest as you need and I hope to hear soon that you are getting better. Nothing else is important.

I want to tell you about the aptitude test. I received a telegram telling me to be in Heidelberg on the morning of February 6. H. wanted to come with me to visit his friend in Heidelberg, but he could not leave until the next day. I went on Friday noon from the lab directly to the Autobahn and arrived after two hours in Heidelberg. It took H. three hours by train. I found a place to stay and wanted to see the town, but the weather was miserable, so I went to the movies. The test was given on Saturday in an American high school. There were twenty seven American students and I, the only foreigner. I don't think that anyone realized that English is not my mother tongue. I copied whatever the Americans did. I also cheated with the questions and peeked at the answers of the students in front or next to me. I then took a guess if their answers did not agree. Sometimes I did not even understand the question. The only problems I could do were those in math. Often I simply took a wild guess since the time allowed for each question was not nearly enough for me. The whole thing was a silly joke and I wonder if I got any points at all. We had to follow the instructions of a "supervisor":

> "Please take the paper.
> Write this number into this field.
> Turn the paper over.
> Write your name and another number.
> Take the pencil into your right hand.
> Put the point of the pencil on the paper.
> Press when you want to make a line."

Do they take us all for idiots? I was glad when it was all over.

Later when I was at Wellesley, I found out that I had gotten the highest SAT scores of all the applicants. If they only knew that I had no idea what I was doing—but I did not say anything.

I met H. in town and we went to visit his friend who is very charming. His "pad" was very cozy, and furnished with wooden crates instead of furniture. He cooked us a chicken, and at night we went dancing in a club with two more students from the "Dolmetscher Hochschule" *[Academy for Languages]*. Heidelberg has many more foreign students than Tübingen. We had a fun evening. The guys took me home to my quarters. H. stayed with his friend. When I went back to see them the next morning at 10 AM, they were still in bed. I chased them out, but there was so much kidding around going on that it took a while before I was back on the Autobahn.

I found a ride with an opera tenor who was going to München. I could ride with him all the way to Stuttgart. I had a "connection" to Tübingen right to the door of my dorm. I am going to bed now. Tomorrow I must be back in my lab. Please, cross your fingers for me and for my trip to USA.

Love,

Hadwig

Tübingen, March 5, 1960

My dear Mother,

I am so glad that you are better, and I can understand that it is difficult for you to get the rest you need.

I have a vacation job at Daimler-Benz in Sindelfingen. I work in the lab measuring the viscosity of lacquer, which I have to get from the plant. When I look out the window of the lab, I can observe brand-new Mercedes driving by or parked in the lot. When I look at these luxurious cars, I realize how poor I actually am, but I will have one of those cars one day.

We start working at 7 AM. I take the bus from Tübingen, which means I have to get up every morning at 5 AM. I go to bed at 8 PM so that I get enough sleep. The daily ordeal (going to work and coming back after work) takes twelve hours, and when I get home I am exhausted and ready for bed again.

H. is in Malta. His mail from there is very interesting. It must be a beautiful place. He is having fun and I work hard, but I have a new admirer who picks me up with taxis for a date. He is a mathematician and comes to see me every other night. I am much too tired for this and I am not really interested in him. I just think of him as a friend, but he is persistent and hard to get rid of. When H. gets back, there will be a jealousy scene again.

I had to borrow the money for my bus fare or else I would not have been able to go to work. I overslept one morning and ran barely dressed, unwashed, and uncombed to the bus and barely made it.

This time it is father who is in the hospital. What are you doing over there, are you not taking care of yourselves? Spring will be here soon and you will not be able to work in your garden. Please, get enough rest, all of you.

I heard they had a major snowstorm in Boston. It sounds like it will be fun over there. I am glad that our winter is over, although this winter was not bad because I have had heat in my room. It was wonderful, not to have to iron my bed or heat my fingers over a hotplate so that I can write.

Love,

Hadwig

Tübingen, March 20, 1960

My dear Mother,

My life consists of three things: working, eating, and sleeping. Helga's visit was a welcome disruption. As we were trying to improvise a dinner from leftovers, we heard from H. that he is back and we should cook for him also. We had great fun together, just like during the semester. H. told us much about Malta and brought little presents for me. Tutte wrote a letter and expects us to visit them. We need a reunion of our clique from Tübingen.

The American Consulate in Stuttgart expects me for an interview on April 8, which is for my Fulbright scholarship. I will try to make the best possible impression. I have not heard anything yet from Wellesley.

The stupid mathematician showed up again. If he does not get it, I will have to throw him out. He is worse than the French.

I can move to a cheaper room in the same dorm in April, which is going to help my finances greatly. I managed to get on the good side of the house manager by being friendly, clean, and neat. You can always score points with a Swabian with those merits.

Lots of love,

Hadwig

Tübingen, April 10, 1960

My dear Mother,

On Friday was my interview with the Fulbright Commission in Stuttgart. There were four of us, and all conversation was in English. They asked me about basketball and my vacation jobs. I have no idea what they thought of me. They assured me that close to Wellesley are also men's colleges. Did they think I am going in order to find a man?

I met Helga and H. in the train back and we decided to cook in my dorm. The kitchen facilities next to my room are constantly used by us, it is cheaper than going out to eat. H's mother sent with him two heads of lettuce, radishes, and herbs from her garden.

H. invited me to a fashion show yesterday. The clothes they showed were much too fancy for backwards little Tübingen. At any rate, I feel best in my jeans and an old sweater or a shirt. H. hitchhiked to Karlsruhe to visit his brother and wanted me to come. I declined because my purse is empty again. I will have to borrow money to pay for the chemicals in my lab course.

I don't know yet what we will do on Easter. We said we will do something together, but I suspect that H. will go home and I will be left here by myself again like at New Year. I don't know why he has never invited me. Many other friends have invited me to their homes on holidays. This is one of the strange things about H. that I don't understand. What is he afraid of?

Tell Ute I will write her soon.

Love,

Hadwig

Tübingen, April 4, 1960

Dear Mother,

Today was housecleaning day. Then I treated myself to a haircut, which I had not had in half a year. I am ready for Easter now. Helga and Peter visited last night, but they could stay only until 10 PM. Helga and I will go to see Ibsen's "Ghosts" in the local theater, which is not very good.

I am reading much these days but not my textbooks. My friends complain about getting sick at the sight of textbooks, and even Peter lost some of his "holy" motivation. It must be due to our great spring weather. Ambitious H. does not work very much either, and he comes to see me every day. He told Helga that he is in Tübingen only because of me. He is thoroughly sick of the place. We have known each other for one year now, but he will have to fight with his bourgeois family in order to spend Easter with me.

I thank you for the dictionary, which gets much use. I received one hundred "pills" *[code for money]*, which I put into the medicine cabinet.

Much love to all at home,

Hadwig

Tübingen, April 21, 1960

My dear Mother,

I heard from Ute that you have problems again with your balance. Please, take good care of yourself. What would we do without you? Thank you for your package and all the goodies in it.

H. and I finally spent Easter together. We cooked in my place and read much. The weather was bad and we gave up on a bicycle trip after a few kilometers. We went to the theater on Saturday and H. took me out for dinner on Monday, after which we took a night stroll across the Castle hill. We spend many harmonious hours together until H. had again one of his "fits." He says he does not want to see me for a whole week, because I occupy his mind too much. He has to think about me constantly and does not get any work done. I don't know what he is afraid of, but it sounds as if he wants to get rid of me. This is a silly situation. Can we not behave like adults and not like teenagers? I will not sit home like a nun and will go out whenever the opportunity arises. I went with Helga and a math major (not the desperate one!) to a recently opened student hangout, a very nice small restaurant.

Don't think that I am not studying chemistry. I do study and have a lot of work. It is just that I write more about my fun times.

I just picked up my mail and found a letter from Wellesley. I am accepted for the assistantship. Hurrah! Now I still need a visa, the Fulbright scholarship, and a medical exam. I am going to work hard on my English. I had almost given up about USA and considered applying for an internship in Glasgow. I am happy it worked out this way. I will be in Wellesley for the academic year 1960/61, which starts in September. I am also a half-time graduate student and don't have to pay tuition. I will try to get back into this dorm here after I return.

I could not work longer at Daimler because I can only earn another 300 Marks or I will lose my scholarship. I could have used some extra money. This is another stupid rule.

H. reappeared already after three days. He cannot stay away for a whole week. We are going to hear the Amadeus Quartet tonight. I will throw myself into my work on Monday, when the new semester begins. I was studying amino acids when the letter from Wellesley came. There is no hope that I can continue to study now. I am much too excited.

Lots of love,

From your happy Hadwig

Tübingen, May 15, 1960

My dear Mother,

All is well except that I am still waiting for the scholarship. Meanwhile I am using some of your "pills." I am happy about every sunny day and am terribly in love with H. while my USA plans are becoming real. I now have all the necessary papers except for the visa.

H.'s father invited me last Wednesday into a café so that we could meet. I was twenty minutes late because of an experiment in the lab and ran as fast as I could to the meeting place. This is not a good situation to meet the father of your boyfriend for the first time. His father is fifty two and very good-looking and also very charming. He was here for an eye exam and took the opportunity to meet the girl who drives his son crazy (my words). We both liked each other immediately. He bought me five pounds of oranges before he left. I believe that he is a little worried about his son and tried to find out how serious our relationship is. H. and I had a good laugh about that and assured each other that we don't want to get married. When I asked him why, he said that I am much too impulsive and spontaneous for him. Hear the "goody-two-shoes" Swabian talking? I could reassure his father by telling him that I am going to spend some time in USA. When we are separated, we will see if this is the great love or not. Both of us need to finish our education, and I want to see as much of the world as I possibly can before I tie myself down. As you see, we are quite reasonable about this.

H.'s boss will be in Boston for a few months and H. thought it would be great if he could come along as an assistant, but this is wishful thinking. Helga introduced me to an English teacher at the "Amerikahaus" where I also study English. I need a transcript about my English knowledge and perhaps I can use him. He has a crush on Helga, which may help me also.

Next weekend I will be in München, where I have a medical exam at the American Consulate. I will stay with Ute M. Helga, her brother, and H. will come also. The stage is set for a fun weekend.

I am working in the lab with compounds highly explosive at room temperature, and I have to work quickly and often have no time to go for lunch in the student cafeteria. I can only leave when all is safely stashed away in the refrigerator.

Please do not tell anybody in East Germany about my USA plans. In case I want to come home before I go across the ocean, I want to feel safe with the Communists. The less they know, the better. I will write a letter to Tante Martha and tell her that she can expect me.

Lots of love,

Hadwig

Tübingen, May 30, 1960

Dear Mother,

I am in the lab waiting for my distillation to finish. I will write this letter while I wait. H. and I went to Heidelberg to visit his friend. It was the anniversary of the fire at the castle. They celebrate this every year with light shows. H., a few friends, and I made a punch, and with a bucket full of this brew we went up on the hill opposite the castle so that we could see the spectacle better. It was a famous place, called the "philosopher's path." Famous philosophers are said to have walked here while thinking about the world. They had fireworks as the finale of the celebration. All of Heidelberg was in the streets.

The next day we saw hordes of abominable American tourists. In case you fear that I will become Americanized, don't worry. I'll be as different as possible when I am there.

I worked hard last week and passed an English exam and have the transcript, which I need. I held a one-half-hour conversation in English. Can you imagine that?

I hitchhiked with H. on Thursday to München. I wondered how it would go when a man is with me. It worked well. We got there okay and I settled with Ute M. We decided to see all our friends in München and had a reunion in a restaurant in Schwabing. We tried to include "Ibicus," but he had a date. We met so many people (München style). There was a lively 72-year-old lady who spoke only French with us, because she had been a governess in France. Then there was a retired dentist who paints, and he invited us to his studio for the next day. Then there were several economics students who drove us finally home. The streetcars did not run anymore because it was too late (or too early in the morning). We continued to party in Ute's place and had a great time. I dragged myself with a bad hangover to the consulate the next day, where I had an appointment for the medical exam. I hoped that nobody would check the alcohol content of my blood, which they gratefully did not do. Instead they told me that my chest X-ray shows problems. I had an exam and chest X-ray a week before in Tübingen as part of my yearly checkup, and I was sure that my lungs are clear. Finally after four more X-rays they were convinced that I am healthy. H. waited patiently for all this nonsense to be over.

We saw a Gauguin exhibit but not the Tahiti pictures, which was disappointing. Our whole crowd drove in the afternoon to the Tegernsee [a lake near München] and rented sailboats. We had great fun until we got becalmed. We finally made it back to land by rowing.

In the evening we ended up in a club in Schwabing and spent too much money. The place was too crowded for dancing and the drinks were too expensive. We made it back to Tübingen the next day in three hours.

Tante Martha wrote a very nice letter. They will pick me up from the boat in New York and I can visit them every weekend if I want to. I am now only worried that I will get seasick on the boat.

H. and I get along again after he was ridiculously jealous in München. When we go out with such a large group of people, naturally I talk also to other men and they often like me. That drives H. crazy. I find it idiotic.

Love,

Hadwig

In Tübingen, 1960.

Tübingen, June 13, 1960

Dear Mother,

If I don't take care immediately of the things you want from here, it is because I am as busy as I would be working at a full-time job. I spend the whole day in the chemistry lab. My dorm and the Chemistry Department are outside town, and I don't get into town during business hours.

I hitchhiked to München on Friday and visited Tutte. H. wanted to come but he is going to see his aunt in Ruhpolding, where she runs a pension. Tutte and I had planned a trip to Vienna for the long weekend. The trip was postponed by one day, and we decided at the last minute to see H. and his brother in Ruhpolding. There is no youth hostel and we had to stay with the nuns. H.'s aunt is charming and we brought her a bouquet of flowers, which we picked on the side of the Autobahn. The next morning we had to get back to München to get a ride with Tutte's friend. He picked us up as promised and drove us to Salzburg, where he treated us for dinner. Unfortunately he was a nerd and not at all interested in the lovely countryside through which we drove. He simply raced and wanted to arrive at his destination as soon as possible. We found him very boring company.

In Salzburg we took off on our own. We loved the town and saw many beautiful churches. A church built by Fischer von Erlach was the best. It is the most beautiful Baroque church and not cluttered with other architectural styles like most old churches.

Mozart's birth house was overrun with American tourists and we did not see much as a result. We climbed the castle on foot, and after we had come down we rested in the Mirabell Gardens where masses of roses bloomed.

On Tuesday we raced with Tutte's bachelor friend to Vienna. The youth hostels were full because of the music festival. We ended up staying in the Catholic mission. We shared an inexpensive hotel room with a Lebanese roommate. We did not spend much money on food. We ate mostly cheese, bread, and milk, which we bought in the stores.

Vienna is even grander than München. We explored it mostly on foot. The Viennese are very charming, and it is probably no coincidence that so many composers and musicians worked here. The atmosphere is hard to describe. It is very relaxed, and musical performances are everywhere. Unfortunately we could not afford to go to the theater or to the opera. We may not have gotten tickets anyway. We befriended a Viennese guy who introduced us to the famous coffeehouses with a violin player, great coffee, and the famous Austrian pastries. One can sit there for hours with one cup of coffee.

We went to Schönbrunn the next day. The palace is still very much the way it was when the Austrian emperors ruled. For an emperor's palace it is relatively simple. I liked Schönbrunn much better than Versailles. We bathed in the Danube that afternoon, and in the evening we visited Kahlenberg, a charming place outside Vienna with many colorful wine restaurants. The next day we saw a Gauguin exhibition in the palace of Belvedere, then the St. Stefan's Cathedral, and in the evening the famous Prater [an amusement park].

We aggravated Tutte's friend by our relaxed attitude and decided not to take any more advantage of him and preferred to go home by ourselves. We had spent all our money and had barely enough left for a streetcar to the Autobahn. We got a ride with a friendly Austrian from Graz. He drove us along the Danube so that we had another opportunity to see his beautiful country. We stopped often and with, "Children, I think we deserve an espresso," he invited us to coffee and pastries. In his generosity he drove us all the way to München, although he had not intended to take this route.

The last day of our vacation we rested in Tutte's place. When I got back to Tübingen, I found the thick letter from you, which contained all my drawings from my childhood. I did not know what talent I had and enjoy having them here.

I am making a tablecloth, napkins, and a matching tea cozy for Tante Martha. Do you think she will like it as a gift?

Much love,

Hadwig

Tübingen, June 27, 1960

My dear Mother,

Thank you for your two letters. I have been busy with work as well as socially. H. and I went to a ball at his fraternity. We had much fun with all the modern rhythms and danced our heels off until the early morning hours. I found H. sick the next day, probably from too much dancing.

Last weekend I went with H. and his parents to Ravensburg. I finally met his mother. My impression was neutral. She is friendly, but I like his father better. He let us use the car on Sunday, and we had an outing into the surrounding area with a dinner of local freshwater fish. On our way back on Sunday, we visited the famous monastery church in Zwiefalten. I was very taken with this Baroque church and will send you a photograph.

I am often together with H., and we are very much in love. Then again, it does not make sense to commit to anything before I go so far away. On the other hand, it will be a test and we will see if we are right for each other. My reason and my feelings are constantly at war and I hope to have more peace when I am far away from here. I am not sure when exactly I will come back.

I have to go back to my studies. This letter is written in a hurry, please excuse any mistakes, I usually don't read the letters again.

Much love to you, Ute, and Gisla,

Hadwig

Tübingen, July 2, 1960

My dear Mother,

I am listening to French on the radio. To hear the melodic language always gets me in a better mood. I don't know yet when I will leave here. The American Consulate is very slow in giving me dates for my departure. It is difficult to make plans to come home in August at this time. I will write as soon as I know anything about it. I would prefer if you could come and see me. If you cannot get a travel permit like last time, please apply for one for me. I can come for only two weeks. I still have much work to do in the lab. It is too stupid that we need travel permits for such a ridiculous distance between us.

I heard Wolf Dietrich Schnurre reading from his works in one of Walter Jens' seminars. I am a regular visitor of these seminars and have heard about Brecht, Kafka, Hemingway, Aichinger, and others. This is a welcome diversion from chemistry.

I am looking forward to my big trip, but I am also a little sad to leave for such a long time. I wish I were there already.

I am going with H. to Nürtingen tomorrow. I cannot wait to see him again. We did not see each other for a whole week.
Love,
Hadwig

My mother was allowed to travel to West Germany, and she came to see me. We took some trips together and visited her relatives.

Tübingen, August 24, 1960

My dear Mother,

I hope you liked your visit with me. I was probably not such great company, because I had my trip preparations on my mind. Our week of vacations together was much too short for me to relax.

We will take the boat to New York. The trip will take ten days. It is a very slow boat. I hope that I can rest aboard ship.

I will tell you about the camping tour with H. and his brother. When we started out it poured but the sun shone in Switzerland. We drove on to Lake Biel and set up our tent for the first time that night. We met American jet pilots and a Canadian family. H. and his brother can converse nicely in English. I tried my best to communicate. We talked English with them until late at night. Some Canadian whisky helped the flow of language.

We drove to Geneva on the next day. The car needed repairs and we had two hours' time to visit the city. There are tourists everywhere. We finally drove on to our destination, Lac d'Annecy in France. The camping place is directly at the lake and we will stay here for some time. The weather was great and we swam daily in the lake. We played volleyball with other campers and cooked our meals on the camping stove. We frolicked and joked around so much that the French and Swiss always talked to us and asked us why we were so happy. The only problem was the French-style toilets. The sight of them alone interfered with my digestion.

We drove around the lake and strolled through Annecy, which is a very picturesque old town with arcades and a "Chateau." "Haute Savois," although French, shows a distinct Swiss influence. We also visited "Aix les Bains," which lies on the "Lac de Bourget." When we arrived there, we found shelter just in time because it began to pour. We did not see much of the place and drove back to our camping place. It kept raining and we had to eat in the car. H. dug a drainage ditch around our tent and got soaked. It was a miracle that we stayed dry in the tent during the night. We returned via Chamonix where we saw the Mont Blanc (from below, naturally). We set up our tent the last time just before Fribourg and took our route home through the Bernese mountains. I saw my beloved mountains again and also the "Jungfrau." We got along famously on this trip and felt sorry that it was over when we entered Tübingen again.

I got my visa on Monday. My suitcase is packed, I have my train ticket, and I am ready to go.

Love,

Hadwig

The Fulbright Commission organized a three-day orientation conference for all students from Germany. We met in Königswinter, a town outside Bonn. We had lectures about the American college system, for example, and an introduction to what we can expect in the new country. This was a great opportunity to meet other students, particularly those who also went to colleges in Massachusetts. Later we met frequently while in the Boston area, sometimes as part of an international student group. From Königswinter we took the train to Bremerhaven, where we boarded the ship "Berlin."

Königswinter, August 30, 1960

My dear Mother,

I did not have time to write any more before my departure. H. helped with everything and lugged my heavy suitcase to the train. He took me out to the movies and to dinner on the last night. He gave me a book and a small seal as a good luck charm. I hoped to find out how he feels about our relationship and wanted to hear some kind of commitment from him. He said nothing and I got upset but felt free to explore the world and meet other men out there.

Eighteen months later after having written a "good-bye letter," he called me in Wellesley and announced that he wanted to take the next plane over and wanted us to get engaged. It was already too late since I had meanwhile met my future husband.

We are 190 students, three of them are from Tübingen. A woman from Wuppertal is also going to Wellesley to the German Department. She is my roommate here. We are very busy and I have to write this letter in stages. The train from Tübingen was very crowded. It was not easy to leave Tübingen, but the company in my compartment distracted me. I had a good conversation with an older gentleman with a PhD in German literature. He knew Gerhard Hauptmann [German playwright and Nobel Prize winner] personally, published many books, and works for the radio now. Not only was he from Erfurt, but he also met with Onkel Köberle the day before and spoke very highly of him. To use the old cliché: it is a small world.

Whatever we learn about the USA in this conference is very interesting and everything is well organized. I keep hearing that Wellesley College is a great school and that I am lucky that I will go there. What can happen to me when I arrive? At worst I may get homesick.

It will take some time before you get my next letter because it has to cross the ocean.

Much love,

Hadwig

Crossing the Ocean to the New World

◆

Adventures at Wellesley College

We spent ten days on the ship "Berlin," also known as the "mother-in-law boat" because mothers of German women who had married American GIs after World War II usually took this safe and slow boat to New York. There were mostly older passengers on this trip and 190 Fulbright students who planned to study at colleges and universities throughout the United States. Since we had met at an orientation conference in Königswinter, we spent most of the long trip by having one continuous party on board. Except for two days out of Southampton, the weather was calm and pleasant, but we arrived in New York while a hurricane was approaching. Thus we were immediately introduced to extreme New England weather. We spent the time before our docking on deck observing the skyline of the city and the impressive Statue of Liberty. My mother's friends, the Rohrbachs, picked me up and drove me through the hurricane back to Andover, Massachusetts. I stayed a few days with them to get adjusted and then was driven out to Wellesley by their neighbor's daughter who was studying there.

Andover, September 14, 1960

My dear Mother,

You must be waiting with much anticipation for a letter from me. So many new impressions and the lazy life on board kept me from writing. We lived like kings on the ship.

The first two days of the trip were very comfortable and I thought myself very seaworthy, but as soon as we left Southampton, where we picked up more passengers, and entered the open Atlantic Ocean many of us became very seasick. September 4 was my most remarkable birthday. My stomach was on strike and at first I thought that humor would cure it, but that was a fallacy. I spent the next two days apathetically in my deck chair. We had winds of force seven, but as soon as the winds abated we all felt fine again. I found a group of very nice students and we spent much time together. I slept in a cabin of four. One of my cabinmates became a friend. I also had the constant company of a student from the Technical University in Berlin. Klaus will go to MIT and work for his "Diplom" in metallurgy. He will be fifteen miles from Wellesley, where I will be able to meet other students. He took good care of me while I was so seasick. As soon as I was well again, we danced every evening on board. Since the non-student passengers were older people, we young ones took over most of the boat. The captain invited us to a cocktail party. We kidded each other with sketches and songs, which we had made up at the last minute. The high point of the evening was a puppet show given by a student who had made the puppets himself. We had competitions in table tennis and chess or we played shuffleboard on deck. The latter game could be played even in bad weather or in the middle of the night. Obviously we did not spend much time in our cabins. The moonlit nights were just too beautiful to stay below deck. The dances usually finished at one in the morning, after which we sang outside until the early morning hours. We had a very talented choir director among us and learned many new songs and canons. Sometimes we had a guitar and an accordion for accompaniment. When we did not eat, play, or sleep, we lazed around in our deck chairs or used the pool or the sauna. Our jokes and playfulness entertained all the other passengers. Without us, the old folks would have died of boredom.

We befriended a passenger in first class who invited us to join him there for an evening. There was definitely more going on in tourist class. I met a chemistry professor from Stuttgart. Many of the Fulbright scholars had their PhDs. It was a very educated group. The food on board was so much richer than student cafeteria food that it was too much for my stomach to take. Nonetheless I enjoyed every minute of our luxurious life.

At our arrival in New York harbor, the immigration service checked our papers when we were still on board. We were a total of 960 passengers and it took too much time. We were all anxious to disembark. Although we arrived in the early morning hours, I did not meet the Rohrbachs until noon. They were waiting on the pier. Klaus carried my suitcase and I introduced him to the Rohrbachs. They knew the professor at MIT who will be Klaus' supervisor and they invited my friend to see them. Luckily our boat arrived in New York before the hurricane hit. We hurried to the car to get a quick start and perhaps outrun the storm. Uncle Heinrich drove us skillfully through the wind and driving rain of hurricane "Donna." We arrived at their pretty little house in Andover in the evening. The Rohrbachs spoil me and I will stay with them for the weekend, later I will go to Wellesley.

I feel as if everything that happened is a dream. I feel as excited as I was when I arrived in Paris. I have a very interesting time ahead of me. I love this new adventure and will write more from Wellesley.

My love to you, Ute, and Gisla,

Hadwig

Wellesley, September 22, 1960

Dear Mother, dear Ute, and Gisla,

I have been here already for a week and am getting slowly used to the new surroundings.

For some reason, it was easier for me in Paris. I got used to the city much faster in spite of my meager knowledge of French. The students in my dorm are all very nice, but I still felt lost the first few days. I had no idea where I was supposed to go and what I had to do to make sure the chemistry department knew that I had arrived. I think the worst is over now and I am registered as a graduate student. I also had my **third** medical exam. They must be afraid that I brought some terrible disease. I had already filled out in the immigration papers that I have no venereal disease and never was a prostitute. I am not kidding.

Today was the opening convocation in the chapel for the new academic year. I was attending in academic garb. We wore black robes and very funny hats and joined the procession after the faculty in their ornate robes and funnier hats. It was very colorful and I wish you could have seen me dressed up like that. The few men among so many women must have felt strange. The convocation itself was not very festive. They talked mostly about business. With all that traditional garb and circus, there was not even one good speech.

I can now find my way around the chemistry department. One of my duties is to set up the experiments for the physical chemistry lab course. It took me two days to set up the apparatus. I will be supervising two groups of girls in a lab course for organic chemistry. I have to teach them simple distillation and other experiments. I anticipate no problems except perhaps with the language. We had a conference today with the head of the department. I find the teaching method very simple. The students find everything prepared for them and have to follow detailed instructions. There is no room for initiative. We, on the other hand, at the university in Germany, had to find out everything by ourselves. I think that our "help yourself method" of teaching is a better academic education; unfortunately we also spent much more time than they do here. I begin to understand why a master's degree in chemistry from the U.S. does not count for much in Germany.

I passed the placement exams and wondered how I did it in a foreign language. I am taking two hours per week of biochemistry lectures with a three-hour lab course, also a course in literature. I will take physical chemistry in the second semester. Perhaps I can use some of the things I learn here later in Tübingen.

The professors in the department are all old spinsters and I hope that I will get along with them. I met all my colleagues at a dinner in the headmistress's house with a chat by the fireplace afterwards.

We are only twelve graduate students and live in a house outside the campus. We each have our own room with bath. There is no Swabian landlady to deal with. The furniture in the house is a bit old-fashioned, but comfortable. We have a kitchen we can use anytime and we have privileges: visitors can stay until midnight, on Saturdays even until 1 AM. However, men are not allowed upstairs in our rooms. We can come and go whenever we wish. Alcohol may be served to guests only with special permission.

We have two Chinese, one Japanese, and one Greek student in the dorm. Some of the women have cars, which means that I get rides to the campus or into town. The Americans are very generous when it comes to offering rides. They don't walk much at all. The drugstore in town carries everything one's heart desires: baby powder, ice cream, chickens, hairspray, baked cakes, and food for takeout. We don't have stores like this in Europe. Everything is sold in large amounts, which makes it difficult to shop for only one person. The only solution is to eat whatever I buy for the whole week until it is gone, and I am thoroughly tired of the same food.

Oh, and the telephone, we have two in the house, which are constantly in use. Good thing, I can call Klaus. He visited me here on Monday and invited me for the weekend to Boston. After he has shown me Boston and Cambridge, I can tell you more about all these new places.

H. writes letters and seems to be sad about my absence. I hope that during my stay here he will understand better what I mean to him. I was disappointed that he did not make his feelings and intentions known to me when we parted in Germany.

Meanwhile I am having fun with Klaus, who bombards me with letters and phone calls. I will keep him mostly as a friend. Sometimes I don't understand why I am so attached to conformist, bourgeois H. when there are so many open and interesting people in the world.

Lots of love to all of you,

Hadwig

Wellesley, October 15, 1960

My dear Mother,

It is 9 PM and I just got back from the chemistry department. Monday is my busiest day. I also have to recover from the weekend. Klaus took me to a party of the German Club at MIT. We met many fun Germans and Swiss. I always have the best time here with German-speaking people. I don't relate as easily to the Americans and often get homesick for "good old Germany." Do you think that will change? H. writes many letters in which he tells me that he is very unhappy without me. It takes much for him to admit this. I read his letters partly with sadness but also partly with a certain satisfaction. The separation seems to do him good.

In the department, they make me take all the idiotic quizzes with the students. They take it all so seriously, but for me it is just a nuisance. I find the courses easy and get "A"s with very little work. The only difficulty is the language, but I am getting much better. I talk and talk and find that practice is the best teacher.

I met my "sponsor" last Sunday for the first time. She is a Wellesley graduate and a mother of six children. Her role is to take care of me. I am not helpless at all and I hope that she does not mind. She took me to a dinner in honor of new international students. I met about thirty women of every age. We all had nametags on our bosoms. When they tried to pronounce my name, they got knots in their tongues. The food was a feast in colors, mostly synthetic I presume. As a chemist, I am always skeptical about food that is too colorful. We even ate from china plates, not the usual cardboard plates.

The French songs I hear on the radio make me miss France, although I have much fun here. Helga wrote from England. She got very seasick during the crossing of the channel. In comparison I did not do too badly crossing the Atlantic.

Too many women in one place are getting on my nerves. They get together whenever there is an excuse for it, like in the many clubs. The only man in the chemistry department is the janitor.

Never mind.

Love,

Hadwig

Cedar Lodge, Wellesley College.

Wellesley, October 29, 1960

My dear ones,

Did you receive all my letters or did some of them get lost?

Perhaps I should number them so that you know that all of them arrive.

I am well and reasonably happy, except that I have to take quizzes all the time. There is no such thing as academic freedom here. All day long and in the evenings I am in the chemistry department. I don't get to meet many Americans that way. When I am with Klaus we are mostly with other Germans. In spite of it, I have learned much English. It was really easy for me to learn the language and I hope that my accent is not so bad that the American ears are hurting. I get compliments all the time about my progress in English. You know I like languages and I am also having much fun with it.

I received your letter on Monday morning and I am so glad to hear from you again. Thank you very much for your good words to soothe my homesickness. You understand me because you found yourself in a similar situation when you were in Amsterdam in your youth. I try very hard to adapt to the people and the new surroundings.

Klaus visited me yesterday afternoon and showed slides of Berlin to me and my housemates. The international audience was impressed. It was an opportunity to tell them about the division of our country, exemplified by Berlin. We have had a very pleasant time and all my housemates liked Klaus very much.

When I go into Boston it takes one hour. I have to take a bus first and then the subway. Wellesley is a suburb of Boston, but the distances here are very large and it is still fifteen miles into the city.

When your letter arrived, I had also one from H. I was very upset about his last letter and wrote him a very unkind answer. Then he wrote me a very loving letter. It speaks for him that he did not do to me as I did to him. I had written him that in his last letter he had an "exquisite vocabulary of caustic viciousness and his sentences boil with anger and cut like a knife." I am not taking all this without defending myself. His mother had given me her address before my departure, just in case I wanted to contact her. Why did she do this, why this sudden friendliness two days before my departure?

It is nine in the evening meanwhile and I just returned from the department. Tomorrow will be another busy day. You asked me about the food. I have never before lived as well as I do here. I am finally not hungry or cold anymore. We make our own breakfast in the kitchen in the dorm. We have lunch in the department. There is also a kitchen. We take dinner with other students in another dorm on campus. The food is very good and so much better than in our student cafeteria in

Tübingen. I am learning about new vegetables such as sweet potatoes, squash, broccoli, lima beans, and sweet corn.

I will send you the new course catalog and also some pictures that I took. Linde wrote me that they miss me.

I will have to tell my boss that I will not stay for a second year. I already booked my return trip. She told me today that my English "improved rapidly." No wonder, I listen to lectures, read textbooks, write papers, and teach, all in English. How can I not learn it rapidly? I wish I had time to read American literature so that I could increase my vocabulary.

Love,

Hadwig

Wellesley, November 8, 1960

My dear Mother,

Thank you for your letter of November 4. You say that I did not confirm having received your letter. I have received them all and thank you very much. I have asked H. to forward to you some of the pictures I sent him.

I have to make a decision about where to spend Thanksgiving. We have four days' vacation. I would like to go to New York with an international student group. It is well organized and very inexpensive. However, Tante Martha has invited me to Andover. I called her yesterday to tell her about the New York trip, and she will be very disappointed if I don't come to visit them. I would prefer to go to New York and be with young people. I am used to doing what I want to do. Too much friendliness is not always a good thing. I cannot get used to those social obligations. I am constantly invited to teas and dinners here where I feel I have to go but I also know I will get bored to tears. I prefer my own "social life" and want to be with my friends. This is not meant against Tante Martha, I only expressed my general feelings about this issue.

You wrote that you thought the teaching methods should be the same everywhere. This is not at all the case here. The students are practically held by their hands while they are here. Then there are those constant quizzes. I got a "D" on the last one. It was in organic chemistry. When I heard that other foreign students had gotten "F"s, I did not feel so badly. I am sure I would have done better if I were used to the format and purpose of these quizzes. Back home we had an oral exam after each course and anything could be asked.

I have not yet seen much of this country. I am imprisoned on this campus and see the same people over and over again. I would love to get out of here sometime. Our life in Tübingen was not as secure, but free.

I am continuing this letter a few days later and my mood is better. I got an "A" on the last quiz. Perhaps I am finally learning the system. I am working harder here than I did in Tübingen. I visited Klaus in Boston last weekend. We have been trying to get tickets for the Boston Symphony, but it is impossible.

I was invited to my sponsor's house last week and finally saw how an American family lives. The houses in this country are overheated. My dorm is so warm that I cannot wear the winter clothes that I brought from Germany. Not much else is new or exciting here.

H. writes stupid letters and looks out for every sign from me that would tell him that I am getting Americanized. What an idiot. Klaus is so much more relaxed and not at all bourgeois. I wish we had more time to do things together, but we have to work during the week.

Much love,

Hadwig

Wellesley, November 12, 1960

Dear Mother,

Your industrious daughter has finally some time to write a letter.

It is Sunday evening and I just returned from the library where I worked on a speech, which I have to give in a seminar. Luckily I had also some fun on Saturday. Klaus and I heard the Messiah in Boston, which was a great performance. We also celebrated a little German Christmas at Klaus' place with music by Bach, candles, and Stollen *[traditional German Christmas bread]*. Tante Martha has invited Klaus for Christmas. I am glad that he has a place to go for the holidays.

It is two days later and I have given my speech. I was told that it was good, but who knows? The head of the department praised me and told me that none of them would have been able to give a speech in a foreign language after only two and a half months in the country. They may be right, but it was stressful for me. I will now rest on my laurels for a while. In the last weeks I have gotten "A"s on all the quizzes, even one "A++." I did not know there is such a grade. I hope to give a good impression for students from Germany and hope to show that an education from Tübingen University is better than one from Wellesley College *[I had not yet understood that Wellesley was primarily an undergraduate school and how it is different from a school that teaches graduate courses also]*.

The weather proved that it can be very extreme here. The temperature is zero degrees F and we had a snowstorm yesterday. We could not get out of our house without sinking into the snow up to our navels (exaggerated) and the traffic is stalled in town. Back home we have this kind of snow only in the mountains. Nobody cares here what people look like and I can pile on the clothes to stay warm. In the buildings it is always very warm. Recently I thought back to those cold winters in Tübingen, where the warmest place to study was in the library.

I want to tell you how one gets into the Christmas spirit here. All the stores have Christmas decorations. Colored lights are very popular. Trees in the town are decorated with these lights. Sometimes they blink off and on and the whole thing looks more like a carnival than Christmas. The best selection of "Kitsch" can be found in the local Woolworth, the worst German "Kitsch" cannot compete with this, the more glitter, the better.

I will have no Christmas presents for you this year. Everything in the stores is relatively more expensive here and shipping it takes forever. A package may not arrive before Easter. I hope you will understand. I wish you all a wonderful Christmas.

We have vacation from December 16 to January 5. I will not be the whole time at Tante Martha's. I have to work here and need the library, and three weeks in Andover would be too much anyhow. Tante Martha is very sweet but also terribly old-fashioned. I count myself lucky to have a mother who has adjusted with the times. This gives us a basis for communication and we don't talk "at each other" but "to each other."

Greetings to you, Ute, and Gisla!

Love,

Hadwig

Wellesley, December 22, 1960

My dear Mother,

The constantly whistling mailman brought your letter with the slides. They are great and I will take them to Andover. I am leaving tomorrow. I stayed here to have time for writing letters and washing laundry, but I mostly "hung out."

We had a party with a bunch of German students. Klaus and I went to hear not only the Messiah but also the Christmas Oratorio. I finally managed to hear the Boston Symphony. I met a chemist from Freiburg at a party in the chemistry department at Harvard. The party was in the afternoon and he invited me to dinner and to the symphony afterwards. We heard music of Beethoven and Brahms. It was a very nice evening.

Imagine, I finally have a record player. Klaus bought one for me. It had always been my wish to have one, but I have only a few records, Tschaikovsky's 6th symphony and Bach's suites No. 2 and 3. I play them over and over again. My sponsor gave me two records for a Christmas present: Brahms' 2nd symphony and the Eroica. I am now the proud owner of four records. My advice is to get yourselves a record player and throw the radio against the wall. I had my terrible headache again and had to lie down.

Whenever the atmospheric pressure changed drastically and suddenly, I would get bad headaches. Later I adjusted better to the climate and they eventually abated.

I have a ride into Boston tomorrow from where I will take the train to Andover. I will write you from there. A very happy New Year to all of you.

So long,

Hadwig

Wellesley, December 27, 1960

My dear Mother,

I managed to get away from Andover. I had to come back to Wellesley to work until school begins. Tante M. was disappointed, but she does not understand that I have to study. I took the opportunity to go back to Boston with Klaus. I got a haircut there and will go back to Wellesley tonight.

Christmas was nice, Uncle H. wrote you already about all the things we did. I was glad to have Klaus there with me. He listened patiently to the same stories that I hear every time I come to Andover. You complained that I did not write much about my visits with the Rohrbachs. I did not write because I was upset about many things and did not want to bad-mouth your friend. Perhaps it is better if I write you what I really think. To begin with, I want to assure you that my relationship with Tante M. is good and she seems to like me.

She likes me mostly because I act the way she wants me to act. If I did not do that, she would surely hate me, she is very good at that. She has a very sharp tongue and can abuse her closest relatives.

I told you already about her being old-fashioned and about her pre-occupation with society. In theses matters she reminds me of our Tante Friedel in Erfurt *[the wife of a Gofferje relative]*.
Uncle H. is generous and very patient. He does not care about money, only about what is going on in his nursery. He loves his plants. Tante M. is the boss and has taken over the financial management. She sees in everything the dollar value and keeps telling me that they live in a very modest house and pay $600 per year in taxes. She does not say how much money they make. When she started to get involved in my money matters, I did not react and she gave me the evil eye. I will never forget that. I told her in my naiveté that I lent a sum of money to the Japanese student in my dorm, which she paid back within ten days.

Tante M. was outraged that I lent out money without interest. She could not understand it at all because she charges her own son interest. She always points out how she has no demands and how modestly they live. The next moment she shows me her fur coat, her precious Meissen china, and her large silver dishes. This is just an example about that sort of thing. She indulges in talking about the charity she handed out to her "dear Germans" after the war. We must appreciate that she really helped, but she did it mainly to secure a place in heaven.

Here is what annoys me the most. She tells me how terrible it was when during the war the planes flew over her house in order to drop their bombs in Germany. She told Klaus in the smallest details how their house was searched, but only once. Should we be sympathetic to their suffering? The bombs were dropped on us while they lived here in safety. Nobody had fun during the war. Perhaps you can understand how I feel when I have to listen to her describing those awful times for them. The best thing is to keep quiet. I heard her say recently: "one can now buy everything in East Germany." I did not comment. There is no point to talk about our miseries to people who don't know what is really going on outside their own lives. She thinks that it is also very useful to show oneself to society as supporters of the museum and in concerts.

Klaus had given them a record for Christmas, a Beethoven piano concerto, played by Clara Haskiel. They did not listen to it while we were there. One day we put the record on and were told that we play too many records. We stopped the record and they put on carnival music from Mainz *[Germany]* and nobody was allowed to talk while this music played. Both Klaus and I found that his present was wasted on the wrong people.

Please excuse me for writing all this. It shows some examples of what happens in Andover and I am always glad to leave. Tante M. has also spoken to Klaus about me and complained about my independence. She probably does not like that she cannot tell me what to do. Please, don't panic when you get a letter from her someday in which she will predict that Klaus and I will get married. Old-fashioned aunts usually see ghosts.

Furthermore, if I would wear all the old lady's clothes, which she wants to give me, I would look horrendous. They are worse than the clothes I left behind in Tübingen.

The Rohrbachs do not understand why we want to see as much as possible of this country. Their argument is: "you have so much time, we did not have those opportunities when we were young" (so why should you?). Why should our youth be the same as theirs? Times have changed.

I worked on my seminar speech at Thanksgiving while I was in Andover. Tante M. told me at Christmas that they had not much of my company during Thanksgiving. I worked on only half of what I needed to do. This time I thought if they don't have much of my company when I study in their place, I might as well go back to Cedar Lodge (my dorm). I don't care for turkey and other amenities and prefer to have my peace.

Klaus is great. He gave me a record of the Beethoven violin concerto. This is my favorite violin concerto and he did not even ask me, he just knew what I like. It is so wonderful that we have the same tastes and understand each other. I think he loves me and we get along so perfectly.

Please excuse me for having written so openly on how I feel about your friends. I like Uncle H. very much and admire his patience with his wife. Klaus got the same impressions as I got while we were there. I am not the only one who feels that way. I must repeat that I am very happy that you stayed "young" and flexible. Old age is no excuse for being outmoded and cranky. I give you my compliments for understanding how young people feel. This is why I can tell you everything.

I hope you had a good Christmas. Even though I should have no complaints, I wish I could have been with you. Tante M. tells me to feel at home in her house, but I cannot help it, I don't feel at home with her.

With all my love,
Hadwig

Wellesley, January 5, 1961

My dear Mother,

I thank you very much for the little Christmas angels; they make my room look much friendlier. I received the praise of our family with gratitude and give the "honor" back to where I came from.

I found your letter as I returned from a talk with the Japanese student. Am I really writing so seldom? I was not aware of it and did not feel guilty. Perhaps it is because the time flies for me. I experience so many new things and don't realize that I have not written for a long time. Meanwhile you are waiting for news from me.

I am well and happy, especially while I listen to my favorite Beethoven violin concerto. A Kenyan student, the Japanese student, and I had a very interesting discussion about people and their countries. I like Yunko, the Japanese girl, who is very sweet. She is delicate and charming and looks irresistible in her Japanese costume. She is also very open, modern, and smart. I have taken her with me to our German parties. She likes all my friends and, of course, they all like her. *[I have found her again. She is living in Japan, and we communicate via email and talk often about our time at Wellesley College].* The most exciting aspect of my stay here is the fact that I meet students of so many different nationalities. In spite of it, I always gravitate towards German students. We have had a wonderful New Year's party. I knew about 80% of the guests and met all the others, among them two chemists from MIT, one very tall, the other very short. The short one is Austrian and the more interesting. He lives close to Klaus' place. We immediately formed an "alliance" and got along very well. Three of the guys at the party visited me on the day after, another one the day after that. I have never been so popular. I think they like me mostly because I am not American. They prefer European women, I prefer European men. They praised my red cheeks (which I find usually embarrassing) and told me they like my fresh looks in comparison to the layers of makeup on the American faces. They also said they prefer unshaven legs (there is nothing to shave on my legs). I think the whole thing is ridiculous, and since it is only such small things that differentiate the German from the American women, I don't understand why they put down American women.

Klaus meanwhile loves me more than I can stand. I begin to feel sorry for H., who I think has missed his chance. It is getting very confusing with all those men. I have not really thought about it all, but when I had a Christmas present from each, I realized the difficult situation I am in. To finish my studies is number one and while I am working on that I am having a good time.

You asked me what I got for Christmas. I will tell you only about the important presents. Klaus gave me the record, which I told you already. H. sent me a large picture of Tübingen and wants to make me an album with photographs of Tübingen *[which he never did]*. Tante M. gave me a silver spoon for my dowry. Someone gave me an evening dress, slightly worn. After I removed the gold ornaments and changed it to European length, it became an attractive dress. I am looking now for an opportunity to wear it.

I hope for all of you that 1961 will be a good year and that there will be freedom to move around the world again for you. I am so grateful for having the opportunity to see new places and meet new people. Life is very easy here, but we study hard. The only thing I miss is the cultural stimulus. It would be so much easier to get a degree here rather than in Tübingen. I will, however, return to Germany. This place is great, but it is not the whole world.

Lots of love,
Hadwig

Wellesley, January 8, 1961

My dear Mother,

The lab I am teaching does not begin until two o'clock and I have an hour's time to write you this letter. I thank you for your last letter, which was very thoughtful as well as interesting. I think I told you that I take only physical chemistry this semester. I have enough to do, get very tired, and look forward to my bath and bed every night. The admirers call and want dates and I have had no time yet to read a book or paint. I am just working and running around.

I want to find a job and stay here during the summer. I hope to be able to get a work permit. I have only a student visa and am not allowed to work, but I need to make a living when I am not at the college. I hope my job applications will go through.

Tante M. has received your book. I have not forgotten her birthday. I gave her a book that I had initially bought for myself but don't have the time to read. I told her that I was looking for a summer job. She reacted negatively again and I don't know what she actually wants from me. She once told me that she would not like me anymore if I stayed for a second year. And if I stay for a second year, it is none of her business. Sorry to talk like that about your friend.

I wish I had my skis here. We have so much snow that it would be fun to go skiing somewhere. I was invited to hear the Boston Symphony yesterday. I did not like the music of Richard Strauss. I prefer "good old" Mozart. I have had a letter from Helga but have heard nothing from Tutte, which worries me.

Love,
Hadwig

Wellesley, January 12, 1961

My dear Mother,

I got up an hour early by mistake and have some time to write letters. Thank you so much for your two letters, especially the one in which you write that you understand me. I have done exactly what you suggested with your friend Tante M. I use my work as an excuse not to spend much time with her and try not to spoil the relationship. I am so happy that you had such beautiful vacation days. You deserved a rest after all your work and I can imagine that it will be hard to get back into the routine. It is such a pity that all of you cannot share my experiences with me directly, only in letters.

When I told the head of my department that I was planning to go back in September, she was very disappointed. The faculty of the whole department tried to convince me to stay for another year. It makes me feel very good to be so wanted. I have switched to independent study and can plan my own curriculum. I will try to learn what I need for the university in Tübingen.

My social life is very lively, more than I have time for. We have a regular "club" of German students here. We have another party tomorrow. It is a send-off party for one of us who will go to the university in Berkeley, California. With him we will lose the apartment in which he hosted all our parties. Anybody who had a friend in Berkeley gave him the address so that he will have instant friends when he gets there. We are a "clique" here. The funniest of us is the Austrian. He is very entertaining with his Austrian charm and tells the most amusing stories in his dialect.

While I am having fun, H. has a terrible time without me. He wrote me about a dream in which he lost me, and in which I was not even speaking to him anymore. He was so shaken that he asked me what I was doing at the time that he had his dream and hoped that I could prove to him that it was only a dream and not a premonition. I think that we always took each other too seriously and we caused our own problems. You are right, Klaus is much more relaxed than middle-class H. and I don't know why I still feel attached to him.

What does father say about all my adventures, or does he not remember me? He never writes. I hope you will benefit for a long time from your nice trip.

With all my love,

Hadwig

Wellesley, February 1, 1961

Dear Mother,

I promised to be better about writing letters, but a long time elapsed again before I write. This time I have an excuse. We had finals, which I finished on Monday. I celebrated the end of the semester by going to dinner with the two Austrian chemists. Today I needed to sleep until noon to catch up on all the sleep I have lost. I have only written two letters today and did nothing else.

It is the ambition of every college girl to be "popular." This means that they want to get many phone calls, letters, and dates. I am lucky enough to have so many friends here that I have a busy social life. I caused great excitement in Cedar Lodge when I received fifteen red roses from an admirer. I was almost embarrassed because the sender not only is looking for a wife but already has his PhD and is nobility from the old country. Unfortunately I like him only because he is very interesting. I now have the reputation of being "popular."

Klaus is gone with his friend John to Florida. Both wrote me a letter. John always hangs out with the German group and he wrote his letter in German. They are going swimming and will come back tanned while my teeth chatter from the cold here. How can one not be envious?

H. has finished his thesis and tells me gruesome stories about the professors in Tübingen who flunk many students in their "Diplom" examinations. The news from my alma mater is not very encouraging. I wonder what kind of fate awaits me there when I go back.

I have not yet found a summer job. This will be my next priority. I promise to write more often.
Love,
Hadwig

Wellesley, February 23, 1961

Dear Mother,

I came quickly back to Cedar Lodge during lunchtime in order to change clothes. We have a department dinner tonight in honor of a visiting scientist. As you know, I don't like those affairs, but I am honored that they are not treating me like a lowly student.

I have gotten new records in the last two days and now I have enough records that I don't have to play the same ones over and over again.

We got transcripts for the semester. I have all "A"s and it looks like I studied hard, but I had really so much fun and did not kill myself with work. The German club is partying again, this time in the house of an American. I have met a Greek student who is working on his PhD at

MIT. He builds some kind of satellite for Venus. He is very nice, tall, and a great dancer. He drives a little English sports car and has to fold himself up every time he gets in and out of that car. We do something every weekend. Klaus is very gallant about it. He always claimed that he is not jealous, but I am sure he does not like it.

I am still looking for a job. I saw a beautiful Modigliani exhibition in the Museum of Fine Arts in Boston. We had a sports event recently at the college. We played a volleyball game, faculty against students. I played on the faculty team and lost with them. It was fun regardless who won.

The winter is still severe here, but I am getting used to the cold. I put on a lot of clothes when I go out and don't care how I look. Nobody cares about appearance here. The Wellesley girls look very frumpy when they go to classes, but on weekend dating nights they transform themselves into beauties, which you would not recognize. Give my love also to Ute and Gisla.
Hadwig

Wellesley, March 2, 1961

My dear Mother,

Today is a "lazy" day for me, which means that I come home in order to study physical chemistry. We have another quiz on Monday. I thought that I would have less work this semester with only one course, but that is not true at all. I don't want to sit around on weekends to study and I have to cram all the work into the hours during the week. Like I wrote you already, to have no date on the weekend is bad for one's reputation around here. We had another German party last weekend. I was not very popular by going home at midnight, but I had enough of partying for a while.

Tante M. called yesterday and wants me to say hello to you. She talked as always too much about her social life. They will go to Bermuda in two weeks, and I thought business was not going well for the poor people.

We have a week of vacation at the end of this month. It is called "spring break." Since I have not yet been able to see anything outside New England, I would like to see Washington, DC. I don't know a cheap way to get there. Hitchhiking is impossible in this country. I wish that lack of money would not keep me here.

Nothing exciting happened recently. I have had no success so far in finding a summer job. H. still writes nice letters and makes plans for the time after my return to Germany (but no serious commitment).

I started to get into the mood for spring and it snowed again. I am slowly getting sick of snow. Spring would begin in Germany by now.
Love
Hadwig

Wellesley, March 15, 1961

My dear Mother,

This morning I planned to write you a letter, but I had one of my bad headaches and rested instead. The German Consul gave a cocktail party for German students, most of which I knew already. Some of them I knew from the trip across the Atlantic. We had a super time. The cocktail party is a great American institution. By standing and moving around one does not get stuck all evening with the same boring person. On the contrary, if there is a group of guests who have the most exciting time, one can join them. After the party, I went with Klaus and some other students to a restaurant, where we continued the fun.

I am sending you some pictures. Junko took them. The pictures with the snow show you what we have to endure here in the winter. It snowed again yesterday. There is no sign of spring anywhere.

Junko's birthday is tomorrow and I baked a cake without a recipe. My American housemates are astonished when I make cakes or food without using a cookbook. I still remember the skills I learned in the hotel kitchen in Switzerland.

I have an interview tomorrow with a professor at Brandeis University. He may have a summer job for me in the organic chemistry lab. Please, cross your fingers for me. If I get the job, I will be able to earn some money before I go home in September.

I have to go to the department now and do some work. Please say hello to Ute and Gisla.

Love,
Hadwig

Wellesley, March 23, 1961

Dear Mother,

Hopefully you have received my letter with the pictures by now. I am recovering from a terrible toothache, which I have had for the last three days. Although I saw my dentist before I left Tübingen, the dentist here predicted that the tooth will have to be pulled, but he is still trying to save it. I am sure that by the time you receive this letter the tooth problem will be solved, one way or the other.

I am not going anywhere during spring break. Harvard and MIT have their spring vacation exactly a week later, which means that Klaus and I cannot do anything together. This is a really stupid arrangement.

I hear in the department that the applying teaching assistants who would replace us in the next academic year are not highly qualified. I had another interview at a university but have heard nothing. I am not even intent on making money. If I would make just enough so that I can live here for another few weeks, I would be glad.

I am envious of your spring. We still have snow. Tonight will be early bedtime for me. I have lost much sleep because of the irritating toothache.

Much love to all of you,
Hadwig

Wellesley, March 26, 1961

My dear Mother,

Today is the first springlike day here. This puts me into the mood for writing letters while I am waiting for Klaus, who wants to come out to Wellesley. We will cook a chicken in our kitchen and go for a long walk, German style. Americans would go for a drive instead of walking.

Peter wrote a letter from Heidelberg and described a beautiful spring, which they have had for three weeks already. I get homesick when I hear about the flowers, which bloom already in Germany at this time.

We have a week vacation at Easter. The Rohrbachs are in Bermuda and I will be the only one left behind in Cedar Lodge at this time. I had to catch up on my sleep and am almost there. My tooth has quieted down and I hope that I can keep it.

I have no plans for Easter yet. I hope that one of my boyfriends will do something with me. Without a car, one is like a prisoner here. The distances are much too long. The train is expensive and the bus connections are miserable. It is better to stay home. I will have to go and see Tante M. after Easter. Otherwise she will be hurt that I have avoided seeing her for so long. I have no more room to write on this cheap airmail letter and have to close.

Love,

Hadwig

Wellesley, March 30, 1961

Dear Mother,

Thank you for the letter with the pressed spring flowers. We have better weather now and I discovered snowdrops and a crocus. I just bought myself an Easter present, two more records with piano music. They were a bargain. It is a pity that you cannot listen with me. It is great to be able to listen to the music of one's choosing.

I have been lucky with the summer job. I will go next week to Brandeis and find out what the research project is on which I will be working. I will start work immediately after the college finishes for the year. As a German, I did not expect to be hired at a Jewish university. Brandeis is in Waltham, which is a little closer to Boston than Wellesley. I would like to live in Cambridge and commute to Brandeis. I am not earning much money, but this is the only job I found and the research sounds very interesting. The academic year finishes on June 5.

I will stay here for Easter. A German student whom I met at the consul's party invited me for a trip next week. He is at Harvard and as I wrote you our vacations do not coincide, so I cannot go.

I am still hooked on my Swabian H., although Klaus claims to love me intensely. I am cautious and don't believe all the love declarations I get. I am still playing around but try to distinguish between what is serious and what is not. I will only worry when I am without a man at age thirty, but until then I still have seven years. I have not yet seen enough of the world and am not ready for family life.

Junko will stay here for a second year and plans to stop in Germany on her way back to Japan. It would be great to have her visit me there.

Lots of love,

Hadwig

Wellesley, April 20, 1961

Dear Mother,

The weather is so beautiful today that I have no motivation for work, but I have to study for another quiz. I will be at Tante Martha's this weekend. I better not arrive with my chemistry books; it would just make her angry.

I found an apartment in Cambridge for the summer. I will share it with three other Wellesley girls. Junko is one of my roommates there. I am still looking for a ride from the apartment to Brandeis every day. Last Saturday was a meeting for international students at Brandeis. We got to see the whole campus. It was interesting to meet students from so many countries. The Asian students were in the majority, but the Europeans were the noisiest. The Japanese, Chinese, and Indians sit usually quietly in the background while the Europeans are up front in all activities. There was a dance in the evening and I met a very interesting English student who had lived for fifteen years in France and one year in Germany. He speaks many languages and is very tall. He called me several times already and next week we plan to do something together.

Klaus meanwhile bought a used car. This means that we can drive around and see more places. With all these activities here, I will have a hard time to get used to frugal and boring old Tübingen again, where every student has to count his (or her) pennies. I don't know either what is going to happen with H. and me after I return. I try not to worry about it, since I still have five months to enjoy life here.

In a few weeks from now the academic year is over, but until then I have still much work to do. I will start to work at Brandeis on June 12. My mailbox has been empty recently. It seems that my friends in Germany forgot me already. H. has plans to go to Greece. He got his "Diplom" and continues to get his PhD. I better go back to my chemistry books now.

With much love,

Hadwig

Wellesley, May 3, 1961

My dear Mother,

The story with my toothache continued. The ache started again on Friday and I had to endure a very painful weekend. My cheek became very swollen and I could not wait to get rid of the tooth, which happened finally on Monday night. I feel better now although a little weak since I could eat only soup and ice cream the last four days.

In spite of this dental "intermezzo," I had to make an important decision. The teaching assistant who was to replace me next year has declined the appointment. The department head asked me again to stay for another year. I asked for a week to think about it. I talked to all my friends, considered all the "pros" and "cons," and decided to stay and get my MA. My arguments for staying were: I will have no problem getting my MA in Chemistry with all "A"s. Although a master's degree is not equivalent to a German "Diplom," I will be able to work with the degree and perhaps shorten my study time. The pay for a woman is usually not the same as the pay for a male chemist in Germany. Why then do I kill myself? By the time I get a "Diplom" and then a PhD in Germany, I will be an old maid. Then there is always the financial problem. It is not yet the end of my education in Germany. I may still go on and study a more specialized field connected with chemistry.

I hope you are not disappointed with my decision. The first year here passed so quickly that the second year may pass even faster. I also feel that I have not seen nearly enough of this country. I have just begun to feel comfortable with the language, the people, and the different culture. We finally have spring.

Love,

Hadwig

Wellesley, May 19, 1961

Dear Mother,

I have just received an atrocious letter from H. I hope you will not react as promptly and negatively as he did to my decision to stay for another academic year. I am very sad. I loved H. and have always hoped that he would in some way commit himself so that we would stay together. It was a miscalculation on my part. We still have a friendly relationship, but I am deeply hurt about his reaction. He has always been a good friend. I wish my life were free from affairs with men. My crying will not help anything, and I was the one who decided to stay longer. This means the end of my life in Tübingen. Nothing will draw me back there. Whereto I will return in Germany is still unknown, but perhaps this will realize my plan to live in München. It is depressing how quickly my friends abandon me, just because I want to stay a few months longer. The only letters that I received from Germany in recent months were yours and those from H. Now there will be only your letters, but they will come forever, regardless of where I am. I have made my decision and must live with it.

Tuesday is the beginning of the last tests in the semester. I have to study for them and my ability to concentrate is gone. I will write when I feel better about this mess.

Much love,

Hadwig

Wellesley, May 29, 1961

My dear Mother,

My first academic year here is now behind me. All my work is done and I belong to the lucky students whose final exams are over. A few poor students in my dorm are still studying day and night for their exams. The last paper was due on Saturday, which I finished on Friday night.

After all my academic work was done, it took me a whole day to clean my room. In this respect I am like all other college students here, once every six weeks is cleaning time, the rest of the time is used for studying or playing.

Junko and I went with my Greek friends to the movies on Saturday and Klaus came on Sunday. We fed him lunch and he drove us through the countryside to a large lake. We had fun observing the American Sunday golfers. I am trying to learn how to play tennis. I inherited a racket from a fellow faculty member and I can use the courts on campus. Michael, the Greek, is teaching me a little. But I think for him it is just an excuse to spend time with me, he is not such a great tennis player.

Klaus and I had a serious talk on Sunday night. I think if he had his degree and finished his studies he would have proposed. He takes our relationship seriously and has talked about it before. He asked me if I could imagine myself as his wife. Honestly, I cannot imagine being anybody's wife at this stage in my life. It is not the first time that he talked about this delicate matter. I realize that I cannot have harmless fun with my boyfriends. This is how it usually was, but now they get serious. I have to be very diplomatic about all this. Klaus and I are very close and he knows much about me. He also knows that I see Michael, who is very jealous and wants to be assured that I don't even look at other men. What a mess!

John, the Englishman, meanwhile calls and writes me letters. I liked him and he is worth getting to know, but how can I handle this at such a time? I wish I could just go away and forget about everybody. It is getting too complicated. It does not look like I came here in order to study, but that is what my plan was. Men or not, I get "A"s in all subjects. I hope I do not bore you with all my silly problems, but I need to talk about it with somebody.

We will have a faculty picnic in Rockport, which is at the North Shore of Boston. I will eat my very first lobster. Later in the week Junko, the Greeks, and I will drive to New York. I am finally going to see the fair city. I will move to the apartment in Cambridge on June 7. I am sorry that I am so late in sending you copies of the photos. We have not taken any new pictures.

Much love,

Hadwig

Wellesley, June 3, 1961

Dear Ute and dear Mother,

I waited with some trepidation for your letter and your reaction for my decision to stay. I was afraid that you would condemn me too like my friends in Germany and even Tante M. I feel that it was the right decision. I thank you, mother, for trying to be just and having weighed what is good and what is bad about my staying here longer.

I will try to explain to you how I came to make the decision to stay on. Half the reason for my American adventure is to study. The other half is to get to know the country and the people. When I left Germany I was aware that by coming here my education would take more time to finish. As you must have understood from my letters, it took me a long time to get adjusted to the surroundings, the different education system, and the way of life here. I have just gotten to the point where I don't see everything with European prejudice anymore. I can imagine that from your side this looks like the beginning of the Americanization process. H. sees it that way. I don't think one can be so easily Americanized after a childhood and education in Germany. Besides,

I spend much time with many European students. Some of them have lived here for six years already and they are still as English, Greek, or German as they were when they first came. This country has such a mixed population that it is accepted to live in any style one chooses without being considered nonconformist. Differences are respected. I felt very unsatisfied with what I expected from my stay in the USA when I thought of having to leave in September. It seems that my "adventure" has just begun.

What did I see in this country? Next to nothing and I know only college life here. My language skills are so much better now that I feel ready for new explorations. I have the opportunity to stay here with very few changes, and it would be a shame if I closed all the doors behind me now.

I remember a talk with a German exchange student who went home after one year because of her boyfriend and told me that she regretted it a thousand times. I don't know if you can understand all this, but I have thought about it very carefully and have talked to my professors and my friends. I think that I can profit spiritually as well as materially from a second year here. I don't believe in an education only in one's field without having the chance to look left and right and learn many other things and widen one's horizon. Of course, I have to finish one day, but for now this is a good compromise between science and other "subjects."

I will work for a master's degree. This is the first place where I have enough to eat and don't have to turn over every penny or even borrow money at the end of each semester, which I had to do in Germany. I feel relatively "rich" here and have even saved some money. I will not lose my scholarship in Tübingen. I ascertained that before I left. I hope that I have answered all your questions. I can understand that on your side of the ocean things look different to you.

My trip to New York was exciting and tiring at the same time. I am overcome with new experiences. New York is an overwhelming city. People and cars race around day and night. It is hard to imagine where all these people come from, perhaps from the skyscrapers. The traffic pattern is very unique; streets lead over and under each other. The subway has three levels and the bridges are very impressive. I admired our Greeks who were driving us through the city. How did they find their way around in this labyrinth? We visited the United Nations and brought home our national flags: Japanese, German, and Greek. We had only two days' time and there is much more to see. We only got a first impression and will have to come back someday. I thank Ute for the pictures in her last letter.

With all my love,

Hadwig

Here is another of my mother's wonderful letters in response to what I had written home after I had received H.'s loathsome letter. Like all her letters in my life, it made me feel so much better and helped me deal with adversity.

Gatersleben, May 30, 1961

My dear Hadwig,

As I returned this morning to the library after three days of vacation, I found your letter of May 19. It took ten days to get here and arrived yesterday. This is a long time, especially when one wants to respond quickly. I am so sorry that it takes almost three weeks before you receive an echo, particularly at a time when you are in pain. I am heartbroken that it is not possible to have you here or for me to be there with you. We could talk to each other rather than communicate insufficiently by letter.

It is very sad that you have your good-byes from H. I assume that you will not respond to it. Of course, he was upset when he heard that you want to stay for another nine months. Let him deal by himself with this decision. Many farewell letters have been written in this world and afterwards everything was right again. This often happens when the writer realizes that his love and feelings go much deeper than he expected. Love is happiness and also pain. I know that such a letter hurts much, but it also clarifies a situation as much as it hurts for the writer as well as for the receiver. Usually such clarity comes much later, but it leads to personal growth and maturity. Nothing is without purpose in our lives. All personal growth is painful, and were it possible to inspect a mature heart, it would be full of scars. We receive such scars throughout our life, when we are in our sixties and probably still when we are in our eighties. I am sure this is no consolation to you.

Time is the great healer. It is a gentle and merciful helper. Healing is a slow process, particularly for an impatient heart. I received such a letter when I was in Holland and it made me feel very lonely in a foreign country. You will feel similarly, although there is a difference of almost forty years. When I went back to Augsburg after almost two years, my night train passed through Ochsenfurth at three in the morning. For a moment I could see the window of father's bedroom and realized that the pain was still fresh. We are strange creatures and suffer easily. And what remained of this great love? I was stepped on and it destroyed me. Not even respect for our life together remains.

I am glad that you have such a good friend in Klaus. He will support you and help you. Try to find consolation in the new work. Don't give yourself so generously to people and things. Let everything come to you, save your energy, keep your calm, and rely on your genuine friends while you are in the USA.

Hawi [*my family nickname*], H. will not forget you so easily. If he does, there is nothing to be done. Believe me, he will not have an easy time of it. Now he can evaluate whether it is and always was the great love. If it was, then the time from October to June should not be the deciding factor. If it was not, be thankful for an early resolution. Why did he never speak about your future? Did you not wait for a word at your departure for America? Why now such a great farewell? It would have been much wiser not to write about it but to wait for your return. Don't think that the time in the U.S. is spent in vain, but it is important that you don't stay there forever. A fatherland and home is a warming shelter, which is needed when it storms outside. All the pain is good for something. I am sure of it, trust me!

I think that your pain will have already abated when this letter reaches you. That would be good. I hope you will write me soon about how you feel. If something develops in München, you could find there a happy and rich life with reasonable people, keep that in mind.

There is still be so much to write about, but the letter is already too long. I assume that you received my last letter. Your semester will soon be over. Let me know what your plans are and where you will spend your short vacations. Please, write me where you are, so that I can write you. You can always count on my letters. The four-leaved clover is from our garden. It rains here all the time. We are cold and have to light the stove. Iris, peonies, and delphiniums wait for sun and warmth.

My dear, I think of you with all my heart.

Your Mother

I found this letter again in 1996, thirty five years later. By then I had received another farewell letter from my husband of thirty three years. My mother's letter was as relevant then as it was when she wrote it.

Wellesley, June 6, 1961

My dear Mother,

I thank you very much for your understanding letter. You are right that I felt very lonesome and abandoned after I received that fateful letter from H. When I have your letters, I don't feel lonely at all. I know you are always there, even if you are far away. You share my happiness and also my pain. Luckily I always "crawl" out of my blue moods. I am not thinking with sadness about Tübingen. I cannot change things and consider myself the luckier one of us. I have so many new experiences and met new people while H. is the one who remains behind and suffers.

I had a very long letter from Helga. It has made me see things clearer, although my first reaction was consternation and disappointment. I see myself continuing my life in München when I return to Germany. H. wrote me another letter and I did not know whether I should be happy or angry about it. Whatever happens, I will enjoy my summer and we will see what lies in the future. Perhaps it makes no sense to make plans at this point.

We had graduation yesterday with the usual procession of professors and students in their academic outfits. It was impressive and I took many pictures, which I will send if they come out. The speeches were about politics and not about wisdom. Honorary PhD degrees were given and I was told that Madame Curie, my idol, was given the first honorary degree from this college in 1921.

I will move to Cambridge tomorrow. I hate to think about all the packing it involves.

With all my love,

Your Hadwig

In July 1961 I started my summer job doing research in organic chemistry at Brandeis University. I rode every day with another research associate from Cambridge to Brandeis. Three other students and I sublet an apartment, which was within walking distance to Harvard Square, a much more interesting place than the small town of Wellesley. The lock of our front door was broken, and we went in and out by going to a porch and then climbing through a window in the hallway. Soon the visitors entered in that way too. I woke up one night with a young man standing in front of my bed asking for one of the girls. The situation was not very safe, but we did not worry about it and nothing happened except that the boyfriends could come and go. This was quite a contrast to the living conditions at Wellesley where the undergraduates were not allowed to bring men into their dorm room. The Wellesley girls enjoyed their new freedom.

Michael and I started an intense courtship in the summer of 1961. By the end of the summer, we had both fallen in love, and the fact that I planned to stay for only a few more months sped up our decision to get married in November. He was afraid that by my going back to Germany he would lose me.

Here are some letters that he wrote home to his parents:

Brookline, November 19, 1961

Dear Parents,

My decision has been made and I am very happy. I am about to marry Hadwig in a small civil wedding ceremony. I hope that this makes everybody happy. We will have a great double wedding in church with Linos *[his childhood friend]* and Vicky in July in Athens with "Koufetta" and all the Greek traditions.

These are our plans: Hadwig will stop school and work at the research center of Polaroid in Cambridge until June. In June we will take a MIT charter flight to London. We want to buy a car in Germany and will sell the MG. We will drive the new car to Greece, and with it we will be able to go on outings together. We will meet Hadwig's parents in Germany and then come down to Greece for the wedding. We may take some trips to the islands later with Linos. Or we may stay in Ekali *[the summerhouse of my in-laws outside Athens]* for our honeymoon. Back in Boston we will both be graduate students at MIT working for our PhDs.

I cannot describe how happy I am now that I made the decision. I could not have chosen a better woman. You will see for yourself this summer. She has begun to speak Greek now and hopes that she will be able to speak it with both of you by summertime *[my in-laws spoke very good English and French]*. I have also learned some German.

Please, do whatever is necessary for the wedding arrangements. Perhaps you could discuss it with Linos and his parents. As far as friends or relatives go, you can tell them whatever you wish. The best thing is to tell them that we will have a civil wedding here first.

If you are still concerned about the speed of it all: In the name of Zeus, I have never been happier. Hadwig wanted to go back to Germany, so that she will not influence my decision. If I judge by my happiness, I did the best thing. I wait for your letter.

Much love,

Michael

Brookline, November 28, 1961

Dear Parents,

I received your letter today and was happy about the things you wrote. Except what disturbed you?

I will tell you that I have made a list of all my former girlfriends. When you compare Hadwig with the others, she is the best of all. She is made for me, as they say in the cheap novels. We are super happy and I have gone through much more difficult decisions than these.

I thought we would get married next September. I thought I should wait until then, but the fact that I could lose her, especially if she goes back to Germany, changed my mind.

I could take more than twenty sheets of paper to tell you about all the attributes of Hadwig, which I weighed before I chose to marry her. I am sure you will agree with my judgment when you meet her yourself next summer. At any rate, like the engineer that I am, I include this list of reasons why I chose her:

The love we have for each other, which now rules everything.

The attributes of the woman:

Her personality: as I have already written to you.

As housekeeper: She cooks perfectly, even Greek food. The house shines, she sews all her clothes.

Socially: She is distinguished and sophisticated and has a beautiful body with lots of grace. Her profile is classical Greek.

Family: She grew up in a very cultured family and refined surroundings.

Are these not the things that impress the Europeans?

I leave some room for Hadwig to write to you.

With much love from your son who is very happy,

Michael

Athens, November 27, 1961

Our dear Hadwig,

I want to write to you a few words and wish you forthwith that you will be blessed with happiness in your marriage with Michael. Together with my wife I am looking forward to get to know you better and to take you in our arms like our second child.

The fact that Michael feels so happy with you must be your achievement and we thank you for it. Michael knows everything we talked about in reference to the wedding. His happiness depends on both of you. We hope and pray that both of you together work for this happiness and I am sure that you will succeed. I hope also that your parents, whom I ask you to greet for us, have agreed to the union.

Many kisses from your second father and your second mother,

Leonidas, Rozanna

Michael talked to the admissions officer at MIT and brought home all application forms, which he filled out. I only had to sign. Before I knew it, I was accepted for the PhD program at MIT. This was another plot to keep me in the country. I had considered going to Harvard, where a famous professor and Nobel Prize winner taught organic chemistry. I never got the chance to even apply anywhere else. The acceptance from MIT came so quickly.

Now that I was planning to get a PhD, it made no sense to get the MA. My courses and thesis at MIT would be the same with or without a master's degree. After we were married, I started to work at Polaroid in Cambridge. I could not start at MIT before the beginning of the academic year 1962, and meanwhile I had to earn some money. We lived in a furnished apartment in Brookline and drove to Cambridge every day together. Michael went to MIT and I to my workplace.

Our civil wedding took place in the city hall of Boston in November. I repeated the words that the registrar read to me without understanding all of it. I repeated phonetically. After the event we went food shopping and continued with our life. A week later we had a party for our friends. Most of the guests were Greek, and when the Greeks are happy they smash their glasses. Weeks later, I still found pieces of our cheap glassware under the radiators and in the corners of our apartment.

Our honeymoon was a trip to Athens in the summer of 1962. We could not buy a car in Germany as planned and rented instead a VW Beetle. We took my mother with us to Athens. We drove through Italy to Brindisi and took the ferry from there to Greece. We had a few mishaps on the road. On the highway out of Rimini, Michael drove the car onto the shoulder, not realizing that the grass was hiding a ditch. Two wheels of the car were in the ditch, the other two still on the road. My mother, who was in the backseat, could not get out. Michael hitch-hiked back to Rimini to get some help. While my mother and I were waiting, a group of Italians congregated and argued lively. Then a car with German tourists stopped. They had seen our Stuttgart license plate and asked if they could help. In a few minutes they had organized the Italians and had them lift the car out of the ditch, mother and all. The Germans had not done anything. They had only given orders. When Michael came back with a tow truck, the car was already back on even ground. We took pictures of the Italians and the tow truck owner with the brand-new Polaroid camera. They had never seen the miracle of pictures coming directly from the camera. That was enough reward for them.

A civil wedding was not recognized in Greece at the time, and as far as the Greek authorities were concerned, we were still living in sin. My parents-in-law wanted us to get married in the Greek Church. The double wedding with Michael's friend did not happen. The couple had already married before we came to Greece. We were disappointed. We had a proper, but small, church wedding on July 14. The whole wedding party consisted of eight people, and my mother was the only guest from my family's side. It was a very hot day in Athens, and the priest blew incense into our faces. I fainted during the ceremony and had to attend my own wedding sitting down on a chair. After that, I blacked out every time I went to a Greek church in the future. Eventually I found out that it was the incense that caused me to faint.

Later my parents-in-law had two receptions in their house. One was for the family of my father-in-law, the other for my mother-in-law's family. This was because the two factions did not get along with each other.

There are not many more letters home in the summer of 1961 because my family fled to West Germany and had no permanent address. They heard rumors that a wall would be built in Berlin, which effectively locked all East German citizens in their country. Up to now, it was possible to cross the borders from one sector to another within Berlin. This tragic building of the wall took place on August 13, 1961. My mother and my two sisters packed whatever they could carry and entered West Berlin just one week before the wall went up. My father was on a business trip, and because speed was of great importance, he could not leave in time. Later he was allowed to move legally to West Germany. My father was retired and the East German government was not pleased to have to pay the pensions of the old people left behind. Most of the younger generation had already left. Miraculously they let my father go.

I am retelling what my sister Ute recollected about their escape to the West. Ute was in Würzburg for medical treatment a few weeks before the building of the wall in Berlin. She read in a Western newspaper that a wall between West and East Berlin was planned in order to keep the many refugees inside East Germany. After her return, my family heard the speech of the head of the East German state, Walter Ulbricht, in which it was confirmed that measures would be taken in order to "increase the productivity" in East Germany. In other words, all citizens would be prevented from leaving. My mother and two sisters decided to pack and go to Berlin, where it was still possible to cross from the eastern to the western sector by subway. My sister Gisla studied pharmacology in Halle and was leaving independently from there. The house of my mother's friends in Berlin-Charlottenburg (West Berlin) was chosen as a meeting place. My mother and sisters stayed with their friends only for a few hours and then went to register at the refugee camp in Berlin-Mariendorf, where thousands of refugees were lining up. Two thousand East German citizens sought asylum every night. The West German authorities were well organized and prepared for many more refugees. My family stayed there for a week, sleeping on cots in the basement of a large building. They were flown from Berlin Templehof (airport in the western sector) to Hanover. Here they took the night train to Hammelburg/Röhn and arrived at a large transition camp. Since the refugees had no Western currency, the West German government paid for all transportation. They spent the night in bunk beds in a large room with about 20–30 other refugees. My mother requested to be transferred to Würzburg. It was important for Ute to be able to continue her treatment for MS with a specialist who had seen her for several years and was an authority in the disease.

The camp in Würzburg consisted of old army barracks. My family lived in one room for a year and then moved to a three-room apartment in one of several new houses built with government subsidy. My sister tells me how happy they were to be free again. My mother found a job in a publishing firm where she worked until her retirement. My sister Ute found work as a medical technician at the radiation department of the university. Gisla took an assistantship in a pharmacy while she was waiting to be able to continue her study of pharmacology.

She was not given credit for the semesters she had studied in East Germany and would have had to restart again. She decided to switch to languages and went to the Language Academy connected with the University in Heidelberg.

When my new husband and I visited my family in the summer of 1962, they were still living in old army barracks in Würzburg. This was not an impressive way to introduce my family to my husband. Whatever money I had saved in the United States I gave to them to help out. It was not much, but it helped to buy a small refrigerator so that they could keep their food from spoiling.

After our stay in Athens we visited my family again on our way back and found them established in a comfortable new apartment. My mother had started life again from scratch for the second time (the first time was in 1945) and told me that if there would be a third time, she would just take her handbag and leave.

After our return from Athens, we lived in Brookline, Massachusetts, and were graduate students at MIT working toward our PhDs. I had a scholarship from NIH, and Michael had a teaching assistantship in electrical engineering. He got his degree in 1964. I got mine in 1967.

And we lived happily ever after—well, for a good many years.

From the Office of Public Relations
Massachusetts Institute of Technology
Cambridge, Massachusetts 02139   For immediate release to Boston newspapers

Ph.D. Thesis, Baby Just Weeks Apart for Wife of Newton Professor

Hadwig Gofferje Dertouzos, wife of Dr. Michael L. Dertouzos of Newton who is an assistant professor of electrical engineering at MIT, received her Ph.D. in chemistry Friday morning (June 9), less than four weeks after giving birth to a 9 lb. 11 oz. baby girl, Alexandra, their first. A research assistant in the Department of Chemistry, Mrs. Dertouzos completed her Ph.D. thesis just a few weeks before the arrival of the baby. Mrs. Dertouzos came to the United States as a Fulbright student at Wellesley College after receiving her B.S. degree in 1959 at the University of Tübingen in her native Germany. Professor Dertouzos earned his Ph.D. in electrical engineering from MIT in 1964. (An article appeared in the *Boston Herald* on June 10, 1967, and in the *Newton Graphic* on June 22, 1967.)

978-0-595-34271-6
0-595-34271-X

www.ingramcontent.com/pod-product-compliance
Lightning Source LLC
Chambersburg PA
CBHW061344280526
45784CB00001B/131